Leach Library
276 Mammoth Road
Londonderry, NH 03053
Adult Services 432-1132
Children's Services 432-1127

MODESTY

ABOUT THE AUTHOR

Hafsa Lodi is an American journalist who has been covering fashion in the Middle East for the past decade. She was born in New York City, and at the age of 14 relocated to the United Arab Emirates with her family, where she attended Dubai American Academy while interning after school with one of the region's leading publishing houses, ITP.

After completing her undergraduate studies at the Ryerson School of Journalism in Toronto, Hafsa moved to London for a year, where she earned her master's degree in Islamic Law at the School of Oriental and African Studies. The relationships between religion, culture and modernity have always fascinated Hafsa, who covered topics like honour killings in Canada's South Asian communities, the use of DNA evidence in rape cases in Pakistan and the industrialization of the Holy city of Makkah, before turning to the fashion journalism beat. While living in Dubai, Hafsa has written for *The National* newspaper, *Luxury* magazine, *Mojeh* magazine, *Velvet* magazine, *Savoir Flair* and *Vogue India*, in addition to working as an online fashion editor for one of the Middle East's largest luxury retailers, Boutique 1. She is a freelance stylist, and also has a part-time clothing line, creating whimsical maxi-cardigans and kaftans during Ramadan, and statement hand-embellished sweatshirts for the winter seasons.

MODESTY

A FASHION PARADOX

UNCOVERING THE CAUSES, CONTROVERSIES AND KEY PLAYERS BEHIND THE GLOBAL TREND TO CONCEAL, RATHER THAN REVEAL

HAFSA LODI

NEEM TREE
PRESS

Published by Neem Tree Press Limited 2020

Neem Tree Press Limited, 1st Floor,
2 Woodberry Grove, London, N12 0DR, UK
info@neemtreepress.com

ISBN 978-1-911107-25-5 Hardback
ISBN 978-1-911107-26-2 Paperback
ISBN 978-1-911107-27-9 Ebook

A catalogue record for this book is available from the British Library

Printed and bound in Great Britain
by CPI Group (UK) Ltd, Croydon, CR0 4YY

This book is dedicated to Noora Sofia, who was the size of a peach in my tummy when I first started on this journey. May we raise you with the best intentions, love and guidance, and equip you with the support, spirituality and self-confidence necessary to become a happy and thriving woman.

CONTENTS

PREFACE

We've gathered in the neighborhood of Motor City in Dubai with some of the region's top personalities in the modest fashion world for a full-day shoot. These young Muslim women work with high-end fashion brands, are dined (not wined, for obvious reasons) at top-tier eateries and are flown across the globe for paid-for travel opportunities. Their egos could be sky-high, and their demands could be of diva status but the group of six are surprisingly easygoing, even when things don't go as planned for our outdoor photoshoot. Though rain is a rare sight in the desert land of Dubai, the overcast sky opens up to an outpouring of fat drops and the women run for cover, lest their mascara run or clothes get wet. Still, their game faces are on and attitudes are positive as they continue to work their angles: smiling, pouting and staring down the camera with the expertise of high-fashion models.

Though they take selfies somewhat instinctually, these are not the frivolous, froufrou fashion bloggers that plague the pages of social media. For these women, faith is a major motivator, guiding their fashion and lifestyle choices, particularly when it comes to dressing without baring skin. Modesty is an ideal that these women strive to portray in their outer appearances, and it's a virtue they work hard to embody too, endeavoring not to get too caught up in the frenzied and fast-paced world of fashion. But while modesty may hold certain unfashionable connotations, these young women are neither frumpy nor matronly. As they pose in their ankle-grazing, and for some of them head-covering, ensembles that they've each styled themselves, lyrics from Drake's hit track "Fake Love" play from one of their iPhones, and they joke about blasting rap music on the Muslim holy day of Jummah, or Friday.

Each lives her own interpretation of a balanced lifestyle, one in which faith is a strong grounding point, but where a passion for fashion also thrives. Saira Arshad (@shazaira on Instagram), a teacher who grew up in Toronto, slips on her Christian Dior heels moments after telling the group about her recent trip to Gambia with nonprofit organization Penny Appeal USA. There, she volunteered on the ground and helped raise awareness for sustainable development, sanitation and safe drinking water. That took place right after her trip to Pakistan, where she was shot for a local shampoo campaign. As a gust of wind hits the group, Saira gives her skirt a quick tug, and starts chatting with Sameera Hussain (@missmulberry on Instagram), who's also a teacher by day, about "haram ankles", a point of contention among their social media followers, who often point out that the show of skin below their midi skirts doesn't conform with strict religious interpretations of modesty.

These young women – teachers, fashion designers, graphic designers, bloggers and mothers in their twenties and thirties – lead lifestyles that allow for both style and spirituality, where they can indulge in contemporary cultural trends enjoyed by this millennial generation without compromising on their religious beliefs. There's an effortless ease to the way in which topics of spirituality are woven into their casual banter. Nabilah Kariem (@nabilahkariem on Instagram), a South African fashion blogger who wears a hijab (a head covering worn by many Muslim women) and has flown into Dubai to attend Dubai Modest Fashion Week, tells Saira that she and her husband are thinking of moving to the UAE the following year. "What's Ramadan like in

Dubai?" she asks, referring to the holy month when Muslims fast daily. Saira says that the cultural norms during Ramadan in the Arabian city require women to dress up in fashionable formal wear and socialize all night. "It's so extravagant – I'm dreading it," she says. The two may get decked out in stylish outfits and masterful makeup for their social media posts, but both recognize that Ramadan is a month of spirituality and inner reflection.

Just like the fashion blogging world may look glamorous to an outsider, Dubai too has a reputation for being centered around glitz and glam. Sameera, who prefers wearing little-to-no makeup during the day, explains that because she lives in Dubai, where women stereotypically cake their faces with beauty products, she feels a certain pressure to put on makeup during meetings with parents, and that when she does, even the children in her class notice and comment on her lipstick colors. She's been watching Korean television shows lately, and has started testing out the latest Korean beauty products. Maha Gorton (@mahagorton on Instagram), a British-Egyptian, tells Sameera that she uses Seoul Kool, a Korean skincare brand co-founded by popular Kuwaiti-American fashion blogger Ascia Al Faraj. Maha, who has her own childrenswear brand, previously wore the hijab, and now wears her blonde hair open in loose waves – a look she says she achieved at home herself, and not at a fancy parlor. "I have three kids and a sick puppy," she says, explaining that her hectic weekend schedule leaves no time for indulging in blow-dries. Maha is a brand ambassador for luxury brand Cartier, a collaboration that over the past year has presented her and her husband with a trip to Jaipur and a spread in *Vogue Arabia*.

Both Maha and fashion designer Safiya Abdallah (@dulcebysafiya on Instagram) started families young – they have three kids each, and reminisce about when their children were babies. Their chatter revolves around training their infants to take pacifiers, and mastering the art of public breastfeeding

– Maha, with twins. When Safiya tells the group that she had spent the previous day at the office of The Modist, a UAE-based e-commerce platform specializing in luxury modest wear, Saira asks her if she'll be heading to the brand's exclusive Ramadan press preview that Sunday – event appearances, after all, are commonplace for these young women, who are accustomed to dropping in on new collection launches and product reveals during lunch or after work, where they mingle, network and get photographed for the pages of local tabloids.

As the rain subsides, Rihab Nubi (@riinubi on Instagram) shows up to the shoot – a few hours late, as the rain had caused standstill traffic in the neighboring Emirate of Sharjah, where she resides. Rihab, with her red lips and winged eyeliner still intact, is meeting everybody for the first time, and gives each a warm hug. Two stylish barrettes are clipped on one side of her printed silk hijab. This style of hairclips is back in vogue, and Rihab's head covering, it appears, will not be a hindrance to her taking up the trend, even though the accessories are meant to be showcased on uncovered hair. But covering up, as these young women prove time and again, is no challenge – nor is it mutually exclusive with looking stylish and attractive.

Our shoot takes place on March 15, 2019 – the same day that forty-nine people were killed after a gunman opened fire on two mosques in Christchurch, New Zealand. Terrorism, violence, oppression: these are stereotypes that often tarnish the reputation of Muslim communities, provoking an overall feeling of Islamophobia – the dislike of or prejudice against Islam or Muslims – leading to hate crimes, and in extreme instances, tragic mass shootings. In the West, images of Muslim women in the mainstream media often show them swathed in all-black, tent-like garments, coupled with headlines that paint them as repressed victims of a tyrannical religion. Though fashion may seem a trivial feature when discussing wars, bombs and gun violence, the attire of Muslim women has been a focal point in a long-standing Orientalist narrative. Women's clothing has played an equally central role in the Islamist agendas of the Middle Eastern nations that have strictly enforced dress codes. But the women on set with me today, who choose to cover their skin in outfits that are both modest and on-trend, and in garments that are shown on European runways and are found in North American high-street stores, are helping to polish the image of "Islamic" fashion. Whether they wear head-scarves or not, their sartorial choices have led to the emergence of a global modest fashion movement – one that has inspired even non-religious women of all types of backgrounds to use clothing to conceal, rather than reveal.

INTRODUCTION

"Earlier this summer in a country pub surrounded by flower-spattered midi and maxi dresses, I was struck that a decade ago the same crowd would have sported whale tails (those thong straps that poked out of the tops of hipster jeans)," observed the *Telegraph*'s head of fashion, Lisa Armstrong, in 2018.[1] Her article asks "Why did demure dressing become the biggest trend in fashion?" which is, in itself, a testament to the global style revolution currently underway.

The modest fashion movement has indeed enjoyed astronomical growth over the past five years, beginning with niche, under-the-radar and faith-led labels and businesses, followed by a celebration of modest fashion among mainstream international fashion houses, and finally cementing itself as a widespread retail norm, attracting shoppers of all faiths and none. In the first quarter of 2019, searches for modest fashion on Pinterest, a popular app used to upload and search for inspirational images, increased by 500 percent.[2]

There was a time not long ago when the mainstream demand for modest fashion was minimal, at best – I remember those days clearly. When I was fourteen years old and living in the small urban town of Morgan Hill, California (which prides itself on being the self-proclaimed "mushroom capital of the world"), I received a gift from a friend that I would come to treasure for many years. Courtney was a Mormon, or a member of the Church of Jesus Christ of Latter-day Saints, and she gave me, her one and only Muslim friend and schoolmate, a gray, oversized T-shirt with the words "Modest is Hottest" written in English and translated into various other languages underneath. Courtney and I were in a similar boat in our California middle school, where there were a handful of other Mormon students, but zero other Muslims. Dates and boyfriends were out of the question, and permission to attend school dances, unchaperoned parties or sleepovers was rarely given by either set of our moderately liberal, yet still somewhat conservative parents. Though we had occasional spurts of rebellion here and there, such as telling our mothers that a birthday party was all-girls rather than the mixed affair it really was, for the most part we accepted and made peace with our house rules, especially when it came to clothing.

That's not to say that all Mormons or American Muslims abide by their parents' guidelines – many teens, and even adults still living under their parents' roofs, would leave home in one outfit, only to shed some layers before reaching school, revealing bare shoulders, knees and more. In the eyes of the mosque and church communities, they would have been the subject of gossip among parents, looked down on as individuals who had "left" the teachings of religion. But must spirituality be so staunchly linked to outer looks? These faiths place God as the ultimate judge, yet humans are quick to ostracize those who fall outside the lines of culturally accepted appearances.

Nonetheless, what Courtney and I really bonded over, as insecure young adults just wanting to fit in with the other girls in our school, was the modest dress code that we were both religiously programmed to adhere to. In gym class, while our peers would roll down the waist lines of their shorts to expose as much flesh as possible, as was the fashion at that time, we would wear ours, which were bought from the boys' section of the school uniform shop, at longer lengths so that they covered our thighs and reached our knees. Our classmates expected no less of us – we were the "goody two-shoes" of the bunch, and known to be more sheltered than the rest. We weren't allowed to go on the overnight class trip to Washington DC, and we were the ones who would show up to pool parties in sporty one-pieces rather than bright and bold bikinis. And when it came time for middle school graduation dress shopping, we scoured the shopping malls for dresses together, and both emerged with spaghetti-strapped gowns for which our sewing-savvy mothers fashioned dainty cap sleeves that covered the shoulders.

But we didn't resent our modesty codes, and we still enjoyed shopping for clothes. Courtney's prom dress was a puffy pink princess dress, while mine was a color-blocked black satin and lavender chiffon design. While our classmates received their grade eight diplomas in mini dresses with bandeau necklines, our shoulders and ankles were covered. It was this shared sense of modesty in a teenage world, where your popularity was also measured by your willingness to flaunt your body, that helped our young friendship flourish, and I proudly wore the T-shirt that she gave me over jeans and colorful leggings before it got relegated to my pajama drawer, and years later, infested with moth holes and ultimately thrown out. Courtney and I fell out of touch, though we recently re-connected on Instagram, where she posts images of her biking escapades, pumpkin patch visits and farmers' market trips with her husband.

A decade and a half later, the words on my old T-shirt no longer hold the novelty they once did. In 2006, the summer after my eighth grade graduation, my family relocated from California to Dubai, where I've resided ever since, and today, modest fashion is available everywhere – here, and in America too. When I was growing up in the US, fashionable modesty was a relatively

3

"It was this shared sense of modesty in a teenage world, where your popularity was also measured by your willingness to flaunt your body, that helped our young friendship flourish ..."

unknown concept and preferred styles of dress included Daisy Dukes short denim shorts and tight tank tops or T-shirts, with skin-tight bodycon dresses reserved for special occasions. Now, much of my work as a fashion journalist involves writing about the global modest fashion movement. I hardly have to seek out the stories, with the burgeoning modest fashion industry constantly bringing new designers to the scene regionally and internationally. The movement isn't restricted to niche, Middle Eastern labels and fashion personalities; rather, it's making waves across the world.

My own style brainstorming sessions have evolved from flipping through endless pages of fashion magazines for evidence of any popular actresses or singers wearing clothing that I could emulate with my personal modesty guidelines (covering the knees and shoulders), to now being spoiled for choice with the variety of modest wear appearing on mainstream celebrities and available in retail stores. Take wedding dresses for instance: the trending bridal gowns of the early 2000s may have been fitted with voluminous skirts, but their top halves revealed bare-shouldered, corset-style bustiers. Recently, former American actress Meghan Markle opted for a demure, conservative Givenchy wedding gown for her marriage to England's Prince Harry, and the fashion world applauded her sartorial selection, which was not only featured in the usual newspapers and tabloids, but inspired trend stories and shopping edits in countless fashion publications as well. Modest fashion has indeed come a long way.

So what is modest fashion? If you ask ten different people to define modest fashion, I guarantee you'll get ten different answers. Everyone's view of modesty is subjective: exact definitions and interpretations of modesty and the subsequent dress codes they inspire are often dependent on and influenced by culture, class, ethnicity and generation. But in the mainstream fashion world today, modest attire refers to garments that, generally, cover the knees (often the ankles too), with sleeves that cover the shoulders (and sometimes the elbows and wrists as well). It is not low-cut or clingy, and is often loose and flowy. It can be stylish, covetable and extremely flattering, whatever your body shape may be, whether you're Muslim, Mormon or hold no religious loyalties whatsoever.

You may wonder if, because of my Muslim faith and multicultural background, I'm especially attuned to the modest clothing trend, perhaps making more fanfare out of it than may be deserved. But I'm hardly the only one picking up on the fashion movement in our midst.

Sitting writing this in Dubai at the dawn of my third trimester of pregnancy in September 2018, I'm feeling terribly left out while key players in the modest fashion realm embark on a major industry moment. I'd give anything to be back in California to celebrate the opening night of the Contemporary Muslim Fashions exhibition at the Fine Arts Museums of San Francisco, where a great number of designers I've met with over the past few years are showcasing their creations. It's America's first major exhibition dedicated to modest fashion and a proud moment for American Muslims, who rarely witness such high-profile celebrations of their culture and faith. Had this exhibition taken place back in 2002 when I lived in Morgan Hill, I would have jumped at the opportunity to make the hour-and-a-half drive to San Francisco to witness history in the making. Hindered by my growing belly, I do what any other millennial in my shoes would do when dealing with a case of FOMO, or "fear of missing out" on a special event: I pick up my smartphone, open Instagram, search the hashtag #ContemporaryMuslimFashions and start scrolling through the images.

I see designs from Indonesian entrepreneur Dian Pelangi, London-based Saiqa Majeed, Saudi Arabian Mashael Alrajhi, and Dubai-based Faiza Bouguessa. Big Western brands like Jean Paul Gaultier, Oscar de la Renta, Yves

Saint Laurent and even Nike are all part of the exhibition too. Fashion designers, models, historians and industry professionals from around the world, Muslim and non-Muslim alike, have traveled to San Francisco to celebrate the opening of the exhibition. High-profile American rapper Neelam Hakeem, a hijabi (a woman who wears a hijab), is also present, dressed in designs from online luxury retailer The Modist. But perhaps what excites me most about the museum's curation is the fact that while it sheds light on the diversity of Muslim fashion, showing different ways the hijab can be worn, it's also flagging up that not all female Muslims cover their hair – a truth often overlooked by the mainstream Western media.

As a fashion enthusiast who doesn't wear a hijab but has always tried to dress modestly from the neck down, I've eagerly awaited a mainstream acceptance of modest fashion for over two decades. I certainly never anticipated seeing a whole Wikipedia page dedicated to modest fashion, or a news story in the *Guardian* titled "The end of cleavage: how sexy clothes lost their allure."[3] Nor did I ever imagine I would type in *vogue.com* and be greeted by an image of two Caucasian models in black jumpers and trench coats, with their faces bordered by tight-fitting black headscarves, topped off with black hats.

It's clear that modest fashion is being embraced by millions of women who have no religious affiliations, as well as Christians, Orthodox Jews and Muslims. Not to mention the style movement that's gaining traction with men, who are eschewing sagging pants and muscle vests for more polished looks, in the name of modesty.

So I can't help but ask – what is driving this trend, and why is it happening now?

The financial incentives fueling modest fashion

While modesty is relevant to consumers of all sorts of faiths and backgrounds, it's retailers' preconceived notions of Muslim and Middle Eastern wealth that is the reason for modest wear skyrocketing into the mainstream over the past few years. Author Shelina Janmohamed, who uses the phrase "Generation M" to refer to the growing group of young Muslim millennials and entrepreneurs who share the characteristics of faith and modernity, points out that while Muslims may welcome the industry's increased focus on modest wear, it's not a black-and-white embracement of diversity. "While reaching out to Muslim consumers might leave their audience with a warm fuzzy feeling, there are financial incentives too," Shelina claims.[4]

In 2015, Muslim consumers worldwide spent around US $243 billion on clothing, with around US $44 billion, or 18 percent, on modest fashion purchases by Muslim women, according to the *State of the Global Islamic Economy Report* from Reuters and DinarStandard. The report estimates that by 2021, Muslim consumer spending worldwide will reach US $368 billion – a 51 percent increase from 2015.[5] Muslims are expected to account for 30 percent of the global population by 2030, with more than 50 percent of that population aged under twenty-five.[6] Their spending power, attributed mainly to Middle Eastern millennials, is what the global fashion industry is now scrambling to attract. In an article about the modest fashion industry for *Bustle,* journalist S.I. Rosenbaum writes, "Financially, its biggest engine is the global Muslim market, particularly in wealthy but devout Gulf nations with money to spend and religious standards to keep up."[7] And so, still reeling from recurring global recessions, more brands are turning their eyes to Middle Eastern wealth.

These population projections and financial motives are no secret – it's widely recognized across the globe that international fashion labels' increasingly covered-up runway presentations are not paying homage to Middle Eastern cultures, but rather to their deep pockets. "It would of course be naive to ignore the fact that modest clothing is another way to market towards consumers from Muslim-majority countries with young populations and many, many petrol dollars," states Kashmira Gander in the *Independent*.[8] Muslim writer and researcher Afia Ahmed has also acknowledged the dollar incentives behind retailers' modest fashion offerings. "D&G, H&M, L'Oréal, River Island and co. care not for our Islamic values so much as they do our pay checks," she writes.[9] It's thus no mere coincidence that high-fashion designers are now heavily influenced by what they view as the Muslim consumer's style preferences. "Almost all of the top fashion houses and high street brands are catering for the 'Muslim pound', or 'Muslim euro', determined to catch the eye and grab the wallets of teenage Muslim girls and working Muslim women," writes Shada Islam for Pakistan's *Dawn* newspaper.[10]

Professor Reina Lewis, British art historian and cultural studies lecturer at the London College of Fashion, has extensively studied the contemporary evolution of modest dress. She found that, before modesty began trending, early Islamic-based lifestyle magazines struggled to convince the press offices of fashion houses to loan them products for their fashion shoots, as they didn't view the predominantly Muslim readerships as target audiences for their fashions. Some stylists and editors had to resort to deceptive devices, like hiding the fact that their publications were in any way aligned with Muslims, to get their hands on these coveted clothes.[11] Now, the tables have turned.

The controversies underpinning modest fashion

It's impossible to ignore the undeniable financial potential unlocked by businesses that take special steps to cater to Muslim consumers. As I reach my thirties, after gaining a master's in Islamic Law from the University of London's School of Oriental and African Studies (SOAS) and working for a decade as a fashion journalist in the Middle East, I'm often finding it difficult to reconcile my two worlds. Though at the age of fourteen, I believed "Modest is Hottest" to be a catchy, clever and relevant slogan that summed up my world view, the social media obsession that many fellow millennials are afflicted with has led me to question the way in which the modest style revolution has used digital means to communicate its message to consumers worldwide. In Islam, modesty is encouraged to promote a certain veil of privacy between men and women. But where's the privacy in sharing selfies – albeit conservatively dressed ones – on Instagram to billions of strangers? If women are using apps like Instagram to show off their skin-covering outfits, are they still embodying the Islamic ideal of modesty?

Plus, there's a whole other dispute brought up by this style revolution. While hordes of fashion bloggers on social media may celebrate it, there are many women for whom the term "modest fashion" feels like an insult. Julie Burchill slammed the concept of modest fashion in an article for the *Daily Mail*. "What I don't like at all is when modesty is used as a shaming stick which women use to beat other women," she writes. "When applied to clothing, the word implies, by default, that any other form of dressing is immodest, that is, tarty, exhibitionist and 'wrong'."[12]

The argument is not a solely Western one. Many women of Asian and Middle Eastern heritages, for whom modesty may have been strictly enforced in their own upbringings, are staunchly against using the word "modest" to promote a certain way of dressing. Gita Sahgal, a prominent Indian writer on feminism, fundamentalism and women's rights, claims, "Whether they know it or not, the global fashion business is marching in step with Islamists when they create lines of 'modest' clothing – as opposed to a range of choices for women and girls."[13]

"Islamists promote hijab for political reasons, the fashion industry complies to make money. It is a nasty alliance," claims Iranian activist Maryam Namazie, who says that "modesty culture" teaches girls from a young age that if they fail to dress modestly, they will become vulnerable to violence from predatory men, who are unable to resist sexual urges. "Women have been fighting modesty rules for as long as the rules have existed, but what is worrying is the return to the mainstream of modesty rules, albeit packaged in a lovely silk-chiffon… Whether via acid attacks or Dolce & Gabbana adverts, the message is clear: a good woman is a modest one."[14]

Some women argue that the modest styles currently in vogue appear overtly elitist, and are only suited to certain body types and budgets. "Only those blessed with the privileges money and slim looks bring, these women seemed to suggest, could get away with wearing a dress that evokes virginal drabness at best and cult-style patriarchal oppression at worst," writes Naomi Fry in a *New York Times* Style Magazine feature titled "Modest Dressing, as a Virtue."[15] She points out that popular television show *The Handmaid's Tale*, based on the novel by Margaret Atwood, uses modest clothing – namely long-sleeved, ankle-length dresses and cloaks, in addition to head coverings for handmaids and servants – to connote obedience and submission.

While it may be true that in some Middle Eastern and Asian communities, conservative dress is enforced upon women – be it by their governments or patriarchal families – many women in the West are adamant that dressing modestly, whether that includes a headscarf or not, can be liberating. Personal interpretations of modesty vary among different women, but the resounding message at the crux of the movement is one and the same: choosing to cover up is a matter of personal choice. Women who opt for more layers and fabrics over the comparatively bare offerings in stores are making the profound decision to take ownership of their bodies, rather than succumb to

Western societal pressures that deem a woman's body – or her hair – to be her ultimate beauty, which she should use to attract men. And the modest silhouettes that are now infiltrating storefronts are providing these women with an abundance of stylish options – their covered-up outfits need not be dull, ill-fitting or uninspiring. Instead, they can exude character and confidence, with the layers, colors, patterns and accessories combining to create an armor that's fashioned from motives far more meaningful than frivolous trends.

CHAPTER 1

THE POLITICS OF COVERING UP

"The idea that modesty can be a secular and feminist option – an individual woman's choice to show less rather than more an act of empowerment – has been anathema," writes author, attorney and political philosopher Rafia Zakaria.[1]

Soon after the September 11 terrorist attacks, New York's Democratic congresswoman Carolyn Maloney donned attire that is worn by a minority of Muslim women, influenced by the countries where they live and the cultural dress norms handed down from extremist governments. Dressing up as a stereotypical Afghan woman, she wore a burka (a loose garment covering the whole body from head to feet) and niqab (a veil covering the head and face) while making a statement in support of attacking Afghanistan. Her argument was one of waging war against the Taliban, yet her sensational wearing of the burka was successful in delivering another narrative: one that claimed, in the interest of feminism, that the West would need to go and save the women of Afghanistan from being essentially locked up in these perilous garments. She made a case for their life-threatening nature in her address, when she said that the mesh veil in front of the eyes made it difficult to even cross the road. She described the burka as "heavy and cumbersome" and stated "the veil is so thick that it's difficult to breathe".[2] As we know, the United States did invade Afghanistan, and the image of the burka became a recurring visual of the war.

"The aesthetic of the veil as repressive – and the premise that giving it up signifies freedom while retention suggests a continued commitment to female repression – is inextricably tied to the history of colonialism and the concomitant emergence of the veil as a visible symbol of what needed to be eliminated from the societies of colonized people such that they, or specifically their women, could be 'taught' feminism," writes Rafia.[3]

This may explain why a number of Westerners, both men and women, are up in arms over the fact that the hijab has infiltrated mainstream fashion. British retailer Marks & Spencer has been at the center of this social debate for years, from the launch of its much-contested burkini line in 2016 to the black headscarves it started stocking in its school uniform section in 2018, prompting many customers to call for a boycott of the store. "I wish they wouldn't call it 'modest'. It implies women not swathed from head to toe are immodest," wrote one user on Mumsnet.com. Another wrote, "They should call it 'covered' or something, not modest. Modest implies horrible things about women who don't dress that way."[4]

Burkini swimsuits, which are favored by many Muslim, hijab-wearing women, were banned in areas of France in 2016, being deemed "the affirmation of political Islam in the public space" by then Prime Minister Manuel Valls. Though the ban was lifted in some areas, it is still in place in some French towns, and the garment remains controversial among Muslims and non-Muslims alike. My own mother, for instance, who identifies as a proud, practicing Muslim, doesn't care for burkinis, believing them to be drab and impractical. "And why are so many of them black?" she asks. "I feel hot just looking at them!"

Personally, I've always felt indifferent to burkinis – while I'd never wear one myself (I'm comfortable wearing stylish one-piece swimsuits with swimming shorts) a trip to Modanisa Modest Fashion Week in Istanbul in 2019 opened my eyes to the vast variety of surprisingly stylish burkinis available on the market. Turkish brand Mayovera, for instance, designs burkini-inspired swimwear that could double as chic clothing. An ensemble consisting of slim houndstooth-patterned pants and a smart black blouse is in fact crafted from swimwear fabric, and technically categorized as a burkini – albeit an aesthetically pleasing one. Some women, like popular modest fashion blogger and author Dina Torkia (@dinatokio on Instagram) have mixed feelings about burkinis:

> I have a love/hate relationship with the "burkini", as it's called. Someone literally took the words burka and bikini, mashed them together and created a word that quite simply has terrified the world in recent years. Somehow, the "burk" bit of the burkini managed to convince those that oppose it that it's a repressive piece of swimwear for Muslim women. What? Muslim women going swimming are now seen as oppressed? Packing swimwear for a holiday has never been so political! Let's get one thing straight, if anyone takes away a person's choice, then you're the one doing the oppressing. I mean, sort it out![5]

Young women who wear some variation of the hijab and have voices on public platforms frequently argue against the stereotypical oppression of women. Sudanese graphic designer and modest fashion influencer Rihab Nubi (@ riinubi on Instagram) emphasizes that women like her choose to dress modestly, yet are labeled as oppressed. "It never ceases to amaze me how a certain fashion style can seem oppressive to some," she tells me. "Oppression occurs when an individual's rights are taken away. If a woman makes a choice to dress modestly, that seems more empowering than anything else because she made a choice that her body belongs to her – and she gets to choose who sees it despite society telling her otherwise. On the other hand, taking away her freedom to dress the way that she would like to, whether that be modestly or not, by placing laws that don't allow certain clothing, is exactly what oppression is."

Gender historian Joan Wallach Scott, author of *Politics of the Veil*, believes that countries like France oppose Muslim veils because having an open, unrestricted approach to sexuality is part of their cultural norm. Covering up one's body with conservative cloaks and head coverings is seen to be an extreme and an affront to their liberal lifestyle, clashing with their perception of freedom. Likewise Reza Aslan – Iranian author of *No God but God* – explains that some Westerners are provoked by the veil because of its clash with the historically rooted European principles of Enlightenment, which promoted individualism over tradition. "Of course, at the heart of this argument, is the profoundly misogynistic belief that no Muslim woman would freely choose to wear the veil … that in fact, Muslim women are incapable of deciding for themselves what they should or should not wear, so it must fall to the state to decide for them," he writes.[6]

Women who opt for modest dress, after all, are often seen as doing so in an act of patriarchal submission. Founder of the online platform MuslimGirl.com, Amani Al-Khatahtbeh (@amani on Instagram) points out that Islam, by definition, means "submission to God", and that Muslim women are not asked to "submit" to anyone else. Yet submission is what is demanded of them when enforced dress codes take away their freedom of choice:

What is it exactly that Western society wants us to do when it imposes an impossible pressure on us to bend, conform, assimilate, submit? When French laws supposedly aim to "liberate" Muslim women from the compulsion of wearing religious garments by ironically forbidding them to wear religious garments [the wearing

of headscarves in schools was made illegal in France in 2004]...
When we are ridiculed and targeted for covering our bodies in
the face of the hypersexualization of patriarchal Western society
that demands we, as women, take our garments off - that is more
comfortable with a pair of naked breasts than covered hair - what
does Western society want from us but our submission?[7]

Reading this entrepreneur's passionately written autobiography, it's clear that stereotypes about cultures go both ways. While Westerners may assume Middle Eastern women are inherently repressed, Middle Eastern views of Western women are often that they brandish their bodies at every available opportunity. When Amani temporarily relocated to Jordan, in her father's attempts to flee from what she said they experienced as rampant Islamophobia in America, she was known as "the American girl" in her new school, where her classmates, upon meeting her, asked, "You're from America? Aren't you supposed to be wearing a miniskirt?"[8]

Celebrities' roles as trendsetters

Feminism, in the twenty-first century, takes a variety of different forms. In the West, mainstream media-driven ideologies promoting empowerment frequently paint a picture of a feisty woman who flaunts her femininity by showing off her body. Popular female role models for millennials include pop artists and reality television stars, who are very often depicted as strong, though scantily clad, icons, with performance wardrobes consisting of skin-tight bodysuits and garments that cover the bare minimum. The Kardashian and Jenner sisters are prime examples of this type of celebrity. But as the modesty movement has gained momentum, those within the fashion industry

"Once we've seen it all – from Emily Ratajkowski's fabulous breasts to Kim Kardashian's monumental butt – now it seems as if the most radical gesture could only involve donning a baggy jumpsuit or a generously cut midi skirt." (*New York Times*) have started to question the domineering "sex sells" mantra that has reigned for so long.

"In a world where the Kardashians seem to strip off their clothes any chance they get, we thought we'd switch gears for a moment and talk about the ladies who actually like covering up," reads the opening line of a 2015 *PopSugar* article.[9] "Once we've seen it all – from Emily Ratajkowski's fabulous breasts to Kim Kardashian's monumental butt – now it seems as if the most radical gesture could only involve donning a baggy jumpsuit or a generously cut midi skirt," states a 2017 story in the *New York Times*.[10] Come 2018, yet further comparisons between reality stars and modest fashion are made such as an article in *Harper's Bazaar Australia*, which states:

> In an era where Kendall Jenner is completely naked sans a strip of glittery fabric and Chopard diamonds on the Cannes red carpet, and Kim Kardashian seems to post a nude selfie every time she's been out of the headlines for more than a week, it's perhaps understandable that women are moving towards an idea of "sexy" that's a little less . . . obvious.[11]

As a teen, before fully understanding the way in which modesty was rooted in my religion, I would often watch films starring Mary-Kate and Ashley Olsen – the strappy lace tops they wore in *Passport to Paris* and brightly colored boob-tubes and halters from *Our Lips Are Sealed* are etched in my memory as clothing I would never be allowed to wear. Everything about the two sisters seemed unrelatable and unobtainable to me, from their whirlwind Vespa rides with handsome boys to their skin-baring wardrobes. Today, the Olsen twins have built their own fashion empire, and their preferred garments of choice are long and loose. Rarely are they seen baring more than an ankle or forearm, almost always swathed in layers of luxury designs that cover them from neck to foot, whether they're spotted by the paparazzi while running to meetings, or on the red carpet for a prestigious awards ceremony.

The elusive Olsen twins aren't the only young women offering up an alternative mode of style. Alexa Chung, Mandy Moore, Blake Lively and Emma Stone have also recently taken to wearing power suits, midi dresses and ensembles consisting of long skirts and blouses for their various press appearances. Amal Clooney is frequently referenced for her demure yet stylish work wear, which often features knee-length skirts and suit sets. At the 2018 Met Gala, Naomi Watts, Sarah Jessica Parker, Rooney Mara and even Bella Hadid donned non-revealing dresses on the red carpet, though their decisions to cover up were likely influenced by the night's theme: *Heavenly bodies: Fashion and the Catholic imagination*. A month later, a *Who What Wear* article about the 2018 Tony Awards credited modesty as the most-followed red carpet trend of the event, noting that actresses like Carey Mulligan, Claire Danes, Rachel Brosnahan and Indya Moore all opted for designs that featured floor-length hems, high necks and long sleeves.

When Kate Middleton married Prince William in 2011, modesty was hardly the fashion buzzword that it would become within the decade. But, perhaps unwittingly, the Duchess of Cambridge quickly became a global style icon of modest fashion. Her style was heralded as chic and covetable through-out Europe and beyond, and dresses from mid- to high-end designers quickly sold out after the Duchess was spotted wearing them. Meghan Markle now dresses in a similar manner, and after she was wed to Prince Harry in 2018, her various knee-length dresses quickly went viral on social media, touted as must-have fashion for the season.

Feminism in the entertainment industry

Some fashion editors will claim that actresses and artists have always worn the latest designs from the runways and that currently, these silhouettes just happen to be conservatively cut. Other fashion journalists have attributed the mainstream rise in modest fashion to be a direct effect of the #MeToo movement, which began in Hollywood in 2017 after prominent American film producer Harvey Weinstein was accused of sexual abuse and rape by more than a dozen women. Many fashion critics' in-depth analyses of the modest fashion movement point out inadvertent links between #MeToo and dressing conservatively. "It's possible to attribute this shift towards modesty as a sartorial backlash to the recent onslaught of sexual harassment and assault allegations," reads a *Harper's Bazaar Australia* article, posing the question, "Are women so fed up with having their bodies objectified that they're using clothing as armor between themselves and the rest of the world?"[12]

A story in the *Guardian* claims, "A recalibration that is beginning to happen after a year of #MeToo is starting to bend the once cast-iron rule of fashion week, that a young supermodel in cleavage and a short skirt is the one and only route to maximizing eyeballs,"[13] and an article in the *New Yorker* states, "It is perhaps no coincidence that this 'super-conservative trendy thing', as one stylist put it, has taken off at a moment when the dynamics of sexual power are being dramatically questioned."[14]

In November 2017, high-end footwear brand Jimmy Choo released an ad campaign that starred Cara Delevingne in a red mini dress and Jimmy Choo boots. As she walks down the streets of New York City, she is catcalled and whistled at, but makes the experience look glamorous and enjoyable. With the entertainment industry still embroiled in the Harvey Weinstein debacle, the ad was deemed inappropriate and sexist and was eventually pulled by the brand. In a 2018 article for *Elle*, Kenya Hunt states:

The #MeToo movement against sexual harassment and assault
heightens the collective "need" to shield one's body. The 2018
awards-season red carpet was the most modest in recent history,
with A-list Hollywood actresses largely wearing high-neck dresses,
black tailoring and long sleeves – which they rightfully refused to
talk about, instead using the opportunity to shine a light on issues of
misogyny and the gender pay gap.[15]

But, as Mormon-American writer Jana Riess points out, many instances of
celebrities clothed in demure evening attire – particularly during the January
2018 Golden Globes, when actresses like Salma Hayek, Alicia Vikander,
Shailene Woodley and more were enveloped in head-to-toe black gowns –
were in fact shows of protest rather than a celebration of modest dressing.
She laments that a number of fashion blogs, some with faith-based foundations, missed the deeper meanings behind these solemn, sober and somewhat
funereal dresses.[16]

"Slut-shaming", or criticizing women for dressing in a way that is deemed
revealing or provocative, has been an issue in and out of news headlines for
years. Fueled by judgements about women who dress in revealing clothes,
it has led to the founding of events like the SlutWalk, which launched in
2011 in Toronto, as a response to a local police officer's sexist public statement on the topic of university campus rape. He advised women to refrain
from dressing like "sluts" in order to avoid similar attacks. More than 3,000
activists gathered to protest this instance of slut-shaming, many dressed in
provocative outfits and swimwear, and some even chose to march topless. The
demonstration spread to other major cities in North America and Europe, as
well as select Asian countries like Singapore, South Korea and India. While
the majority of reports from the mainstream media acknowledged that the

message presented by the SlutWalks is important, some conservative publications and news outlets argued that educating young women to shed their clothes to defend victims of assault was counterproductive.

Although initiatives like the SlutWalk are designed to fight the narrative that claims that the more skin a woman shows, the more vulnerable she is to assault, many Muslim women who dress modestly, and choose to cover their heads, have countered with the argument that even the wearing of loose, non-revealing clothing and a headscarf provides no shield against sexual harassment, assault or rape. An article in the *Independent* tells the stories of a Yorkshire-based woman named Farzana, who says she's had her crotch grabbed while wearing a niqab, and another anonymous source, who stated, "As a hijabi woman covered head to toe, [modest clothing] didn't stop my rapist."[17] The experiences shared by these women, who dress in skin-covering garments, ironically echo the messages promoted by the SlutWalks – that what a woman chooses to wear cannot be used to justify her assault or rape.

Clothing for comfort and protection

Although some may presume that the increasing popularity of modest fashion is a response to high-profile sexual harassment cases, others argue it's about women calling their own shots in terms of the clothing they feel most comfortable in. "Women of all faiths are demanding clothing that is actually wearable. Comfort, once the domain of the unstylish, has become *à la mode*, and even Italy's biggest designers are having to take note," writes Selina Denman, editor of the *National*'s lifestyle section. She, too, however, acknowledges the movement's connection with #MeToo. "In a post #MeToo era, runways that once served up hefty doses of fantasy are finally having to get real."[18]

French-Algerian designer Faiza Bouguessa also takes a non-religious approach to her interpretations of modest fashion, focusing instead on the feelings of comfort and protection that clothing can provide for women all over the world – not just those who identify as Muslims. "Today I feel even women in the West want to feel protected," she tells me. "I think that because there has been so much sexualization of women's bodies for many years, with the porno-chic of Tom Ford and these kind of moments in fashion, women are now re-appropriating their bodies – they want to feel like they own their own bodies and they want to show that they have an appreciation for fashion but at the same time, they won't let other people control them; they want to be in control."

Having to make an effort to seek out clothing that's practical, offers coverage and aligns with mainstream fashion trends is a shopping struggle that men are, for the most part, unfamiliar with. Whether or not a blouse has a plunging neckline, a skirt has a too-short hemline or a shirt has long enough sleeves are hardly a part of the average man's shopping considerations. Take swimming shorts, for instance – while they're bountiful in the summer collections of men's sections, you'll rarely find them in the women's sections, even though many women, like myself, prefer to pair their swimsuits with shorts. Some do so to achieve a more modest appearance, while others are insecure with their body shapes and need extra coverage to feel confident. However, women's swim shorts have become synonymous with modesty – not with comfort or protection. The same goes for suits – while they're a staple in the wardrobes of working men, blazer-and-pants ensembles for women are often stamped with the word "modest", even though the garments in question are the same as their male counterparts.

At a time when female entrepreneurship is being championed, and the use of the phrase "girl boss" to denote ambitious and confident working women has been normalized, the modest fashion movement also offers a new form of power dressing. A 2018 *Racked* article about dress codes for women in politics implies that they often resort to wearing conservative and covered-up clothing because according to studies, those seen in shorter skirts or unbuttoned shirts may be deemed less intelligent and less competent. "Muted colors, long hemlines and covered shoulders, and perfectly coiffed hair" make the unofficial uniform for women in or seeking to hold political office, states the article.[19] But the trending styles on offer now are a departure from the dowdy skirt suit ensembles that defined previous feminine work wear: designers' and retailers' increased attention to modest wear has allowed for a greater variety of clothing that's both stylish and polished.

While you wouldn't bat an eye when seeing females in certain professional positions dressed modestly, some women who have long dressed this way for faith-based reasons – the real muses of the modest fashion movement – are still expected to justify and explain their reasons for covering up. In 2018, American-Muslim political activist and fashion blogger Hoda Katebi penned an opinion piece for *Glamour* magazine titled "When you wear a turtleneck, you're elegant; when I wear one, I'm oppressed". In it, she states, "I've become acutely aware of a painful double standard generated by what I choose to wear from the neck up: Non-Muslim women can sport modest clothing and be called professional or elegant, yet when Muslim women dress modestly, our taste and style is often overlooked… This plays into something that's quite common in fashion – the phenomenon of trends seeming to only get the rubber stamp of approval when Western, white people embrace them."[20]

When modesty first started surfacing on the runways, designers were the ones who were applauded for going against the grain and covering up their models, and celebrities were commended for choosing to wear high-necked, full-sleeved gowns on the red carpets, but the stylish millennial trendsetters who took to social media to flaunt their modest styles, often completed with a hijab, weren't as frequently referenced in mainstream fashion reports – even though many credit them for being the backbone of the modest fashion movement that has now gone global.

CHAPTER 2

HOW DRESSING MODESTLY BECAME A MAINSTREAM STYLE TREND

Winter 2018 is right around the corner, but in the various storefronts on London's Oxford Street there's a recurring theme of light layering, rather than a showcase of the usual winter jackets and coats. At Zara, models wear printed midi skirts paired with athletic hoodies and chunky trainers. Underneath a hoodie is a white turtleneck, and beneath a below-the-knee skirt, black leggings are worn. "The buzzword of the coming season is 'protection' – whether it's from the mean streets, or just from the elements, the options for cosseting and swathing yourself in layers of coverage are endless," reads *Marie Claire*'s trend report for the season.[1] A couple of blocks after Zara, the windows at Evans showcase glitzy, full-sleeved, calf-length kimonos over all-black ensembles. "Cover up: £40" (US $48) reads the accompanying sign. "Cover up" has been somewhat of an unofficial slogan of recent seasons, and it's hardly just a high-street styling trend. In fact, the groundwork had been set more than a year earlier by luxury fashion houses.

Rewind one year to autumn 2017 in the United Arab Emirates, where fashion magazine *Harper's Bazaar Arabia* has partnered with Dubai's Mall of the Emirates for its annual House of Bazaar event. The itinerary includes talks by prominent fashion designers and personalities, and I'm here to meet Serbian designer Roksanda Ilinčić, who launched her eponymous label in 2005 and has since excelled in creating dresses that celebrate demure glamor and have been shown each season on the runway at London Fashion Week. Her signature color-blocked kaftans and dresses have been donned by celebrities and high-profile women like Lady Gaga, Michelle Obama, Kate Middleton, Sonam Kapoor, Cate Blanchett and Jessica Biel. Today, the designer has chosen to respect the Dubai mall's conservative dress code without sacrificing her own style – she wears a bright yellow maxi dress from her upcoming spring/summer 2018 line, and tells me why conservatively cut fashion appeals to her: "It's actually something that is protecting us from the outside world," she says, mirroring a sentiment that I know is shared by many Muslims. "I don't like to expose too much skin, and I feel that actually covering the body feels much more mysterious and appealing than showing too much flesh."[2]

When I return to the mall later that evening for her runway show, I see that Roksanda now wears an ankle-length coral dress over a pair of wide-leg pants, achieving a look of sophisticated elegance. Five years prior, the pairing of a long dress with bell-bottom pants would have certainly been deemed "frumpy" at best by fashion critics.

"Frumpy" is one of the many words that were commonly used to describe modesty in fashion in the past, along with "matronly", "aged", "conservative", and "shapeless". Connie Wang, senior fashion features writer at *Refinery29*, explains that when women shop for garments for a new job or special occasion, many often subconsciously seek out modest options:

The thing is: I can't say it that way. If I tell these women that "modest fashion" is what they are actually looking for, most would recoil, as if I'm also telling them that they're old-fashioned or uptight... To anybody who doesn't prescribe to a conservative religious ideology, "modesty" evokes images of Muslim women cloaked in head-to-toe burkas, Mormon sister-wives in prairie gowns, or Orthodox Jews in long skirts and wigs.[3]

Modest fashion is feted at fashion weeks

There's one international fashion house that perhaps singlehandedly stripped modest fashion of its negative associations on a global scale and ushered in a new era of covered-up dressing on the catwalks: Gucci. When Alessandro Michele took the reins as creative director of the brand in January 2015, he gave the Italian label a whole new identity. Over the next few seasons, his collections displayed an array of seemingly Victorian-inspired long hemlines, high necklines and loose, voluminous cuts. Pleated midi skirts in leathers and metallics suddenly became all the rage, paired with printed pussy-bow blouses and layered knits. Gowns crafted from luxurious silks, chiffons and laces featured ruffled necklines and tiered skirts, and patterned suits gave female power-dressing a whole new meaning.

All of a sudden, the eclectic librarian look – baggy cardigan, high socks and all – was something to be emulated, rather than ridiculed, and "granny-chic" became a trending buzz phrase in the industry. Paired with smash-hit accessories like quilted bum bags (also known as fanny packs or belt bags), crystal-studded sunglasses, pearl-emblazoned leatherware and logo-adorned backpacks, the styles spoke to both nostalgic baby boomers and millennials.

It all climaxed at Gucci's autumn/winter 2018 show, where models wore clearly hijab-inspired headwear fashioned from the brand's silk scarves. Some wore ski masks that covered their faces (inspired by face veils, perhaps), and others turbans. Many critics admonished Michele's use of hijab- and niqab-inspired head coverings, labeling it as a disrespectful form of cultural appropriation. The Italian fashion house, from 2015 onwards, was just one of many high-end brands starting to take inspiration from, and at the same time to target as consumers, women in the Middle East.

"Brands' increasing tendencies to cater to Eastern markets were not purely inspired by aesthetics, or any newfound appreciation of Muslim culture or religion for that matter."

"Fifty years ago, few envisioned a day when Islamic fashions, including the burka, would be hot items on haute couture runways," writes Middle Eastern Studies professor and author Faegheh Shirazi.[4] Luxury brands' awareness of the abaya dates back to 2009 when John Galliano, the then artistic director of Christian Dior, debuted designer abayas in Paris worth between £4,000 and £8,000 (US $4,836 and US $9,671), alongside brands like Nina Ricci, Carolina Herrera and Alberta Ferretti, as part of a project commissioned by Saks Fifth Avenue's stores in Saudi Arabia. In 2012 alone, garments shown at fashion weeks by Yves Saint Laurent, Azzaro, Alice Temperley, A.F. Vandevorst, Zac Posen, Etro, Carlos Miele, Emilio de la Morena and Alexis Mabille all appeared to pay homage to Middle Eastern silhouettes, with kaftan-inspired cuts and hooded garments – some models' faces were even entirely covered on the catwalk.

Many women in the Middle East were overjoyed, believing that their heritage was finally being appreciated by designers in the top echelons of the industry. But brands' increasing tendencies to cater to Eastern markets were not purely inspired by aesthetics, or any newfound appreciation of Muslim culture or religion for that matter. As Faegheh points out, "Using Islam as a portal for selling modest yet highly stylish attire has proven a shrewd business decision."[5]

In 2016, Dolce & Gabbana debuted, rather unexpectedly, a line of abayas. Though the designs in question were neither new nor revolutionary, simply replicating, in many cases, styles already found at traditional Arab souqs (marketplaces) – with much costlier price tags – the move nonetheless marked a turning point in high fashion. These new, luxurious Italian-made abayas made headlines around the world, accompanied by the brand's photographs of Caucasian models covered head to toe in the black lace, embroidered and floral-printed fabrics, complete with Dolce & Gabbana leather handbags, stilettos, wedges and statement sunglasses. Models' heads were all wrapped in matching shaylas, or scarves.

In an article discussing the spring/summer 2019 fashion weeks, the *Guardian*'s associate fashion editor Jess Cartner-Morley observes that Milan hosted collections that were far more modesty-conscious than those previously shown at its historically titillating runway shows. "For decades, the mantra of Milan fashion week has been that sex sells," states the fashion editor. Labels like Prada, Salvatore Ferragamo and even Roberto Cavalli, whose entire brand DNA is centered on sex appeal, took a decidedly demure approach to their summer designs for 2019, spearheaded by Gucci:

> This recalibration away from banking on sexy pictures is backed up by the success of Gucci... It is about energy and modernity and individuality. It is sometimes geeky, sometimes lavish, sometimes sporty, sometimes costumey. Sexy is the one look it never does. I don't recall any fashion brand reaching the size Gucci is in fashion right now, while being so very deliberately not about sex.[6]

And when these new, covered-up offerings from Gucci were lapped up by wealthy, trend-conscious consumers, competing brands and more affordable labels were quick to follow in the fashion house's footsteps. Following the path of all retail trends, modest dressing started trickling down from runways to accessible luxury brands and, eventually, to the high street.

The Ramadan rush

Many international labels decided to test the modest fashion waters during Ramadan, the holy month when Muslims fast daily, celebrating the end of the month with the Eid al-Fitr holiday. Part and parcel of Ramadan, especially in the Middle East, are lavish buffets and all-night soirees where women dress up, feast and socialize with family and friends. British retailers have taken to calling it the "Ramadan Rush", as they witness a spike in sales due to Middle Eastern tourists shopping in their luxury boutiques – some even hire Arabic-speaking staff specifically for this month, which has been likened to the Christmas shopping season in the West.

New York label DKNY was the first big Western brand to announce a Ramadan-specific collection in summer 2014, when it showcased a collection of belted gowns, long blazers, floral separates in loose cuts and lightweight, open jackets. Sleeves reached elbows, and dresses covered the knees. American fashion label Tommy Hilfiger followed suit in 2015, when it released its first Ramadan capsule collection for women, featuring silk maxi dresses, pleated skirts and elegant blouses in jewel tones. Caterina Minthe, features editor at *Vogue Arabia*, points out that the brand "tiptoed" around traditional silhouettes of abayas and kaftans: "Ultimately, the entire collection displays a Western design house's off-kilter interpretation of Middle Eastern modest dressing."[7] In 2015, popular Spanish high-street brand Mango also debuted its first official Ramadan line, which again focused on Middle Eastern consumers, though silhouettes were not entirely in line with the conservative dress codes of some Arab countries. Year after year, sleeveless tunics and strappy gowns and jumpsuits feature in the brand's Ramadan collections, which seem to prioritize glamor and occasion wear over hijab-friendly silhouettes.

In 2018, Michael Kors jumped on the bandwagon, offering a limited-edition range of kaftan-inspired dresses for the Middle East market, along with a range of sparkling handbags suited for evening festivities. The same year, Swedish high-street retailer H&M also forayed into modest fashion. Unlike its predecessors on the high street, H&M didn't focus solely on the

Middle East; the range launched in sixty-nine different countries and was timed to release just before the month of Ramadan, although the word "Ramadan" wasn't used in any of the brand's marketing or campaign strategies, likely in an effort to appeal to a variety of shoppers. Designs included a pastel pink kaftan, a long tunic-and-pants set in a mint green jacquard fabric, a shimmering wrap skirt with ruffles in mustard yellow and a red kimono-inspired midi dress. The garments were priced slightly higher than those in the store's ordinary range, perhaps in efforts to target the spending power of wealthy Middle Eastern customers.

Another way mainstream retailers have incorporated modesty into their product ranges and marketing initiatives is by roping in famous faces in the Muslim fashion blogging world to help create limited-edition collections for their brands. In 2015, Japanese clothing label Uniqlo teamed up with British-born designer Hana Tajima (@hntaj on Instagram) to launch "Hana Tajima for Uniqlo". Hana, who converted to Islam at seventeen, wears the hijab, and the collection launched with a variety of overcoats, dresses, skirts, blouses and head coverings. Printed midi dresses, elegant turtleneck tunics, roomy wide-leg pants and kimono-style cardigans featured the brand's signature modern and minimalist aesthetic, and the garments acted as modest wear staples, yet were equally wearable for general consumers. Scarves were produced with the brand's special AIRism technology: a smart and breathable textile that releases heat and moisture. The designs first debuted in Southeast Asia before making their way to Europe and North America, and since then Hana has been designing seasonal collections for the label.

This collaboration was widely deemed more successful than other retailers' attempts to attract Muslim markets with flashy renditions of modest wear. "Instead of trying to capitalize on the market without engaging with Muslim communities (something other brands have drawn criticism for), the retailer enlisted Tajima to design a collection for them and star in its accompanying campaign," notes *Dazed* writer Ted Stansfield.[8] The strategy of employing famous influencers to help design and sell clothes has also been utilized by Middle Eastern labels. Kuwait-headquartered fashion brand Riva partnered with fashion blogger Ascia Al Faraj (@ascia on Instagram) in 2017 on a collection called "Modest by Ascia". The resulting sporty bomber jackets, slogan sweatshirts and jersey dresses embellished with iron-on patches were noticeably streetwear-inspired, targeting the brand's millennial shoppers. And, in 2019, Turkish e-commerce platform Modanisa teamed up with hijabi model Halima Aden (@halima on Instagram) to launch her first-ever design collaboration, which consisted of glamorous turbans and shawls.

Online e-commerce sites selling general luxury fashion (without any previous modest wear focus) were quick to follow high-end and high-street brands. In 2017, American high-end e-tailer Shopbop partnered with online Middle Eastern fashion magazine *Savoir Flair* and Dubai-based hijab-wearing fashion blogger Saufeeya Goodson (@saufeeya on Instagram) to promote its Ramadan offerings. Oriental rugs and bedouin-inspired props made up the backdrop of the shoot, which featured Saufeeya in decadent outfits such as a printed Diane von Furstenberg maxi dress, a Tibi shoulder-cut-out dress paired with a white turtleneck and white pants and a Melissa Odabash kaftan with embellished Rochas shoes. The same year, UK-headquartered luxury goods site Farfetch recruited New York-based hijabi influencer Maria Al-Sadek (@mariaalia on Instagram) to create a Ramadan style guide using products from its site, and the blogger picked out Valentino dresses and Sara Battaglia separates to model in a photoshoot that was accompanied with an interview about how she celebrates the religious holiday and what she looks for in an Eid outfit.

British luxury fashion e-tailer Net-a-Porter started promoting localized fashion campaigns during Ramadan in 2015, and in 2018, debuted its biggest

Ramadan campaign to date. It teamed up with ten international brands: Jenny Packham, Elie Saab, Reem Acra, Erdem, Zuhair Murad, Marchesa Notte, Safiyaa, Etro, Mary Katrantzou and Oscar de la Renta, who each created limited-edition Ramadan evening wear pieces just for Net-a-Porter. While the campaign may have been shoppable for a limited time only, the website has retained its dedicated modest wear section. When browsing the site's drop-down menu, you'll find "modest" nestled between "lingerie" and "pants". That same year, British high-street e-tailer ASOS celebrated Ramadan by sending out 20 percent discount codes to its customers, with a caveat: the code was only applicable to customers ordering from select countries in the Middle East and Asia.

In 2018, American multi-brand department store Macy's also launched modest wear, by American label Verona. As the partnership was neither seasonal nor tied to Ramadan, this signaled a more permanent step in cementing modest fashion as a regular retail category. "The need for modest clothing, especially everyday wear, is in such demand and many brands only saw the opportunity for occasion wear," the co-founder of Verona, Lisa Vogl, tells me. Maxi dresses and skirts, asymmetrical tunics, tiered collared blouses, bell-sleeved maxi cardigans and stylish pants are all in Verona's exclusive range for Macys.com, accompanied by satin, chiffon, pleated, printed and hand-dyed headscarves.

And, in 2019, Verona partnered with ASOS, which in May again took steps to recognize Ramadan. At the beginning of the holy month, the home page of the London-based e-commerce site featured a brown-skinned model in a tangerine-colored suit, python handbag and metallic heels, accompanied with the title "The Ramadan Edit". Just underneath was an image of London-based hijabi model Asha Mohamud, wearing a plaid maxi skirt, blue hoodie, white trainers and black turban. Clicking the photo took users to a page of exclusive-to-ASOS designs by Verona (including a range of headscarves), as well as a selection of modest pieces by ASOS's own in-house label.

Headscarves have their moment in the limelight

While the veil, or hijab, may not be a fixed part of every Muslim woman's wardrobe, it has nonetheless come to symbolize modest fashion on a global scale. American Eagle made a savvy business decision when it released its denim hijab in 2017, which sold out just two weeks after its launch. American Eagle is known for its jeans and distressed denim wear and its hijab campaign, titled "I can", also starred Halima Aden: the quintessential American-Muslim model. In 2018, Nike became the first major athletic label to release an activewear hijab. The fitted hood was crafted from lightweight sport material with holes for breathability, and designed with a length that allows the wearer to tuck it into the neckline of their clothing. The Nike Pro Hijab was introduced through a campaign that starred Emirati figure skater Zahra Lari, Emirati weightlifter Amna Al Haddad, Lebanese-German boxer Zeina Nassar and American fencing Olympian Ibtihaj Muhammad. This also marked a departure from previous brands' dependency on conventional Caucasian models for their modest wear imagery.

A household name when it comes to global brands, Nike's endorsement of modest fashion sealed the deal, paving the way for Muslim creatives to start reaping the benefits of a now worldwide fashion phenomenon. Knowing the target market better than their Western competitors, and inherently motivated to portray modest clothing in a truly fashionable light, the time was ripe for Muslims to claim the modest fashion retail space as their own.

Indonesian fashion designer Anniesa Hasibuan, for instance, made global headlines in 2016 when her brand became the first to showcase a modest wear collection at New York Fashion Week that featured all of the models wearing hijabs. Creamy silk gowns, enchanting capelets, elegant draped blouses and velvet pants were elevated with bold satin sashes, shiny silver, cream and salmon-toned hijabs, and the occasional pair of embellished aviator glasses. The moment was described as historic by the *New York Times*, CNN and the BBC. Hijabs weren't her only political statement – when casting her models for the following New York Fashion Week season, she selected only immigrants, or models born to immigrants, for her show.

In 2017, American-Muslim designer Ayana Ife was selected to compete in season sixteen of the prime-time reality TV series *Project Runway*. Throughout the weekly design challenges, the Utah-based, hijab-wearing designer stuck to her forte of modest fashion, even when it required her to create a couture gown out of unconventional safety materials. She made it all the way to the finals, bagging second place after showing her spring/summer 2018 collection at New York Fashion Week, where she cast an array of models reflecting different ethnicities and body types, including some who were styled with hijabs. And in 2018, Netflix documentary series *Follow This*, which shadows *BuzzFeed* journalists as they research niche news stories, released an episode called "Cover-up Couture", shedding light on the up-and-coming modest fashion industry. The episode follows the journey of BuzzFeed's senior culture writer Bim Adewunmi, who identifies as Muslim but doesn't adhere to strict modesty guidelines, as she interviews key players shaping the industry in America.

Grassroots modest fashion

Reina Lewis has observed that "a global modest fashion infrastructure of competing modest fashion weeks, fairs, and expos has grown out of what were once low-key, community-run gatherings."[9] One of the very first events founded to celebrate modest fashion in the United Kingdom was "Smoky not Smudgy", organized by the Islamic Society at Imperial College London. The first edition was held in 2007 as part of the university's annual charity week, and the one-day, women-only pampering event featured a fashion show, makeup classes, beauty treatments, hijab-styling workshops and a souq-style bazaar where modest fashion brands could sell their designs to visitors. Though Smoky not Smudgy was a student production, the platform highlighted a number of emerging local modest wear brands. It also hosted soon-to-be-famous modest fashion influencers, just a few years ahead of the global modest fashion boom, like Dina Torkia (@dinatokio on Instagram), who became one of the most famous Muslim fashion bloggers of the decade, Russian-Algerian modest fashion influencer Nabiila (@nabiilabee on Instagram), and Birmingham-based Saima Chowdhury (@saimasmileslike on Instagram), who presented the fashion show that year.

Doctor and former medical student Minaal Khan, an organizer of the event between 2011 and 2012, and fashion show volunteer between 2012 and 2017, observed that most of the participating brands, and attendees of the event, were Muslim. Embarking on new territory, where Islamic commodities would be shown on a modern, Western platform, organizers had to take into account traditional religious and cultural sensitivities, and balance these with the mainstream factors that go into producing a runway show. "We didn't have specific requirements and let the brands be creative and original – in one year the fashion show included modest swimwear, bridal wear and even niqabs," says Minaal. The only two rules laid down by the university's Islamic Society, she says, were that no men be permitted entry to the event, and that the only music playing during the runway show be a cappella, to appease the traditional Muslim view that instrumental music is "haram", or forbidden.

For the 2017 Adelaide Fashion Festival in Australia, Technical and Further Education in South Australia (TAFE SA) teamed up with the Islamic Fashion Institute in Bandung, Indonesia, to bring over six Indonesian fashion designers to participate at the festival. According to TAFE SA fashion and costume lecturer Jane Hardacre, "The economics suggest that it's a growing population – there's a growing demand for modest fashion and we're responding to that."[10]

The International Fashion and Design Council (IFDC), a global platform headquartered in Dubai, launched a program called iFash in 2015 to help instill modest fashion as a permanent retail category in major department stores. The Dubai branch of French fashion school Esmod has incorporated this into their curriculum, and teaches fashion students how to create modest garments.

In summer 2017, the IFDC partnered with Italy's Torino Fashion Week to introduce a modest wear category on Italian runways for the first time – the unprecedented occasion brought together modest wear labels from all over the world, including the UAE, Oman, Bahrain, Malaysia, Indonesia, Turkey, Canada and America. While Torino may not be a fashion capital at the level of Paris or Milan, some of the labels were recipients of awards from sponsors like LVMH, Debenhams and AT Films. Australian designer Ilham A. Ismail won the AT Films award and stated, "By coming to Torino, I've accomplished spreading my message of coexistence and peace up north of the globe. Coming all the way from Australia, we've been united with other amazing Muslim designers from all over the world. We've made new friendships and as a group we delivered a message about how powerful us Muslim women really are."[11]

A year later, the IFDC hosted an event at the Milano Fashion Library called the Milan Fashion Week Modest Soiree. Bow Boutique from Saudi Arabia, Al Nisa Designs from the United States, Chantique from Brunei and Luya Moda from the United Kingdom were all highlighted at this event which took modest fashion a step further into being recognized and celebrated on a mainstream European platform.

Modest fashion weeks

Franka Soeria and Ozlem Sahin were two of the first entrepreneurs to recognize a major gap in the worldwide fashion week market and the immense potential for modesty-themed events. In 2015, the duo started conceptualizing Modest Fashion Week, which they launched in Istanbul in 2016, followed by events in Jakarta, London and Dubai. Realizing they would need a great deal of glamor to be taken seriously, they hired a team from Mercedes-Benz Fashion Week. "We were the first to use the term 'Modest Fashion Week,'" says Ozlem, adding that modest fashion was previously tied to "hijab" or "Islam", and that modesty can be a lifestyle irrespective of religion.

I meet the duo at a beachside teahouse a few weeks ahead of their Modest Fashion Week in Dubai in 2019. Franka is Indonesian, with a background in fashion journalism, and Ozlem is Turkish, with experience in fashion-related start-ups. "Me and Ozlem are the perfect representation of modest fashion: she doesn't wear hijab, I wear hijab; she's European, I'm Asian," says Franka, who accessorizes her all-black outfit and fitted black hijab with a mustard floral-printed scarf tied loosely around her neck. Ozlem wears her curly blonde hair open, and oversized pearl earrings, a gold septum nose ring and bejeweled black heels complement her monochrome outfit. The two operate under their company Think Fashion and created ModestCatwalk.com to give their designers an online e-commerce outlet. While Think Fashion flew out bloggers and paid for their hotel stays in the past to help spread hype and awareness for the events, it's a practice they say they won't be continuing. "Now it's not about the numbers – the most important thing is the designers," says Franka. "We are self-funded," adds Ozlem. It helps to partner with brands that have big budgets – Think Fashion recruited Turkish modest fashion e-commerce platform Modanisa to sponsor and host

Istanbul Modest Fashion Week in 2016, London Modest Fashion Week in 2017 and Jakarta Modest Fashion Week in 2018. In 2019, Modanisa parted ways with Think Fashion and hosted its own Modest Fashion Week in Istanbul, which I had the opportunity to attend.

Turkey is situated between Europe and Asia, the prime location for a celebration of modern Muslim fashion. Pastel suits completed by printed silk scarves, patterned maxi dresses with oversized belts and sequin-studded kaftans, all worn with head coverings, were some of the outfits I saw at the city's Zorlu Center, where Istanbul Modest Fashion Week took place. Modest fashion influencers and bloggers like Australia's Yasmin Jay (@yasssminjay on Instagram), Canada's Hanan Tehaili (@hanantehaili on Instagram) and England's Basma Kahie (@basma_k on Instagram) flew in to attend the event, where they were dressed by some of the brands showcasing there. Along with runway presentations from designers hailing from London, Indonesia, Malaysia, Kazakhstan, Spain and Turkey, the event featured panel talks, including one suggesting that Turkey is the world's capital of modest fashion. While the event brought in brands with no affiliation to Modanisa's e-tail website, it also featured brands and personalities who had collaborated with the online platform – like Halima Aden, who debuted Halima X Modanisa, her first-ever design collaboration, on the opening day of the event, and Dubai-based Rabia Z, who created a sustainable fashion collection with Modanisa.

Haute Elan, the first European e-commerce platform dedicated to modest wear, launched its own London Modest Fashion Week in 2017. The company's founder and CEO, Romanna Bint-Abubaker, followed a model similar to the one conceptualized by Think Fashion's Franka and Ozlem, and recruited over 200 designers to participate. Mirroring the traditional runway setup of mainstream fashion weeks, London Modest Fashion Week was different in that its strict vetting process allowed only brands that conformed to loose modesty guidelines to participate. "No backs showing, no deep necks, no sheer garments and no extremely fitted designs. Short sleeves are okay, because we say there are levels of modesty, as long as it's not sleeveless and not with cap-sleeves – they have to be longer than that," Romanna explains when I visit her office in Wimbledon.

Franka and Ozlem have similar modesty guidelines for brands participating at Think Fashion's various modest fashion weeks. "Nothing transparent or sleeveless, and lengths up to the ankles. If it's shorter we always advise leggings," says Ozlem. Modesty-themed fashion weeks also deviate from their mainstream counterparts when it comes to charges incurred by designers. Franka explains that while a designer may have to pay upwards of US $200,000 to host a show at New York Fashion Week, Think Fashion's runway spots are sold to designers for US $4,000. "We wanted to make it cheaper, but production is expensive," she says.

Front rows of the runway shows at these modesty-themed fashion weeks appear much like the major international shows, filled with stylish fashion personalities but, in contrast to mainstream fashion weeks, with distinctly modest appearances. A range of trending outfits, featuring white leather ankle boots, sporty trainers, gold pointed heels, bright yellow culottes, fitted plaid pants, boyfriend jeans and even luxe tracksuits are visible, along with many head coverings (and a few face veils) tied in a variety of different ways. Bloggers sit with their smartphones held up high, documenting the catwalk shows for their blogs and social media pages.

At Haute Elan London Modest Fashion Week in 2018, the front row included an unlikely guest: Lindsay Lohan, wearing a black hijab. The press coverage of the week was extensive: "First ever Muslim-friendly modest fashion week held in London",[12] "London Modest Fashion Week: Faith can be fashionable",[13] "Modest fashion crosses cultures",[14] and "Lindsay Lohan

"While modesty-themed fashion weeks may have a predominantly Muslim audience, and are largely painted by the media as 'Muslim' events, they're attracting women of all faiths."

shocks with hijab at London Modest Fashion Week"[15] were some of the headlines published by the *Huffington Post*, the *Telegraph*, *Arab News* and *Business Insider*.

And while modesty-themed fashion weeks may have a predominantly Muslim audience, and are largely painted by the media as "Muslim" events, they're attracting women of all faiths. I learn this in my adopted city of Dubai, within a few seconds of being seated in the front row at Dubai Modest Fashion Week in March 2019.

"Everything's just so beautiful," says a young woman in a strong American accent, as she holds up her iPhone to film the models passing along the runway in front of her. Robed in a knee-length red dress with an attached cape, pearl-emblazoned sunglasses and a white Gucci handbag, Alexa Sue-Anne Dudley (@1998miss on Instagram) embodies the excitement of a child in a candy shop, as she oohs and aahs over the floor-length gowns and abaya-inspired ensembles on the rooftop of the Emerald Palace Kempinski in Dubai. It's the American blogger's first time in the Middle East, and she traveled here just to attend Dubai Modest Fashion Week. Alexa is an Apostolic Christian, pre-med student and modest style blogger living in the state of Tennessee. Her modesty guidelines, she tells me as we chat in between shows, are that garments must cover her chest, shoulders and knees. "And I don't wear pants, I only wear dresses and skirts, because in the Bible it says that it's a shame for a woman to dress like a man," she says, referencing a verse in the Bible that commands that women should not wear distinctively male clothing, and vice versa. "Whatever it is that I choose to wear, I want to make sure that it's pleasing to God," says Alexa.

Alexa agrees that it's Muslim women who are currently fronting the modest fashion movement, even though modesty is central to other religions as well. "We have a lot of common ground, that's why I'm so happy to be here. All that I've encountered is inclusivity, and I think that modest fashion is a bridge for all women," she tells me. It's the eve of the young blogger's twenty-first birthday, and her mother, who came along on the trip as her chaperone, is equally in awe of all the glamor. She too dresses conservatively. "In our faith, growing up, we had no television, [but] this has completely changed the conversation," says Alexa's mother, gesturing to her iPhone.

Fashion weeks aren't the only platforms celebrating this global style revolution. During autumn 2018, modest wear enjoyed its moment in the American limelight when the Contemporary Muslim Fashions exhibition launched at the de Young Museum, part of the Fine Arts Museums of San Francisco (FAMSF). "'Contemporary Muslim Fashions' is an overdue, much-needed exploration of a multifaceted topic as yet largely unexplored by museums," stated former director of the FAMSF, Max Hollein, to the *National* newspaper in the UAE. "The Muslim fashion scene is extremely vibrant and influential, with some of the most stunning works I've recently seen; it seemed like a blatant omission that this topic had yet to be explored by a major institution."[16] The exhibition, which ran until January 2019 in San Francisco before moving to the Museum Angewandte Kunst in Frankfurt, Germany, conveyed the message of Islam as a multicultural faith, encompassing a diverse array of fashions inspired by different interpretations of holy texts. Key modest wear designers – and not just Muslim ones – from across the globe were highlighted in the exhibition, which even included mainstream Western brands like Nike and Dolce & Gabbana.

Visitors could also shop modest fashion-themed paraphernalia, including a coffee-table book co-written by Reina Lewis entitled *Contemporary Muslim Fashions*, Michigan-based photographer Langston Hues' book *Modest Street Fashion*, a promotional poster featuring American model Halima Aden, a T-shirt decorated with the word "beauty" in Arabic script and a scarf by New

York activist label Slow Factory, emblazoned with the words "Banned Countries", in reference to Donald Trump's 2018 travel ban, which prohibited residents of certain Muslim countries from traveling to the United States. This was symbolic of the dichotomy at play – on one hand, the nation's president was pushing to build walls to keep immigrants out, and on the other, a prestigious institution within his borders was celebrating the very diversity he was hoping to eradicate.

Max Hollein told the *New York Times* that although the aim of the exhibition was to share cultural fashions, rather than provoke anti-Muslim sentiments, the museum did witness some strong reactions over email, proclaiming that the timing wasn't right to celebrate Muslim culture in America, and that the exhibition would endorse the oppression of women. Nonetheless, tons of positive press accompanied the opening of the exhibition. "Ten years from now, we may look at 'Contemporary Muslim Fashions' at the de Young Museum as a turning point in American history, where mainstream America, despite an angry minority, embraced its 'others' at the highest institutions," writes non-Muslim founder and designer of Slow Factory, Celine Semaan.[17]

Muslim models go mainstream

Fronting the campaign for the Contemporary Muslim Fashions exhibition at FAMSF was hijab-wearing model Halima Aden. In the years leading up to 2020, Halima has been perhaps the most frequently featured face of modest fashion in the West. The American-Somali teenager's success story is widely celebrated among many millennial Muslims. Born in a refugee camp in Kenya, Halima moved to the United States with her parents at the age of six. In high school, she was voted Homecoming Queen, and she competed in the Miss Minnesota USA Pageant in 2016. Halima wore her hijab throughout the beauty pageant, donning a burkini during the swimwear segment of the competition. Though she didn't win the crown, she made national headlines and was instantly heralded as a national face of diversity. It still came as a shock to most industry professionals when she was recruited by renowned international model management firm, IMG Models, and an even bigger surprise when she made her fashion week debut at Kanye West's Yeezy Season 5 presentation at New York Fashion Week in February 2017, enveloped in an ankle-length fur coat and a fitted black headscarf.

What could have been a one-off opportunity didn't end there – Halima was booked for the runway shows of fashion labels like Max Mara and Alberta Ferretti in Milan, for which she wore her hijab throughout, while robed in luxe trench coat and pants ensembles. She was also the one hijabi face in a beauty campaign for Rihanna's Fenty Beauty brand. Later that year, she became the first hijab-wearing model to star on a *Vogue* cover, appearing on the cover of the June edition of *Vogue Arabia*. She also impressed French fashion editor and former editor-in-chief of *Vogue Paris*, Carine Roitfeld, and starred on the cover of the tenth edition of her *CR Fashion Book*. Not only did Halima take the fashion industry by storm, she also used her newfound fame to shed light on world issues of substance far beyond fashion. In 2018 she became a UNICEF ambassador, advocating for refugee children and their rights at a time when President Trump was separating children from their parents at the Mexican border. That year, she also spoke at the first-ever TEDx event at a refugee camp, which took place at Kenya's Kakuma Refugee Camp – the same camp Halima herself was born at in 1997.

While the model has traveled often to Dubai and Abu Dhabi, the first time I see her is in Turkey, at Modanisa Istanbul Modest Fashion Week in April 2019. It's the first show of the first day, and uber-stylish women dressed conservatively but glamorously sit huddled along the raised benches on either side of the catwalk. Most of the women, who are modest fashion bloggers and influencers, have their smartphones in hand – some are snapping photos of the runway, but many are taking selfies. That is, until they catch a glimpse of Halima at the back of the catwalk, strutting down the runway in a black, sequined design by Refka – the in-house label from Modanisa. The phones are instantly flipped, as guests focus on the world-famous face of the modest fashion movement.

As the first mainstream hijabi runway model, Halima had to educate those within the industry about her modesty guidelines – and while she brought her own hijabs with her for her first few fashion-week trips, designers soon started making headscarves especially for her. As we chat over Turkish coffee while I interview her for Abu Dhabi-based *Luxury* magazine in a quaint hotel off the coast of the Bosporus River in Turkey, she tells me that for her first time walking for Max Mara in Milan, she brought her own headscarf. The second time, the designer had created one for her to wear. "And coming back the third time, he had ten or twelve of us girls – I wasn't the only one with her hair covered, it became part of the look," she says.[18]

Was Halima herself a muse? It's possible. For spring/summer 2018, all of Marc Jacobs' models donned headscarves wrapped as elaborate turbans on the runway at New York Fashion Week. "Head pieces were being celebrated – it's no longer a 'Muslim women head covering' thing, you know, turbans are in," Halima tells me excitedly.[19]

A spotlight on Halima and headscarves allowed more hijabi women to try modeling. Belgium-based Algerian Feriel Moulai, who I also meet at Modanisa Istanbul Modest Fashion Week, became the first hijabi model to walk at Paris Fashion Week in September 2018. "It was a huge thing for me, because it was a first time for a girl with hijab, and I was proud because France is not really comfortable with the hijab," she says. Feriel tells me that since she was a child, she had always dreamed of modeling, but was afraid of being near-naked and exposed. It's only after she started wearing hijab at the age of twenty that she began to seriously pursue modeling. For the Muslim holy month of Ramadan in 2019, Feriel starred in her biggest job to date – a global fashion campaign by UK-based luxury e-tailer, Farfetch.

Another acclaimed Muslim model in the limelight is hijab-wearing Mariah Idrissi. Born to Pakistani and Moroccan parents in London, Mariah was working in retail at London's Westfield Shopping Mall when she was approached by a casting agent. A few weeks later, she was recruited for H&M's "Close the Loop" campaign to promote recycling clothing, along with a group of other diverse models. When the campaign released in autumn 2015, Mariah became an overnight celebrity, making international headlines as the first hijabi model.

I meet Mariah during one of her trips to Dubai, when she is in town for shoots with *Harper's Bazaar Arabia* and *Grazia Middle East*. Given her Instagram profile bursting with edgy portraits and high-profile industry event attendances, I'm slightly intimidated – will the world's first hijabi model be stuck up and snooty? But the young woman who walks into the café is warm and exuberant, immediately apologizing for being a few minutes late. She wears a green printed blouse tucked into high-waisted mom jeans; large silver hoop earrings and a salmon-pink headwrap frame her face, which has hardly any makeup. Mariah is down-to-earth – she wears sporty trainers, and asks if there are any budget-friendly nail salons in the area. Prior to landing her first modeling job with H&M, she never imagined that she would be a model, and instead aspired to pursue film-making, to help put a spotlight on under-represented communities. "I wanted my specialty to be telling stories that have not been told, about our people [Muslims] in the West – there's no positive representation at all," she says. "And then when the H&M thing came up I thought, okay, it's fashion, that's still creative arts, I can tell my stories as a model by just promoting the message of representation."

Rather than taking on every exciting modeling job that comes her way, Mariah chooses those that reflect her message. "I've always had a voice attached to every shoot I've done," she says. In September 2017 for instance, she was the cover girl of the UAE's *Emirates Woman* magazine, decked out in luxury brands like Gucci, Hermès, Prada and Miu Miu. The cover story addressed Mariah's thoughts about the lack of diversity in the fashion industry, and discussed her status as a positive role model for Muslim women. Mariah's Islamic beliefs, she says, guide her in every area of life, even when it comes to modeling in the fashion industry. "Being a Muslim, as much as fashion is a very secular industry, my faith is what drives me in every decision I make," she says. "I couldn't call myself a real Muslim if my day to day job that I put so much time and energy into, didn't have anything deeper – there has to be meaning behind it."[20]

Halima and Mariah helped pave a path that other Muslim women would soon take, wearing their faith with pride in the form of a headscarf while being photographed for some of the world's top fashion publications. "2017 was definitely the year of the hijabi model," notes online Arab women's lifestyle magazine *About Her*, in an article introducing yet another London-based hijab-wearing model, Shahira Yusuf.[21] Shahira was scouted by Storm Models – the same agency that first discovered supermodel Kate Moss. Before even booking any modeling jobs, Shahira was paraded in the press as the next Halima Aden, nabbing interviews with *Vogue*, the BBC and the *Guardian*, and featured on the covers of *Grazia*, *Emirates Woman* and *Observer Magazine*. "The fashion industry is a patriarchy," she told the *Guardian*. "Mine is a conversation all women should be encouraged to have, about how comfortable they are showing their skin and their bodies, how comfortable they are being portrayed as sexual objects. I shouldn't be listened to just because I'm religious. This conversation isn't just for Muslim women."[22]

They have opinions, they have voices and they have social media platforms where they can reach their millions of followers. Like plus-size American model Ashley Graham, who raises awareness for body positivity, the hijab-wearing models emerging on the international fashion scene will not settle for the traditional role of being likened to a clothes hanger – though Halima tells me that her aunt once jokingly called her "Halima the hanger". "She's like, 'so, in America, walking around in heels is considered a job?' But I feel like what's considered modeling has changed so much with social media," says Halima. "Modeling has become so much more, it's no longer about photoshoot–model–buy. I speak at schools and at university campuses, there's some work that I do with UNICEF – it doesn't pay me but it's advocacy, it fulfills me in the places that really matter."[23]

Models who cover their hair may never experience the normalcy enjoyed by their white-skinned, bare-headed peers in the industry. Their hijabs are identifying markers on their heads that are more than just conversation-starters – they put these women on a pedestal that celebrates diversity and inclusion, and at the same time, makes them particularly vulnerable to critique. When American clothing label Banana Republic launched a line of hijabs in 2019, it recruited New York-based hijabi model Fatuma Yusuf to model the designs for its website. In one image, Fatuma wears a ribbed T-shirt with sleeves cut above the elbow, and in another, she wears a dress with a slit that exposes some of her leg. While many of Fatuma's social media followers applauded her modeling feat, other Muslim women took to Instagram to express their disdain that the hijab wasn't being represented in line with its traditional guidelines (all skin covered except a woman's hands, feet and face). The controversy quickly went viral, after which Banana Republic deleted or cropped the images that had sparked debate.

CHAPTER 3

WHY COVER UP?

When I was a child, I used to be in awe of women who wore bikinis while at the pool or beach. They were almost naked, yet were lounging in a public space, and in my childish mind, that was the ultimate antithesis of modesty. These women were asserting their femininity in a way that was rebellious and alluring, and I wanted in – but I kept my secret fantasy to myself. Then, when my baby cousin received a micro-mini bikini on her first birthday in New Jersey, it all erupted, and my elder cousin and I both confronted our mothers, arguing that we too should be allowed to wear bikinis. My mother and aunt sat us both down and explained that the private parts of our body should be covered, not accentuated. "When you're married, you can wear whatever you want," our mothers told us, explaining that until then, we would need to safeguard our bodies and our reputations, ensuring we stayed moral and pure. Wearing decent clothes was crucial to this, and bikinis, like shorts, tank tops and mini dresses, didn't make the cut. While allusions were made to "good Muslim girls", we weren't then made aware of the actual religious stipulations regarding modest dress – we naively thought we just had strict mothers.

When a woman chooses to dress modestly, her decision is often influenced by her religion, which may refer to covering up – be it explicitly or implicitly – within holy texts. It's clear that there are far more similarities than differences in the foundations of the three Abrahamic religions – Islam, Christianity and

Judaism. Firstly, they all place a focus on female modesty: though the terms may differ, "haya", "modesty" and "tzniut" are all intended to safeguard the chastity of women. Men are assumed to be easily vulnerable to sexual temptation, and for this reason, women must cover up. And while semantics may vary, with some texts advising women to cover their "adornments" and others specifying the prohibition of "gold" and "pearls", the overall message in the scriptures is one and the same: don't show off, be it your body parts or your material riches. From the neck up, meanwhile, it's evident that the concept of veiling had a place in the early traditions of all three religions.

What the holy books say

Islam

There is no single definition of modesty that all Muslims adhere to. In the Quran, the best-known verse pertaining to modesty is Surah An-Nur 24:31:

"And tell the believing women to reduce [some] of their vision and guard their private parts and not expose their adornment except that which [necessarily] appears thereof and to wrap [a portion of] their headcovers over their chests and not expose their adornment except to their husbands, their fathers, their husbands' fathers, their sons, their husbands' sons, their brothers, their brothers' sons, their sisters' sons, their women, that which their right hands possess, or those male attendants having no physical desire, or children who are not yet aware of the private aspects of women. And let them not stamp their feet to make known what they conceal of their adornment. And turn to Allah in repentance, all of you, O believers, that you might succeed."

The other often quoted verse in the Quran is Surah Al-Ahzab 33:59:

"O Prophet, tell your wives and your daughters and the women of
the believers to bring down over themselves [part] of their outer
garments. That is more suitable that they will be known and not be
abused. And ever is Allah Forgiving and Merciful."[1]

While many Muslims consider the headscarf to be mandatory for a Muslim
woman's appearance in public, many others contend that it isn't a binding
requirement, or believe that the rules were intended for a time and place,
or for a particular group of women like the Prophet Muhammad's wives.[2]
Reza Aslan goes so far as to argue that "during the Prophet's lifetime, no
other women in the Ummah observed hijab," and that the veiling was neither
required nor practiced by Muslim women until many years after the Prophet's
death, as a result of the Quranic interpretations of male authoritarian legal
and religious scholars.[3] But most Muslims are in overall agreement about the
requirement for modesty in general, for both men and women. In Islam, the
Arabic word "haya" is most commonly used to represent modesty, and traditional interpretations of the term include the avoidance of perfume, cosmetics
and jewelry in the presence of men who are not of close kin. More general
definitions of haya include being respectable and reserved with members of
the opposite sex, without any verbal vulgarity or physical contact.

Overall, the concept of haya is intended to shield or separate the male and
female genders from one another, to prevent temptation and safeguard against
illicit sexual activity. This religion-rooted concept of retaining a sense of
modesty when in the company of the opposite gender is why many conservative
Muslim parents forbid their children from dating and attending mixed-gender
events (and sometimes even mainstream schools). Religious families living in

non-Muslim-majority countries especially struggle with implementing these values in their children's teachings. *Muslim Ink* journalist Umm Rashid writes, "For a generation that has been brought up on risqué offerings from Hollywood and Bollywood, music channels, TV soaps and talk shows, suggestive advertisements and explicit content on the internet, the Islamic concept of haya might seem like an outdated, impossibly archaic ideal."[4]

It's this tradition of haya that is used to justify segregated social events in Arab and other Muslim cultures, and it's also the faith-based reasoning behind the cultural usage of the abaya, which is a typically black outer garment intended to cover the female form. There's a widespread misconception, especially in the West, that the plain black abaya is the sole garment in the traditional Muslim woman's wardrobe. This is far from the case – Middle Eastern women certainly indulge in other forms of fashion, be it under their abayas, or for female-only events, where they're permitted to wear clothing and swimwear that show more skin, meaning that the otherwise taboo garments of mini dresses, backless gowns and bikinis become permissible for these all-women occasions. At traditional Arabic weddings, for instance, functions are usually segregated, with women arriving to wedding halls cloaked in abayas, only to remove them once inside, revealing glamorous gowns and dresses, perhaps with backless designs, bare shoulders, plunging necklines and above-the-knee lengths. Just before the groom and male family members enter the venue, an announcement is made and the women quickly put their abayas back on. And in terms of swimwear, many water parks in Arab countries, such as Dubai's Wild Wadi, host dedicated ladies' nights, where staff, lifeguards and guests are all female, allowing conservative Muslim women to dress in the swimwear of their choosing.

In Muslim cultures, females, rather than males, are usually the ones tasked with embodying the concept of haya in their families and communities, as Reina Lewis explores:

Though concepts of modesty, and attendant codes of honor and shame logically require modesty from both genders, it is most often women who have borne the burden of representing and protecting family and by extension community morality, especially as mothers charged with transmitting Muslim/community values to the next generation.[5]

But it's important to note that the celebration of feminine beauty is not wholly discouraged in Islam. Egyptian anthropology professor Fadwa El Guindi, who offers a thorough interpretation of Surah An-Nur in her book *Veil: Modesty, Privacy and Resistance*, claims, "Within Islam, a woman's sexuality does not diminish her respectability. Islam in fact supports this combined image in womanhood. What Islamic morality forbids is the public flaunting of sexuality."[6] She points out that one verse in Surah An-Nur prohibits women from "stamping their feet", to refrain from making noise with their anklets. The verse, she claims, is a response to the practice at that time when women may have jingled their anklets to attract men – which is impermissible as it could be arousing. She believes that within this context, it is the act of stamping and jingling one's anklets with the intention of attracting men that is forbidden, rather than the general wearing of anklets.

Many Muslim women who dress fashionably and indulge in cosmetics believe that they are operating within the parameters of Islam, since beauty is appreciated by God. "Allah is beautiful and loves beauty" is the hadith (a tradition or saying of the Prophet Muhammad) used to justify this belief. This quote is one of the chief arguments presented by millennial Muslim bloggers who refute the argument that modesty is contradictory to the fashion world; it's even used as the opening text for the fashion section of *Modestly*, the autobiography written by modest fashion blogger Dina Torkia. In Islam, women are thus encouraged to look beautiful, just as long as they don't flaunt their sexuality in front of men. And while women may be the perceived vessels through which values of modesty are embodied and passed on, Muslim men are also advised to keep up modest appearances, particularly through the avoidance of wearing gold, big rings, colorful patterns (so that other men are not distracted during group prayers) and fabrics made from silk, according to various hadith.[7]

Exact definitions of modesty and subsequent dress codes differ from culture to culture. And while there's a focus on physical appearance, the term haya also refers to inner modesty. In fact, this idea is common across the Abrahamic faiths of Judaism, Christianity and Islam, but because the black burka that engulfs a woman's body from head to toe has become synonymous with Muslim dress in the mainstream media, other faiths' beliefs about modesty, both the outer and inner kinds, are often overlooked.

Christianity

The Quran is to Islam what the Bible is to Christianity. But unlike the Quran, which is believed to be the direct word of God as narrated to the Prophet Muhammad, parts of the Bible are thought to have been written by a variety of authors, disciples of Jesus Christ and early Christians. Female modesty is mentioned in numerous places in the Bible. A verse in the New Testament reads:

> And I want women to be modest in their appearance. They should wear decent and appropriate clothing and not draw attention to themselves by the way they fix their hair or by wearing gold or pearls or expensive clothes. For women who claim to be devoted to God should make themselves attractive by the good things they do.[8]

Another reads:

> Don't be concerned about the outward beauty of fancy [elaborate]
> hairstyles, expensive jewellery, or beautiful clothes. You should
> clothe yourselves instead with the beauty that comes from within,
> the unfading beauty of a gentle and quiet spirit, which is so precious
> to God. This is how the holy women of old made themselves
> beautiful. They put their trust in God and accepted the authority of
> their husbands.[9]

Like the Quran, verses of the Bible mentioning female modesty are linked
with patriarchal family systems, which were typical of the cultures of those
historical times. Today's followers of these religions often interpret the verses
and adapt the general messages they convey to present-day circumstances.

The Bible also mandates the covering of hair for women under certain
circumstances:

> A man dishonors his head if he covers his head while praying or
> prophesying. But a woman dishonors her head if she prays or
> prophesies without a covering on her head, for this is the same as
> shaving her head. Yes, if she refuses to wear a head covering, she
> should cut off all her hair! But since it is shameful for a woman to
> have her hair cut or her head shaved, she should wear a covering.[10]

Early depictions of Christian saints feature women with covered heads, and
yet veiled Christian women are a rare sight today. Texas-based New Testament Studies professor Daniel B. Wallace considers the head covering to be
symbolic and argues that when the message of Christianity was just starting

to spread, the wearing of female head coverings was already widely practiced. "The important thing to note is that the early church adopted a convention already in use in society and gave it a distinctively Christian hue," he writes.[11] Veiled women, he argues, would not have felt out of place during the time of early Christianity, whereas today, they would stand out. Still, while head coverings may not be worn by the majority of modern-day Christians, relatively modest dress codes are still generally adhered to by all people when attending religious events and visiting churches, where women are often encouraged to wear longer skirts and dresses, and men are advised against wearing shorts or jeans, which may be seen as disrespectful.

Mormons, or members of the Church of Jesus Christ of Latter-day Saints (LDS), are usually classified as a branch of Christianity, as they generally follow the teachings of Jesus Christ and regard the Bible to be the word of God, though they follow a special LDS edition of the King James translation. Modesty is integral to the faith, and the church's official website advises:

> In addition to avoiding clothing that is revealing, we should avoid extremes in clothing, appearance, and hairstyle. In dress, grooming, and manners, we should always be neat and clean, never sloppy or inappropriately casual. We should not disfigure ourselves with tattoos or body piercings. Women who desire to have their ears pierced should wear only one pair of modest earrings.[12]

Carol F. McConkie, former First Counsellor in the Young Women General Presidency in the LDS Church, describes female modesty as being vital to avoid illicit sexual behavior. "Immodest appearance and behavior will often arouse sexual feelings and will break down barriers and invite increased temptation to break the law of chastity," she says.[13]

Judaism

In Judaism, the Hebrew word "tzniut", meaning "to conceal", is used to connote modesty in both dress and behavior, and is similar to the Arabic word haya, which also doesn't restrict its definition to the bodily appearance. The framework for the concept of tzniut is rooted in the *halakhoth*, or laws of the Torah. According to fashion editor and *Vogue* contributor Michelle Honig, who considers herself an Orthodox Jew, basic modesty guidelines in Judaism include the covering of the knees, elbows and collarbone.[14] American Rabbi Norman Lamm has stated that tzniut is a defining characteristic of the Jewish religion, and that the term has three dimensions: striving "for hiddenness as a prerequisite for holiness", a sense of personal dignity and self-respect and "respect for the inviolability of the personal privacy of the individual."[15] In terms of attire, Orthodox Jews believe that trousers are forbidden garments for women, who must wear long skirts and dresses instead. Veils have a place in Jewish dress codes, too: women are typically encouraged to start covering their hair once they are married, as the sight of a woman's hair can be a sexual stimulus for men.[16] Practicing Jews who classify themselves as Hasidic are generally more rigid in their followings of sacred Jewish texts and command-ments, and some Hasidic Jews in Hungary and Ukraine even shave their heads after their weddings, so that it will not be possible for any of their hair to show and cause potential temptation among other men.[17]

Some modern Jewish Rabbis have imposed stricter, more literal inter-pretations of tzniut: British Rabbi Eliyahu Falk for instance, has written, "even a minor exposure is provocative and a serious shortcoming in tzniut. It is therefore forbidden for the neckline of the garment to extend even half a centimetre beyond the permitted level."[18] Rav Yitzchak Yaakov Fuchs meanwhile, believes that tzniut forbids the wearing of bright colors, especially red.[19] A more colloquial definition of tzniut is presented by Jewish author

"Though recent proposed headscarf bans in places like France and Quebec and niqab bans in countries like Belgium, Austria, Denmark and Sri Lanka have triggered international headlines, the symbol of the veil has been equally divisive within Muslim-majority countries."

Gila Manolson, who says its purpose is to "look good, but without flaunting yourself. It urges you to downplay your body in order to reveal your soul. This doesn't mean wearing shapeless, drab clothing. It means being attractive in a way that draws attention past your physicality to your personhood."[20] As with Muslims and Christians, there is a diverse spectrum of the religion, and not every follower practices modesty in the same way. Many liberal Jews, Muslims and Christians dress in ways that may not stand out as modest at all, but these individuals may identify as religious in other ways nonetheless.

How Muslim women's dress codes evolved in the twentieth century

It's spring 2014, and I'm seated in one of the front rows of the auditorium in the main university building of University of London's School of Oriental and African Studies (SOAS). I'm enrolled in the Islamic Law master's program, and my professor is currently outlining the rules of child custody in the event of a divorce, according to the different schools of Islamic jurisprudence. While the word "shariah" has become somewhat of an umbrella term for all Muslim legal issues, Islamic law, my professor emphasizes in almost every lecture, is by no means a simple set of divinely ordinated written rules that are unquestionably followed by every Muslim. The main sources of Islamic law are the Quran, and the Sunnah, or sayings and traditions of Prophet Muhammad. But neither cover every single possible legal issue that might arise in the twenty-first-century, let alone in the time period that the Prophet lived in. In fact, it was hundreds of years later – during the ninth and tenth centuries – when the four major Islamic schools of jurisprudence were established. The Hanafi, Shafi'i, Maliki and Hanbali schools are the main authorities followed by Sunni Muslims, while Shiite Muslims are broken into further sects and schools, so you can imagine why Muslims around the world have differing and often opposing beliefs not only about legal matters, but spiritual practices too.

I'm surprised to learn that even when it comes to the topic of custody rights among parents, there are major differences between the different schools of thought, and the different Muslim countries that implement some form or other of Islamic family law. As I scribble my color-coded notes, Mariam, a student seated next to me, with pale skin and long brown hair, asks if she can borrow a pen, and I hand over a black one. She smiles, and at the end of the lecture, returns it. Over the first few weeks of the term, Mariam and I often sit in the same row and sometimes compare notes, but our interaction is limited to the classroom. Towards the middle of the term, she seems to stop attending the lectures, though I don't think much of it – it's common to drop out or change programs in university, and not everyone is cut out for the complicated and at times frustrating reality of studying Islamic law. One day towards the end of the term, a woman wearing an all-black burka, complete with a veil across her face, sits down next to me. I don't pay any attention, and wait for the professor to take the podium, but notice that the woman seems to be staring at me. As I turn to my right and offer a friendly smile, she waves her hand, and it hits me – this is Mariam. The student who I knew to wear skinny jeans and T-shirts was now covered head-to-toe in a loose black cloak.

I often think of Mariam when debates about Islam take place in news articles, or in conversation with my friends. She's a reminder that not only are there countless opinions about how to practice and portray Islam, but also that an individual's own relationship with their faith is always open to changing interpretations and influences.

While veiling has become somewhat synonymous with Muslim women, it's clear that the concept of covering one's hair was not invented by Islam.

Veiling was a pre-Islamic practice followed by women and even men in Greek, Roman and Byzantine cultures, and it was also an aspect of religions like Christianity and Judaism. Though recent proposed headscarf bans in places like France and Quebec and niqab bans in countries like Belgium, Austria, Denmark and Sri Lanka have triggered international headlines, the symbol of the veil has been equally divisive within Muslim-majority countries. For a long time, it was neither enforced nor was it the norm among middle- and upper-class communities; and people are often unaware that for many years in the twentieth century, hijabs and niqabs were actually banned in Middle Eastern and Muslim-majority countries. But with the politicization of Islam, and a perceived need to protect Muslim nations from some Western ideals, the political climates of some Muslim countries were reversed, and many Muslim women emerging from these social revolutions took to covering up their bodies and hair even though headscarves may have never been part of the culture within their families. The historical experiences of each nation are unique and complex, but the political policies of a few countries in particular set the tone for neighboring nations to follow, leading to a widespread adoption of the styles of dress that have now come to represent Muslim women worldwide.

Turkey

After the modern state of Turkey was established in 1923, President Kamal Atatürk passed reforms to convert the new Republic into a secular, modern, nation-state that looked to the West, forcing a break with its Ottoman, Islamic past. Headscarves were worn casually by a minority of women, and by the 1960s and 1970s hijabs came to connote lower-class status. Following the 1980 military coup, headscarves were banned, and in 1987 the country applied to join the EU. The ban was particularly harshly enforced from 1997 until it was lifted in 2013. As Islam re-emerged in the political sphere under

President Erdogan, a new, Islam-influenced middle class arose, with women adhering to a distinctly modest form of dressing.

In Turkey, the term "tesettür" signifies the covering of bodies and hair, and early designs were dark, loose and boxy overcoats coupled with printed headscarves. When the conservative clothing style grew in popularity, being adopted by educated, middle-class women, it began shedding its previous link to the lower class. As more female university students took to dressing in this markedly Muslim way, institutions began implementing headscarf bans across the Muslim-majority nation, fearful of the possibility of radical Islam spreading in the country. In spite of this, tesettür became a thriving retail category and has remained so since, serving a segment of the Muslim middle class whose lifestyles are religiously influenced. Marked by long, tailored dresses and tunics, contemporary Turkish tesettür, which caters to the nearly 60 percent of women who reportedly wear headscarves in the country today, often appears utilitarian-inspired, with detailed belts, collars, lapels, fastenings and embellishments. Feminine dresses and robes, decorated with whimsical chiffon panels, ruffles and lace are also popular styles. Modern-day tesettür designs are trend-based and change seasonally, just as mainstream industry styles do.

Iran

In 1935, inspired by the westernization policies in Turkey, Iran's leader, Reza Shah Pahlavi, began implementing a nationwide hijab ban, even though religious groups strongly opposed his secular approach.

Women wearing scarves over their hair weren't allowed to work in professional capacities and weren't permitted entry into theaters and restaurants; those found disobeying this policy in public had their headscarves forcibly removed by soldiers. Some of these women took to eschewing the traditional Iranian "chador", or black cloak, in favor of a more Western-inspired "manteau", or overcoat, with a headscarf. After World War II, however, the Shah was removed from power and bans were lifted. Some women took to covering their hair again, and a burgeoning Islamist group, discontented with Western-inspired capitalist, socialist and nationalist ideologies, set the framework for the Islamic Revolution of 1979, during which many women took center stage, donning the historic chador as a show of resistance. The next year, the new zealous governing authorities in power took steps to make hijabs mandatory for Iranian women, and once again employment policies were changed – whereas women wearing hijab were once not allowed to work, now those who were bare-headed could not be employed.

Since the early 2000s, dress codes in Iran have become more moderate, and while covering your hair and wearing loose-fitting clothes is still a legal requirement for women, many now don colorful outfits with printed silk scarves. Today, a manteau-inspired blazer or cardigan, for instance, may be paired with skinny jeans and a light silk headscarf that still reveals the front portion of the wearer's hair. Mojeh Izadpanah (@mojeh_i on Instagram), the founder and editor-in-chief of Middle Eastern fashion magazine *Mojeh*, is the epitome of the modern, fashion-conscious Iranian woman: one need look no further than her Instagram photos from her visits to Tehran, where she styles slogan T-shirts with tailored pants and light duster jackets, completed with a non-committal approach to wearing loosely draped headscarves.

Egypt

A similar political pattern ensued in Egypt. Throughout the twentieth century, westernization flourished in the country, which was increasingly exposed to European cultures, and many women who had previously worn the hijab took to wearing lighter forms of it, or removing it from their wardrobes entirely, according to author Leila Ahmed, who was raised in Cairo in the 1940s. Veiling, according to the author, became synonymous with "backwardness". Yet in the 1970s, rather than being mandated by authorities, the veiling movement was bottom-up: headscarves started gaining popularity within university campuses before spreading into the rest of society. This, according to Leila, was a gradual response to Egypt's defeat in the 1967 Arab–Israeli War. Disheartened with the government and its secular ideologies, many Egyptians, both male and female, were attracted to the religious ideals being imported from the Muslim Brotherhood and Saudi Arabia. Islamist movements that grew at these university campuses offered students a special sense of kinship and community, recognizable by a markedly Muslim way of dressing that included hijabs. Within a couple of decades, women who had never worn the hijab began to do so:

> And young girls were soon growing up unaware that there had been a time when Muslim women - devout, mainstream Muslim, and not merely secular women - had not worn hijab. The entire era of Muslim women going bareheaded was being quietly erased from Muslim memory, and even Muslim history.[21]

Before this resurgence, the veil was so far removed from normal life in Egypt that it was seen as an unorthodox, rather than mainstream, symbol in the media. Mohja Kahf, an Arab-American poet and comparative literature and culture studies professor, says:

> In Egyptian cinema's golden age from the 1950s to the 1970s, there is nary a hijabed women to be found, unless it is a poor old farmwoman... Not until the 1990s, after it had become clear that veiling was making a massive comeback across Arab societies, did

Egyptian film grudgingly include an image of a woman in hijab, and at first only on villainous characters.[22]

Fadwa El Guindi says that the first form of "Islamic dress" in Egypt, which was donned by activists in the 1970s, was an "innovative construction" with "no tangible precedent".[23] Interestingly, these veiled Egyptian women were not embraced by the rest of society. In fact, fellow Egyptians were puzzled as to the cause of this renewed trend of veiling. "Was this an identity crisis, *our* version of America's hippie movement, a fad, youth protest, or ideological vacuum? An individual psychic disturbance, life-crisis, social dislocation or protest against authority?"[24] Some were so perplexed and uncomfortable with the emergence of young women donning head-to-toe abayas that they took to ridiculing them, brushing them off as women who only covered their hair because they could not afford to visit a hairdresser. By the 1990s, a period in Cairo also known as the "mosque movement", new clothing companies emerged to cater to the newfound demand for ultra-conservative attire, and the activist women who were donning it. Still, it has not become a compulsory form of dress in Egypt, and many women take to wearing popular Western attire instead.

Fadwa notes that the modern veiled Egyptian woman that emerged in the 1970s was not the same as the older, veiled Arab woman of the early 1900s:

This is neither a return to an early veil nor a return to an early Islamic community. It was not the same veil or the same woman or the same community... The contemporary college woman adopting a conservative appearance and demeanor continued to be active and visible in mainstream society, competitively enrolled in higher education, majoring in "nonsoft" professional fields, asserting her Muslim identity, career-oriented, modern and veiled.[25]

This could describe the modern British or American Muslim woman who wears her hijab proudly to signify her faith and also her disdain for stereotypes about Muslims that are propagated by Islamophobic beliefs.

Saudi Arabia

The Arab States, or countries of the Gulf Cooperation Council (GCC), include Saudi Arabia, Oman, Bahrain, Kuwait, Qatar and the United Arab Emirates (UAE). These are the countries where the abaya has long enjoyed its status as national dress, often influenced by the "Wahhabi", the strict, orthodox Muslim policies of Saudi Arabia. Up until the Islamic Revolution took hold of Iran in 1979, Saudi Arabia was the only Muslim country in the world where veiling was legally enforced upon women.

And while the abaya, with a mandatory headscarf, has been the national dress in the country since the monarchy was founded in 1932, in 2018 – the same year that the Kingdom started permitting its women to acquire driving licenses and lifted its ban on movie theaters – a senior council member of Saudi Arabia's leading religious authority questioned the country's requirement of the abaya. "More than 90 percent of pious Muslim women in the Muslim world do not wear abayas," was Sheikh Abdullah Al-Mutlaq's statement that quickly went viral in February 2018.[26] The following month, the Kingdom's crown prince, Mohammed Bin Salman, confirmed that the abaya need not be worn, as long as women were to dress in clothing that was "decent" and "respectful". Perhaps sounding like a revolutionary ruling to traditionalists who have followed the country's strict interpretations of Islamic law for almost a century, the prince's reforms are part of a wider plan called Saudi Vision 2030, which aims to diversify the economy and develop public sectors, including offering more job opportunities to women.

Even a design as simple as the abaya has evolved over time in Arabia. According to UAE-based fashion historian Reem El Mutwalli, only wealthy bedouins, such as the wives of sheikhs, would wear abayas in the pre-oil period of the UAE. The necklines of these early versions were traditionally decorated with gold trims. Sheer fabrics began being used for formal, occasion wear abayas in the 1970s, and by the 1990s, it became common to see abayas bedazzled with embellishments, lace and embroidery.[27] While abayas remain the norm among local women in GCC countries, modern styles include colorful versions, open fronts and sometimes no headscarf. "In the Arab world, Turkey and Iran, it is a new veiling, distinctly modern in both tailoring and ideological trappings," writes Mohja Kahf. It's a "veil tailored for getting out *into* the modern world, not one designed for retreating from it like the older, more formless abaya."[28]

Indonesia

Although the Middle East may be viewed as the epicenter of Islam among Westerners, Indonesia has the world's largest Muslim population. "Even in Indonesia, Muslim women are symbolic representatives of political Islam, and 'jilbab', as pious fashion is called there, plays a role not only in personal moral formation but also in national politics," writes Elizabeth Bucar in her book *Pious Fashion: How Muslim Women Dress.*[29] The nation gained independence from Dutch colonial rule in 1945, and its first leader, President Sukarno, pushed for men's national dress to appear westernized and sophisticated, and women's to be authentic and culturally inspired. The country's next leader, President Suharto, was more radical, and banned the wearing of the headscarf in schools and government offices. But in the late 1980s and early 1990s, the notion of an Islamic lifestyle began attracting the young middle class, particularly university students. "This period also saw the first display of religious identity via modest dress among young women, as a sign of personal transformation and in-group identity", writes anthropology professor Carla Jones. Muslim dress came to be called "Busana Muslim", and popular

Indonesian fashion designers who had previously rejected the Busana Muslim market started catering to them in the early 2000s with diffusion lines from their main collections, as well as with fashion shows and launches that were often timed to release just before Ramadan.[30]

The veil as a political symbol

Through this brief outline of historical dress codes in predominantly Muslim countries, it's clear that neither abayas nor headscarves have been fixed, mainstream modes of dress. Rather, the increase or decline in popularity of Islamic dress codes have oftentimes been tied to the policies of various government regimes, or to political resistance movements or campaigns against colonialism, westernization and even nationalism. In a section of her book titled "The Politics of Clothing", Elizabeth states, "Since Muslim women were regarded as the receptacles and conveyers of religion, they disproportionately bore the burden... The headscarf, as the most visible symbol of Muslim women, became the target of political reform as part of agendas that often had very little to do with Muslim women themselves."[31]

And while veils, including full face veils, are frequently used to convey piety and adherence to traditional interpretations of Islam, in some countries, like Pakistan, where neither hijabs nor burkas are mandated by the government, veiling can be used for other purposes entirely. "Prostitutes are often fully veiled. Many such burka-clad women are known to frequent busy bus stops in Karachi where they can whisper to clients and quickly clasp a strange man's hand from underneath the all-covering burka, their intention and proposition clear to all parties," reveals author Rafia Zakaria. She also describes how the veil allows for anonymity: a sort of invisibility cloak that a woman may throw on as she leaves her house for a secret date with a male, ensuring she won't be recognized by any relatives or community members, thus keeping her "moral" reputation intact. Women's motivations for donning the burka in such cases, she writes, are "for the freedom it offers from social mores and from being identified."[32]

Hijabs have evidently been worn and taken off for a multitude of reasons, religion being only one of them, but over the past few decades they've made a considerable comeback.

Fashion historian Daniel James Cole believes history is repeating itself, he tells me over the phone from New York:

> Throughout the twentieth century, until the Islamic Revolution of 1979, we have seen, starting with President Atatürk in Turkey and Reza Shah in Iran, a lot of discouragement of the hijab. I have a student from Iraq who showed me a picture from the 1960s of her mother and she looked like she was from suburban America. The outfit was by my standards completely modest but it wasn't necessarily Islamic. I think we're seeing a movement back into more adherence to those traditions on an Islamic level - I think more women are wearing hijab whose mothers did not, and that we're seeing a cultural pendulum swing.

The emergence of a new, modern veil

Although tesettür, jilbabs, chadors, abayas and other forms of dress have come to represent Muslim communities across the globe, the contemporary Muslim woman often looks strikingly different from her predecessors. She may, for instance, cover her hair with a scarf tied like a trendy turban or beanie-style hat. Worn often by millennials, these new head coverings may show the neck or some hair, and are seen as a middle ground. "For hijabis, we enjoy the privilege of being able to style our headscarves like turbans, which evoke a kind of religious ambiguity for us – they're seen as more trendy on women than religious," says hijab-wearing American entrepreneur and author Amani Al-Khatahtbeh.[33] Similarly, a Moroccan-American student at New York University, Romaissaa Benzizoune, has written that because she covers her hair, her peers often make certain judgements about her and are shocked, for instance, to discover that she too has crushes on boys, or has the lyrics memorized of popular, though explicit, Pitbull songs. "Ditching my classically wrapped headscarf for a turban style has helped, but not entirely," she writes, emblemizing the turban as a signifier of a more modern, liberally aware Muslim woman.[34]

London-based writer Afia Ahmed has described the turban style of hijab as "a symbol of the modern Muslim woman", but points out that in representing women of "neo-Islam", it marginalizes traditionally dressed Muslims. While countless photoshoots and campaigns championing modest fashion and showcasing the diversity of Muslim women have gone viral, they tend to fixate on those who wear turbans or more modern head coverings, rather than traditional headscarves. "Commercialization didn't make hijab easier, it changed what it is. People no longer ascribe to the hijab, they ascribe to a fashion trend," she claims.[35]

When it comes to the dress practices of Muslim women, debates are almost always centered on how they cover their hair, even though there are millions who wear modest clothing without choosing to wear headscarves. The emergence of a new, millennial Muslim woman who may adhere to a loose, stylish mode of covering her hair and don distressed denim jeans with fitted tops departs dramatically from the image of the female activist engulfed in a chador, protesting on the streets during Iran's Islamic Revolution.

CHAPTER 4

HOW WE SHOP NOW

As a teenager living in the United States, trips to the mall were spent browsing accessories stores like Claire's, and speed-walking by the window displays of Macy's, JC Penny and Sears, where mannequins sported clothing that wouldn't work for modesty-conscious consumers. Dresses were rarely both stylish and long, and tops that had long sleeves and high necklines were labeled as "peasant tops" – so I stayed far away. And though the layering of strappy tops and dresses over long-sleeved turtlenecks and blouses is considered stylish today, it certainly wasn't ten years ago. Unless I was in need of new jeans, clothes shopping was for the most part uninspiring, as retailers simply didn't offer designs that would suit customers with modesty guidelines like mine.

Today, that's all changed. I'm a shopaholic when it comes to clothes, guilty of a wardrobe that closes with great difficulty due to all of the garments I have squished inside. Whether they're bought on the high street or from online retailers, my clothes cover most of my skin while mirroring trends from the runways and fashion magazines. Shopping for modest fashion has never been easier, as retailers have realized the business value of catering to women who seek more coverage with their clothing.

One way brands earn the loyalty of modest shoppers is by offering specialized alteration and bespoke services – a custom engrained in the Arab world, where many high-end boutiques make requested changes to garments to suit the needs of customers. It's a cultural practice that luxury and couture designers are growing increasingly aware of when it comes to the Middle Eastern market. Tom Ford, for instance, began producing made-to-measure versions of the Arabian dishdash, a traditional garment for men also known as the thobe or kandoora, to his Middle Eastern clients in 2007.

At the end of 2017, Middle Eastern concept store Sauce launched its first online, made-to-measure evening wear collection to coincide with the festive season. Visitors to the website could choose between three sample silhouettes, and then customize the look in terms of hemlines, sleeve lengths and ruffle placements. With the click of a button, a mini dress could become a maxi dress, and a strapless or off-the-shoulder design could be given long sleeves. Ten to fourteen days after placing their order, a customer could expect to receive their delivery. Zayan Ghandour, designer and creative director of Sauce, said that the growing demand for modest fashion was one of the inspirations behind the launch.[1] If this type of service had been available in my teens, shopping for graduation gowns and prom dresses would have been a much more enjoyable experience.

Easy and affordable alteration services, however, are not a part of the mainstream retail culture in the West. And while Western brands' Ramadan-specific or limited-time-only collections may be aimed at Middle East shoppers and their stereotypically excessive spending habits, many modest fashion shoppers lack the budget to shop for designer brands, and seek wearable, versatile and affordable garments all year round.

Soon after modesty began influencing the high-fashion runways, pleated maxi skirts, floral prairie dresses and wide palazzo pants emerged at high-street stores such as Zara, River Island, New Look and Miss Selfridge, and layering strappy dresses over T-shirts and blouses was championed as a modish styling trend. But as the weeks turned into seasons, modest options such as these didn't disappear from stores as did other trends, like cropped tops, bicycle shorts and micro-mini sunglasses. Rather, modest fashion has been deemed a "macro trend" by industry professionals such as Ghizlan Guenez, founder of luxury e-tail website The Modist.[2]

Fashion-conscious, modest-dressing millennials may have previously succumbed to unstylish ethnic wear or men's oversized garments to fit with their faith-based dress codes. But for many female Muslim shoppers, runway-inspired, affordable pieces that even their non-Muslim comrades are wearing are easily preferable to the traditional, cultural garb worn by elder genera-tions in their families, which they would have to source from abroad or from religious shops within their communities. The go-to high-street destinations for London-based modest fashion designer and blogger Zinah Nur Sharif (@thezirkus on Instagram), for instance, are Zara, Mango and Primark. "I never bought or even considered buying clothes from Islamic stores, as I do not consider them stylish or suitable to my personal style," she stated in an interview with Emma Tarlo, who co-wrote *Islamic Fashion and Anti-fashion* with Annelies Moors.[3] In the introduction of their book, the authors say that the high street is the shopping destination of choice for millennial Muslim women.

Ultra-affordable and stylish modest wear mass-produced in China is now readily available in cheaper souqs and markets too. In the UAE, for instance, weekend trips to Dubai from neighboring Emirates and Arab countries like Oman and Saudi Arabia often include taking a car with a large boot for a visit to Dragon Mart – a massive shopping complex comprising more than 4,000 outlets selling goods imported from China. Nestled within its sprawling alleyways are an abundance of clothing shops where you'll find embellished tulle maxi skirts (complete with lining) for £12 (US $15), full-length baroque dresses that make for glamorous evening wear for £54 (US $65), and beautifully embroidered two-piece tunic and pants sets priced at £28 (US $34), commonly favored by Middle Eastern millennials who sport them as travel wear (instead of donning their abayas) when journeying abroad. Distressed denim jackets with long hemlines, pearl-adorned dresses cut in kaftan-inspired silhouettes and long-sleeved pinstriped jumpsuits galore hang on racks. It's fast fashion at its prime, with a decidedly modest vibe.

Prior to the influx of modest fashion offerings on the high street and in souqs and marketplaces, style-conscious women on budgets would simply purchase ordinary clothing and layer it to achieve a look of overall modesty. Canadian modest fashion blogger Saira Arshad (@shazaira on Instagram), who wears her hijab in the trendy turban style, tells me that she doesn't find shopping easier today than it was perhaps ten years ago:

> I shop the same way I used to, in the same stores that I used to shop
> at. Recently a lot of brands have taken up on the hype and want
> to cater to the Muslim population, so a lot of stores are picking up
> on that and it just happens to be what's on the runways, but at the
> same time it comes down to how you style your clothes. You can
> pick out whatever: a T-shirt and layer it with a jacket, it just comes
> down to finding certain pieces in different places. If you were to say,
> "give me a store where I can go shop modest fashion", to be honest,
> it's where everyone shops – Topshop, River Island and H&M, I don't
> think you need to be confined to this whole "modest fashion" label.

When we meet in Dubai, Saira is dressed in a yellow floral dress from H&M cropped right above the ankle, paired with light gray leggings and a matching gray turban. Silver hoop earrings reaching almost to her shoulders along with a quilted leather bum bag by Gucci complete her stylish outfit. While her wardrobe includes a few statement splurges, and a host of cultural accessories picked up along her various travels, Saira tells me that most of her garments are from the high street. "I shop like everyone else and I'll pick up pieces and try and put them together in my mind, and that's what fashion is, isn't it? It's just an expression of your own style," she says.

The fashion blogger points out that high-end labels and platforms that may claim to specialize in modest wear don't always appeal to her personal taste – not to mention her budget. "I don't even shop at any of these 'modest fashion places' because A) they're super expensive and B) it's something I can just find at the souq," she says. Popular UK-based online retailer ASOS, she says, is one of her favorite shopping destinations for garments that can be worked into modest fashion looks.

Along with Topshop and Zara, ASOS is a personal favorite shopping destination of modest fashion blogger Sameera Hussain (@missmulberry on Instagram) too. Sameera doesn't cover her hair but makes a conscious effort to cover up from the neck down, and part of her unique modest fashion charm involves her out-of-the-box approach to styling. She explains that she'll often shop from the "ASOS Tall" section on the website, which launched in 2014 to cater to women who are 5'9 and above. "Often I buy dresses from ASOS Tall just because they give me extra length – yes it's an option for tall women, but it's also a great option for women looking for modest clothing," she tells me.

The rise of e-commerce platforms
dedicated to modest fashion

A hallmark of this generation of digital-savvy millennials is their reliance on the internet and demand for instant gratification. This makes e-commerce a convenient and often preferred way to shop. Turkish investor Kerim Türe set out to diversify the clothing options available to women in the nation in 2010. "Walking around Istanbul, I would regularly see uniform types of clothing – young women dressed in the same style clothes as their mothers. It was unfair and there was clearly a gap in the market," he tells me. In 2011, he launched Modanisa (the sponsor behind many of the world's Modest Fashion Weeks), whose name is a combination of the Turkish and Italian word for fashion, "moda", and "nisa", which means "woman" in Arabic. The CEO explains that religion or adherence to Islam wasn't really a motivator in launching the website, but that the target market was certainly Muslim women. "We did want to help give more choice to Muslim women who preferred to dress modestly but were constantly ignored," he says. "Fashion [in Muslim-majority countries] was a man-made space and consequently women's clothing needs were not addressed for years and years. When we looked around and talked about 'Muslims and fashion', there was nothing there. 'Islamic clothing' had been reduced to a black burka."

Today, Modanisa carries more than 70,000 products from both established high-street brands and emerging designers, with categories including elaborate evening gowns, semi-formal dresses, casual attire, coats, pants, tunics, activewear sets and burkini-style swimwear options, as well as sections dedicated to lingerie and loungewear, in addition to a separate section for plus-size designs. There is a wide variety of head coverings, including scarves, shawls, turbans, bonnets, athletic hoods and separate neck covers, in the form of turtleneck pieces and collared bibs, for women who follow conservative interpretations of hijab. In this same section, you'll find a range of gloves and colorful sleeves – essentially tubes that can be worn under short-sleeved tops to ensure the wearer's arms are covered. Visitors to the website are met with so many different options that it can almost seem like a visual overload. But creating a mecca for modest fashion was always the plan for Kerim.

Though based in Turkey, Modanisa delivers worldwide, and Kerim says that Europe and the Middle East closely follow Turkey in terms of order numbers. "The business became a pan-global affair almost instantly," he says. "We were sending goods to customers in the Middle East, Europe and North America pretty much from day one. We decided early on to use express couriers, which ensured we could quickly ship packages across the world." The CEO's decisions to stock affordable fashion and extend the website's offerings to the global modest consumer paid off, and in 2015, the Reuters and Dinar-Standard *State of the Global Islamic Economy Report* named Modanisa as the world's most popular conservative fashion website.[4] "We have enjoyed an average of double digit growth since we launched, averaging about 70 percent year-on-year growth," he reveals.

Kerim says that the website targets women aged sixteen to twenty-five, but that the average customer is around twenty-nine years old. Social media is heavily utilized for marketing purposes, and the brand has three official accounts on Instagram alone, including one localized Turkish one, one in English and one in Arabic. "Social media has been vital for our sales. These visual platforms give us the opportunity to directly engage our target audiences," says Kerim. "We work with over 150 influencers worldwide, who between them have millions of followers. They are an integral part of the modest fashion sector." The platform also collaborates with fashion designers – in 2017, it partnered with Turkish designer Raşit Bağzıbağlı. His evening wear collection was shown at Jakarta Modest Fashion Week and Dubai Modest Fashion Week, before making its way to the Contemporary Muslim Fashions exhibition in San Francisco.

In the UK, Haute Elan was the pioneering modest fashion e-commerce platform in the country, which is home to more than 4.1 million Muslims – a number that is expected to triple over the next three decades, according to the Pew Research Center.[5] In autumn 2018 when I meet the website's founder Romanna Bint-Abubaker at the company's headquarters located in central Wimbledon, London, it's clear that she's a passionate and driven entrepreneur. Unable to sit still for very long, the Haute Elan CEO has her finger in many pies: she's planning a photoshoot campaign for the website, finalizing dates for the Haute Elan London Modest Fashion Week, checking new samples for her in-house label, Nur, and overseeing a customer service request, all while making herself a cup of tea and chatting with her mother who pops into the showroom to drop off some new abayas. Our meeting comes only a few months after Haute Elan received new funding, and the business has moved to a new office space, which is currently filled with floor-to-ceiling industrial shelving units packed with stock. Abayas and dresses hang on nearby racks and even from industrial pipes, and a white bookshelf in the room stores rainbow-hued copies of the Quran and bottles of colorful halal (an Arabic word used by Muslims meaning "permissible") nail polishes. These nail polishes are breathable, meaning that they allow water and oxygen to pass through and reach the nail, so that they can be worn during Muslim prayer.

When the company first launched, under the name Haute Arabia, it was purely to provide European exposure to Middle Eastern labels. "Originally we started off consulting for brands in the Middle East who wanted to grow and expand into the European and international markets," she explains. "This was in early 2011 when e-commerce was still very young in the Middle East, and even with more developed brands it was also quite nascent. These brands didn't know how to reach the international consumer, so they wanted us to consult and take them to the Harrods level."

With her background in banking and private equity, and a particular interest in Islamic investment markets, Romanna decided to create a single platform to introduce consumers to these Arab brands instead of spending time strategizing separately for each one. The website, Haute Arabia, launched with a grand kick-off party at the Bulgari Hotel in London's posh Knightsbridge district in 2012. "After that we grew with more designers. We focused a lot on luxury at that point and bespoke orders and it was all drop shipping, so we didn't stock any products; customers would order and they'd be delivered from the designer's atelier," explains Romanna.

The target niche for the entrepreneur, who wore the hijab at the time but has since taken it off, was luxury modest wear, and many of the initial designs on the website took the shape and form of the Arabian abaya. "We like to wear abayas in our culture and at our family social events here in the UK too, and there was a need for modest dress that wasn't available in the kind of standard or elegance that we would have liked," she says. Romanna then decided to diversify the site's product ranges to appeal to more customers. Haute Arabia became Haute Elan, and the website started stocking more affordable brands, as well as brands from other parts of the world too, including local London labels. For a while, Haute Elan also had a brick and mortar store in London, which closed in 2018 so that the company could focus on its e-commerce strategies, with improved content like photoshoots and video campaigns.

"We were ultimately the first that had any kind of modest product in a multi-brand concept space," says Romanna. And while Haute Elan was one of the first major global online platforms to curate chic and conservative clothing, when awareness about modest fashion entered the mainstream, the company no longer enjoyed the monopoly it once had over the market, and it became difficult for Haute Elan to stay afloat in a now-saturated industry filled with competing modest fashion brands and websites. After facing challenges with funding and investments, Haute Elan's time in the e-commerce realm seemingly came to an end. By the end of 2019, the website had disappeared, along with any mention of future editions of Haute Elan London Fashion Week.

In Asia, e-commerce businesses centered on modesty are thriving, especially in Muslim-majority countries. Indonesia's largest online platform for modest fashion is Hijup.com – a name derived from the words "Hijab up," intended to signify a fun and positive approach to wearing the hijab, like the phrase "dress up." It was founded in 2011 by Diajeng Lestari, who aimed to provide consumers with stylish clothing while promoting an Islamic lifestyle. More than 200 different fashion labels are sold on the site, mostly characterised by a distinct Indonesian flair. Tiered floral maxi dresses and tunics with waterfall hemlines are styled on models with scarves tied so that not a single strand of hair is visible. While much of the clothing offered on the site has a markedly Muslim aesthetic – think prayer covers, long tunics, ankle-length shirt-dresses and headscarves galore – there's also a range of contemporary designs that are modernised with androgynous cuts and tartan overlays.

Hijup sells athletic wear and swimwear, and there are even garments specifically designed for breastfeeding, featuring discreet panels and concealed zippers, masked with layers and chic ruffles. A section on the site directs visitors to a group of brands named Hijup Basics, Hijup Daily, Hijup Essentials and Hijup Scarf. From trendy deconstructed shirts and pleated skirts to ornate hijab pins, these are all Hijup-branded items. Hijab sets from the Hijup Scarf range come as packs of three, in colorful, printed pouches stamped with Hijup's logo and the hashtag, #empowerchange.

Developing in-house labels under the umbrellas of multi-brand online platforms has proved a clever business decision for e-tailers. They have more flexibility in determining prices, and receive a larger share of profits, when they are designing and producing garments themselves. Modanisa's own line is called Refka, and offers shoppers modest garments marketed as "affordable luxury", and Dubai-headquartered website The Modist launched its own label, Layeur, just over a year after its website went live in 2017. Layeur presents shoppers with longline tuxedo jackets, A-line skirts, shirt-dresses, turtleneck tunics and palazzo pants in an array of metallic, jewel-toned, silk and sequined finishes. Prints range from youthful polka dots to sophisticated houndstooth and color-blocked patterns, and the silhouettes are loose, elegant and, as the name of the brand suggests, easily layerable.

The Modist's timely website launch coincided with the global modest fashion boom, and it quickly became the most talked-about modest wear e-commerce platform in the world, even though its products may not be compatible with the budgets of the masses. The Modist carries only luxury brands, such as Valentino, Burberry and Marc Jacobs, to name a few. It's rare to find a garment costing under £200 (US $242) on the website – typical finds include a gold tailored blazer by Haider Ackermann priced at £2,415 (US $2,922) or a £4,675 (US $5,656) lace gown with sequined appliques by Jenny Packham. Even the packaging is luxurious – garments are wrapped with scented black tissue paper inside sturdy monochrome boxes, within thick cardstock bags. With their orders, customers also often receive hard copies of *The Mod* – a glossy fashion magazine published by the platform. The website even offers same-day delivery within the UAE at no extra cost, and in 2019, the platform introduced its "Try, buy, treasure" service where customers could order items to be delivered to their homes, where they could try on garments before deciding to purchase them.

Poised, elegant and remarkably stylish, The Modist's founder and CEO, Ghizlan Guenez, has been the face of the business since its inception. With an Algerian background, Ghizlan was raised between Beirut and Dubai, and she worked in private equity for over a decade before launching The Modist.

"Islam is an all-inclusive religion. It is something that invites everybody. And if you want to invite everybody, you've got to keep the conversation open, by not telling or dictating what modest fashion should look like but by allowing people to have the freedom to choose what modest fashion is for themselves. That is why I wanted to keep it open and not just focus on Muslims."

In 2018, she was one of the few women in the Middle East featured on the *Business of Fashion* 500 – an annual list of prominent personalities shaping the industry. The other members of The Modist's strong founding team hold high credentials in fashion, including its chief operating officer Lisa Bridgett, who has experience in senior marketing roles at Net-a-Porter and Ralph Lauren. The team's marketing efforts have been hugely successful, taking root even before the website went live: notable modest fashion influencers around the world, including New York City-based Maria Al-Sadek (@mariaalia on Instagram), posted images of The Modist's minimalist white shopping bag with the brand's logo weeks ahead of its launch, setting the foundation for the soon-to-follow hype around the website.

One of The Modist's first campaigns post-launch starred Halima Aden. Against a colorful woodland backdrop, Halima is featured alongside two other models, though she's the only one with her hair covered. The trio is styled in kaftans and dresses crafted from pastel jacquard fabrics, sequins and chiffons from The Modist's first Ramadan range. Though it had only been a few months since The Modist's launch, the platform commissioned prominent international labels like Mary Katrantzou, Adam Lippes, For Restless Sleepers and Osman to create exclusive Ramadan designs for them, and these are the garments modeled by Halima in the campaign, winning both parties extensive international coverage in the press.

Part and parcel of its luxurious, high-end appeal are the glamorous events that The Modist has organized, in Dubai and internationally. It hosts exclusive press events and VIP meet-and-greets for its designers who visit Dubai and throws lavish dinners to celebrate ground-breaking partnerships – like its 2018 tie-up with London's luxury fashion retail platform Farfetch. During the kick-off of the Contemporary Muslim Fashions exhibition in San Francisco in 2018, The Modist loaned some of its designs to the museum for the showcase, and also held an intimate luncheon with key players and influencers in the modest fashion industry. Although the market it caters to may be small relative to the high street, The Modist is frequently referenced by fashion journalists in articles about the modest fashion industry.

While Haute Elan, Modanisa and The Modist may have been launched for Muslim shoppers, they all avoided branding their sites as religious ones, in attempts to attract a wider range of customers. Kerim shies away from classifying Modanisa as a website for Islamic clothing: "Religion is personal," he says. "We are very careful about sacred values. We know Modanisa predominantly, but not exclusively, caters to modestly dressed Muslim ladies. They shop with us because they want choice and style, religion doesn't need to come into it."

Religion and faith were personal motivators for Romanna when she founded Haute Elan; however, she was also cautious and abstained from discussing Islam on her site, though, as she admits, this strategy seems to go against common-sense target market protocol, since only around 10 percent of her customers were non-Muslim. "You think, shouldn't it be very clear and very targeted, but I've always thought this is the right marketing strategy for us," she says. "Islam is an all-inclusive religion. It is something that invites everybody. And if you want to invite everybody, you've got to keep the conversation open, by not telling or dictating what modest fashion should look like but by allowing people to have the freedom to choose what modest fashion is for themselves. That is why I wanted to keep it open and not just focus on Muslims."

And though The Modist is headquartered in Dubai and feeds the wealthy, fashion-hungry consumers of the Middle East, religion isn't mentioned anywhere on its website either, and Ghizlan rarely discusses Islam in interviews with the press. "I think that when you speak to modesty, sometimes there are certain perceptions that modesty is this certain religion, this certain region, a particular age and particular look," Ghizlan told *Vogue*. "We want to change those perceptions. We are saying that modesty can be so many different things, can be coveted by so many different women, and that it can be cool and beautiful and elegant and everything a woman wants."[6]

(Clockwise from top left) fashion blogger Sameera Hussain (@missmulberry), fashion designer Safiya Abdallah (@dulcebysafiya), childrenswear designer Maha Gorton (@mahagorton), fashion blogger Saira Arshad (@shazaira), fashion blogger Nabilah Kariem (@nabilahkariem) and graphic designer Rihab Nubi (@riinubi) each showcase their own interpretation of modest fashion. Photo taken by Kochkarova Tamila (@kochkarovatamila).

An image from Nike's 2017 Pro Hijab campaign featuring American-Muslim fencer Ibtihaj Muhammad. Courtesy of Nike.

A modest activewear outfit by British-Egyptian designer Yasmin Sobeih of Under-Rapt (@under_rapt). Courtesy of Under-Rapt.

CEO of Haute Hijab, Melanie Elturk (@hautehijab), at New York Fashion Week in 2017. Courtesy of Melanie Elturk.

Halima Aden (@halima) ends the runway show at the launch of her turban collection created in collaboration with Turkish e-commerce platform, Modanisa (@modanisa), at Istanbul Modest Fashion Week in 2019. Photo taken by Rooful Ali (@rooful).

Antwerp-based modest fashion blogger Sarah Dimani (@saraahdii). Photo taken by Marie Bouly (@marieboulyphoto).

Palestinian-Irish modest fashion blogger
Marwa Biltagi (@mademoisellememe)
at New York Fashion Week. Photo taken
by Moeez Ali (@moeez).

New York-based modest model Wafeeqa Azeem (@wafeeqaswardrobe) wearing a design by Abaya Addict (@abayaaddict). Photo taken by Nicole Najmah Abraham (@najmdesignsphotos).

A burkini designed for lifeguards by Lebanese-Australian designer Aheda Zanetti (@ahiidaofficial). Courtesy of Aheda Zanetti.

Modest swimwear by Turkish brand Mayovera (@mayovera_com), available online at Modanisa (@modanisa). Courtesy of Modanisa.

Pioneering modest fashion blogger Dina Torkia (@dinatokio) during London Modest Fashion Week in 2017. Photo taken by Rooful Ali (@rooful).

Palestinian-Irish modest fashion blogger Marwa Biltagi (@mademoisellememe) at New York Fashion Week. Photo taken by Asaf Liberfroind (@thestreetvibe).

American-Jewish fashion blogger and co-owner of modest fashion label Raju, Rachelle Yadegar (@rachelleyadegar). Courtesy of Rachelle Yadegar.

Apostolic Christian fashion blogger
Alexa Sue-Anne Dudley (@1998miss)
at Dubai Modest Fashion Week in 2019.
Photo taken by Rooful Ali (@rooful).

Mexican-Emirati modest fashion influencer
Ashley Al Busmait (@desert.vogue).
Photo taken by Marrwan Elhussein
(@marwanonthemoon).

Designs from the Raşit Bağzıbağlı X
Modanisa collaboration (@rasitbagzibagli).
Photo taken by Mustafa Çetin.

Models backstage dressed in Luya Moda, styled by The Cactus Agency (@thecactusagency), at the Muslim Lifestyle Expo 2018 in Manchester. Courtesy of The Cactus Agency.

UK-based male modest fashion influencer and personal shopper Zaahid Ahmed (@zaahidma). Photo taken by Just Nayeem (@justnayeem).

A model dressed in Luya Moda (@luyamoda) during the Islamic Fashion & Design Council (@ifdc_org) Milan Fashion Week Modest Soiree. Courtesy of the IFDC.

A design from the fall/winter 2017 collection by Dubai-based label Bouguessa (@bouguessa). Photo taken by Mariah Jelena (@mariahjelenak).

Niqabi photographer and henna artist Shagoofa Ali (@mamoii_). Photo taken by Madi Rae Jones (@madi.rae.jones).

New York-based modest model Wafeeqa Azeem (@wafeeqaswardrobe). Photo taken by Tennyson Aldane Brown (@tenapix).

(Left to right) Fashion designer Safiya Abdallah (@dulcebysafiya), childrenswear designer Maha Gorton (@mahagorton) and fashion blogger Nabilah Kariem (@nabilahkariem). Photo by Kochkarova Tamila (@kochkarovatamila).

(Left to right) Fashion blogger Sameera Hussain (@missmulberry), fashion blogger Saira Arshad (@shazaira) and graphic designer Rihab Nubi (@riinubi). Photo taken by Kochkarova Tamila (@kochkarovatamila).

CHAPTER 5

FOR WOMEN, BY WOMEN

For e-commerce platforms serving a global audience, keeping religion outside of the fashion sphere makes business sense, as potential non-Muslim customers can then feel included. But an undeniably revolutionary spirit has been a driving force behind bringing modest fashion to the limelight, spearheaded by a group of young Muslim women who seek to fight Islamophobic sentiments and are straying from previous, traditional norms while forming their own definitions about what being a Muslim woman may look like today. This new group of millennials is widely being referred to as "Generation M". The title was used by author Shelina Janmohamed in her book *Generation M: Young Muslims Changing the World*, which was published in 2016, and states:

> Beneath the dark shadow of 11 September, our young Muslims have grown up under intense global scrutiny. But instead of hiding, the generation that have resulted are passionate about their faith and proudly self-identify as Muslims. They are ardent about defending themselves against what they believe are the misconceptions about Muslims, at the same time as seeing their faith as something that empowers them. They see it as their role to be ambassadors for their faith.[1]

There's also another group of Muslims that have been bred within this post-September 11 environment in the West, according to Leila Ahmed, author of *A Quiet Revolution: The Veil's Resurgence, from the Middle East to America.* "Against this backdrop of intense national and international (and primarily Western) interest, the subject of women and Islam also took on now a new burst of liveliness among religiously committed Muslim American feminists, giving rise to a new level of Muslim feminist activism," she writes.[2]

Many female Muslim entrepreneurs are transparent about the impact the September 11 terrorist attacks had on their Western upbringings, and admit that it sparked their drive in launching businesses aimed at correcting stereotypes about the religion. Jordanian-American founder of the online platform MuslimGirl.com, Amani Al-Khatahtbeh explains in her memoir of the same name, "That day has become crystallized in my memory not just for how harrowingly scary it was… but also because I deeply believe that my generation of millennial Muslims has, whether we like it or not, come to be defined by it."[3]

Though a renewed sense of their commitment to Islam, linked inextricably with negative backlash towards their faith, may be a driving force behind Generation M's intentions in many matters of life, they are neither traditionalists nor tied to old-world, established interpretations of Islam. Rather, they're forming their own opinions about what conforms to an Islamic lifestyle, including within the realm of fashion.

Hand in hand with the birth of Generation M has been the advent of Brand Islam – a phrase coined by Faegheh Shirazi. "The commodification of Islamic dress is here to stay as a multibillion-dollar business," she states. "With young Muslim women designers rising in the ranks to support increasingly innovative styles, Islamic fashion is maturing as a hot commodity and entering a new entrepreneurial phase."[4] These designers are not content with images that have come to represent "Islamic" fashion – namely, the abaya, paired with the tightly wrapped black headscarf, which can come across as intimidating, old-fashioned and off-putting for young Muslims in the West. "Fashion is one of the means by which these young women are asserting their self-expression and identity. Part of the motivation is to overtly demonstrate that they are 'normal' like everyone else, that they are not oppressed or anonymized," writes Shelina.[5]

Creating fashion that shatters stereotypes

Some Muslim labels are motivated by a desire to combat anti-Islamic icons propagated by the mainstream media, often driven by the new wave of "religious feminism" that Leila contends emerged post September 11.[6] "Shorthand visuals are often used to signify 'Muslim', and Generation M are fed up with the laziness of this," explains Shelina.[7] So, these Muslim-owned brands have taken prevalently used icons and have turned them on their heads, embracing the images that may have previously connoted negative symbols in the media. Australian label Sanat Craft, for instance, has reversed the words "Muslim extremist", selling T-shirts emblazoned with the words "extreme Muslim", accompanied by an illustration of an abaya-clad woman with a motorcycle and a bearded man in sunglasses doing the rock-on hand sign. There's also Toronto-based label Black Orchid, which describes itself as a pop culture brand "aimed towards positive Muslim and ethnic representation".[8] Its signature illustration is of a hijab-wearing young woman with a side-swept fringe, glamorous sunglasses and colorful lipstick, sometimes wearing a halo of flowers on top of her headscarf. Variations of this icon appear on sweatshirts, T-shirts, denim jackets, backpacks, cosmetic pouches, phone cases and enamel pins by the brand. T-shirt Policy London also specializes in quirky,

Middle Eastern-inspired graphics that feature digitally illustrated renditions of culturally inspired visuals like niqabs and henna-painted hands. Though based in the UK, the brand sells its T-shirts through ASOS Marketplace, and has many clients in the Middle East, who welcome the upbeat, tongue-in-cheek depictions of their heritage.

Texas-based streetwear brand Next Ummah Apparel is another brand focusing on T-shirts to shed a fun-loving, fashion-meets-faith light on religion. "Muslims have a problem. And that problem is a cultural problem. Islam is a huge part of our identity, but our culture doesn't allow it to contribute to what it means to be cool or proud," stated founder Ali Mahmoud. "In some cases, we even distance ourselves from Islam in our art or clothing to seem 'cooler'. That needs to change, and we're here to do that through clothing… We want Muslims to feel empowered about their religion when they wear their clothes, and we want them to look good while doing it."[9] One of his designs is a parody inspired by Grant Wood's iconic 1930 painting *American Gothic*. Ali's version, titled "American Muslim Gothic", features a black hijab on the woman pictured and a white prayer cap and long white beard on the man. Other T-shirts by the brand include designs depicting prayer-mat patterns and scattered dates, which Muslims traditionally eat when breaking their fasts during Ramadan.

There's also Emirati fashion and accessories label FMM by Fatma Al Mulla. While Fatma now creates home decor, stationery and clothing in addition to tech accessories, her quirky "niqab lady" phone cases were a hit when they were first released in 2015. The oversized silicone phone cases were made for both Apple and Android phones. In addition to black, peppy colors like mint green, pastel pink and sky blue were also available, each featuring the frame of a face veil, revealing a winking set of eyes with bold lashes. Fatma's iconic designs glamorized an image frequently portrayed as threatening by Western media, and inspired a host of knock-off phone cases produced throughout the Middle East and China.

These are just some examples of Generation M's skills in combating negative stereotypes with fast-selling, optimism-driven products of commodification. This generation's brands utilize the marketing potential and global reach of social media, along with their own e-commerce platforms (or in some cases, third-party platforms like Etsy or ASOS Marketplace), and many participate in runway shows, secure connections with celebrity stylists and partner with international retailers to further expand their labels. "These Muslims are not rejecting modernity, they are shaping it. They are turning their aspirations for freedom, security, employment, and engagement into a concrete and formidable reality, and they are doing it at a frenzied pace," writes Shelina.[10]

Muslim modest fashion labels make their mark in the West

Most Muslim modest wear labels based in the West are founded by women who have struggled to find stylish attire that fits with their personal dress codes, and turned to designing pieces for themselves instead, only to realize that there was huge demand from their peers. Such was the case with Chicago-based label Abaya Addict, founded by Deanna Khalil. "I wore hijab fairly young, at the age of seventeen, and always struggled with finding clothes that were 'just right'," she tells me. "I'd love a dress only to discover it had huge slits; I'd love a print on a short-sleeved shirt but would have to keep it hidden under a long-sleeved cardigan. Myself and the women around me got so good at layering to fit the bill. But by the time I turned twenty-five, I was sick and tired of it. Shopping was a hassle, and getting dressed was like a puzzle."

Deanna and her husband moved to Dubai, where the plenitude of fabric markets and tailors inspired Deanna to start creating her own clothes.

"I'd love a dress only to discover it had huge slits; I'd love a print on a short-sleeved shirt but would have to keep it hidden under a long-sleeved cardigan. Myself and the women around me got so good at layering to fit the bill. But by the time I turned twenty-five, I was sick and tired of it. Shopping was a hassle, and getting dressed was like a puzzle."

"I'd find fabric in the local markets and take it to my tailor and show him sketches of the long-sleeved, high-neck, slit-less, non-transparent items that I needed. I wanted to throw a dress on and not need to add a single extra thing besides the hijab on my head," she says. Deanna started wearing her designs and received so many compliments from friends that she decided to test out a business idea. She invested in making a collection of ten pieces, photographed them on a friend and posted them on a simple Facebook page that she set up. "Within a few hours I had sold out, and within a week, grew to 7,000 followers. At that point I knew I had gold in my hands," she says.

"Modesty never looked so good" is the tagline of the brand, which sells online at AbayaAddict.com and ships worldwide. In 2019, the label landed at select Macy's department stores in the United States. Apart from a range of versatile abayas, matching sets, such as a printed kimono with wide-leg pants, or a pleated skirt with a sweatshirt in the same color, are also sold on the website, along with trendy separates. Solid, printed and embroidered maxi dresses, below-the-knee dresses and tunics styled with leggings or pants, jumpsuits and cardigans are all on offer, along with a variety of jersey, chiffon and viscose hijabs. The brand also sells prayer covers, which are tent-like shrouds with holes for the face and hands, meant to be worn while praying. Though Abaya Addict was born in the United Arab Emirates, it moved its headquarters to Chicago in 2017 after Deanna realized that the strongest demand for her products was from North America. "We took a step back and looked at our numbers, and we found that 75 percent of our customers were based in the United States, so it made sense to establish our brand closer to them," she says.

In the same way that Abaya Addict uses alliteration to combine an Eastern cultural word with a catchy English term, Melanie Elturk decided to name her modest fashion label Haute Hijab. This American brand, however, is centered on head coverings rather than attire. "We actually started as a modest clothing company and then five years in we pivoted, and focused solely on hijabs," says Melanie, who is both the founder and face of the brand. "We looked at the figures and realized that 70 percent of all of our revenue was coming from hijabs, when the hijab had [originally] been kind of an afterthought." She explains that in America, finding suitable hijabs is no easy feat, and that many women source theirs from overseas, or struggle with what she calls "makeshift hijabs" bought from the high street. "They go to fast-fashion stores like Forever 21 or H&M and buy neck scarves which aren't meant to be worn on the head, and aren't meant to be washed," she says. Seeing a clear gap in the market, Melanie set out to make Haute Hijab a leading American headscarf label. Luxe, minimalist, visually appealing and user friendly, the brand's website has a high-fashion appearance, featuring bold headlines and striking imagery. Visitors can shop by category of hijab: everyday, formal or professional, or, alternatively, by fabric.

Like Deanna of Abaya Addict, Melanie spent some years living in the UAE, before she and her husband quit their jobs in 2016 and moved the brand's base back to the US, which is where they discovered around 90 percent of their orders were originating from. At that time, the label sold primarily everyday scarves priced at around US $20, but soon expanded to offer luxury and silk designs, as well as underscarves, which are often worn beneath headscarves. Melanie says that Muslims account for more than 95 percent of her customer base, namely because of the brand's emphasis on the hijab, and that she's driven by the desire to empower Muslim women with stylish scarf options. "It's 100 percent motivated by faith and the only reason I'm doing this, to be honest, is because of the contribution that I'm trying to make to our community," she explains. "Having a side hustle in fashion is cool, but I don't think that I would have done it if it wasn't modest or faith related."

Haute Hijab has spread awareness for Muslim head coverings even among non-Muslim Americans. In 2019, cult beauty brand Glossier used scarves by Haute Hijab for an advertisement that was featured in the *New York Times*, and starred hijabi makeup artist Rafiqah Akhdar. The same year, Haute Hijab video campaigns were played on the screens at New York's iconic Times Square. Though non-Muslims account for no more than 5 percent of Haute Hijab's customers, the designer says that many of the brand's social media followers are non-Muslims, and that Orthodox Jews and conservative Christians will occasionally purchase her headscarves. And while the brand has seen an increase in sales and social media exposure over the past two years, Melanie says that this is not because of any global modest fashion movement, but because of the brand's efforts to diversify its designs and ramp up its marketing reach. "Whether or not the mainstream takes notice had no bearing on whether or not our customers needed products that we provided," explains the designer. "We've always catered to the very specific demographic of Muslim women and they've always had a need for hijabs, so it's just up to us to reach as many of those women as we can regardless of what the trends might be in the mainstream."

Syrian-American Marwa Atik is another entrepreneur who has made a business out of selling headscarves, and like Melanie, she also models her designs herself on social media. Echoing Melanie's observation about the lack of suitable hijabs in the mainstream market, Marwa launched Vela Scarves in 2009. "There was a huge modesty gap that was not being met," she says. "The scarves sold in major stores were often thick Pashmina scarves that were uncomfortable to style around the head." Unlike Melanie, Marwa's motives for selling hijabs weren't outright religiously inspired. "My adherence to modesty did play a role, however when I launched the brand, I wasn't really thinking much about that because it is so embedded in me that I don't have to outwardly think about it. When I launched Vela, it was more of a way for me to showcase my creative designs and express my style in my own way while still being modest," she explains.

Marwa says that the majority of her customers live in the US and Canada, followed closely by the United Kingdom and Australia. The brand's website showcases a host of scarf designs in a range of materials and patterns, including satin chain-printed scarves with a luxurious, Hermès-esque appearance that are stamped with the word "Vela", which she explains is the Latin word for veil. Marwa also collaborates with other creatives, like popular Toronto-based South Asian artist Babbu the Painter. Viscose scarves from this collection feature depictions of camels, evil eyes, Arab women with the pop culture phrase "yallah habibi" (Arabic for "let's go, my love") written within lenses of sunglasses, and Indian women with elaborate nose piercings and the sarcastic Hindi word "bakwaas" (meaning "nonsense") featured in their black lenses.

"Vela has always been an advocate for interfaith," says Marwa. "About a year ago we posted a video campaign showcasing a Muslim, Orthodox Jew and Sikh and it was all to show and tell the story that regardless of the religious or modesty choices we make, we are all connected and choose to cover." Diversity is key to the brand's ethos, and this is apparent from a quick look at the Vela Scarves Instagram page, which features a multitude of ethnicities and approaches to modesty. Many images show Marwa herself, wearing her headscarves draped elegantly over one shoulder, while other pictures show models and customers wearing their scarves around their necks, without covering their hair, or even tied around their torsos as halter tops. This approach helps the brand appear versatile and wearable across a multitude of cultures and style preferences, rather than being bound to religious guidelines.

American fashion photographer Lisa Vogl grew up in a Christian and Catholic household, but in 2011, she converted to Islam and started wearing the hijab. She found it difficult to find stylish but affordable attire and so in 2015, she and designer Alaa Ammuss co-founded Verona, a Florida-based fashion business. A year later, they applied for The Workshop at Macy's – a competitive, week-long course targeted at helping boost women- and minority-owned businesses. Verona was one of eight brands given the opportunity to sell at the flagship Macy's store in New York and in 2019, the label landed on UK-based site ASOS. Lisa's diverse background gives her insight into the different definitions of modesty, and this is reflected in her designs:

> Everyone has a different interpretation or level of modesty they like to adhere to and we like to make sure we cater to everyone's needs in that area. That is why you'll see some tops that are longer than others as well as some dresses being looser and some not. We also like to recognize that modesty is not just for Muslims. It's important to many other women in other faiths that wouldn't necessarily follow the rules of hijab but want to dress modestly with their arms and legs covered.

Designers excel in modest activewear and swimwear

Whenever the words "modest" and "swimwear" are used together, the word "burkini" will likely follow. Having become somewhat of a buzzword when it comes to Muslim swimwear, the burkini essentially refers to the coupling of leggings with a hooded long tunic or swim dress, both produced from swimwear fabric. It was designed by Lebanese-Australian Muslim Aheda Zanetti in 2004, as a way for all Muslim women to enjoy the Australian beach lifestyle and partake in activities like surfing. Prior to the advent of the burkini, many Muslims would simply wear leggings and a loose top over a normal swimsuit, but due to health and safety regulations, street attire is not allowed at many pools and water parks, and wearers will often get turned away.

In 2011, British television personality Nigella Lawson wore a burkini while vacationing in Sydney in an effort to shield her skin from the sun. (Her burkini was bought from Muslim swimwear brand Modestly Active, and according to the designer, Kausar Sacranie, approximately 15 percent of her customers are non-Muslims.[11]) This sparked much debate over whether Westerners should tolerate what was perceived to be another symbol of female oppression. Pierre Bergé, co-founder of French fashion house Yves Saint Laurent, vocalized his outrage when British retailer Marks & Spencer started manufacturing burkinis for its European stores. "Designers are there to make women more beautiful, to give them their freedom, not to collaborate with this dictatorship which imposes this abominable thing by which we hide women and make them live a hidden life," said Pierre.[12] Marks & Spencer had released its burkini line in UK stores in 2016 after having offered it in its Middle East stores for three years, and the £49.50 (US $60) burkini swiftly sold out in UK stores over the summer season.[13]

A year later, Hollywood's Lindsay Lohan was spotted sporting a burkini while vacationing in Thailand. But while it may have continued to be the butt of ridicule for some Western spectators, countries in the Muslim world were reaping the benefits of this now-mainstream swimwear design. As Faegheh Shirazi points out, "Not one to miss out on profits, China has also flooded Muslim nations with ostensibly Islamic bathing suits. As might be expected, these bathing suits are generally more affordable and have saturated the swimwear market. The more intensely these bathing suits, which quickly emerged in bright hues, are marketed with the imprint of Islam, the stronger their sales."[14]

In the UK, modest swimwear brand Lyra Swim launched in 2016, founded by Ikram Zein. While appearing like conventional Muslim swimwear, her creations are far from drab burkinis – they're simple but elegant, usually taking the form of tunics with fitted long-sleeved bodices and zip-up neck-lines, attached to thigh-length tulip skirts and worn with leggings. The brand's summer 2019 collection features muted tones of brown, grey and peach with steel-coloured leggings, achieving a style that's both sporty and sophisticated. With prices starting at US $92, Lyra Swim delivers worldwide and even offers speedy 4-day delivery internationally.

Another European modest swimwear label is Munamer, which launched in 2018 at the London Muslim Lifestyle Show. Its exotic, burkini-inspired designs will resonate with South Asian customers, as many of its pieces feature prints reminiscent of Indian and Pakistani ethnic wear. That's because Chiara Taffarello, the brand's Italian founder, spent time in Pakistan and observed the lack of women entering swimming pools in hotels, before embarking on a business idea centered on modest swimwear for Muslim women. Her tropical, geometric and traditional prints are all inspired by cultural textiles and the actual swimwear, which comes in the form of tunics paired with leggings and matching hoods or turbans, is all produced in Italy. The label is a high-end one, with prices starting at US $260, and designs are available through Munamer's website.

Aside from head-to-toe-covering burkinis, relatively conservative swim-wear styles quickly started trending as a response to the modest fashion prop-agated by labels like Gucci. Long-sleeved, surf-inspired one-piece swimsuits began emerging in high-street stores like H&M, and some swimwear brands, particularly in the United States and Australia, launched to cater to women seeking more conventional one-piece suits, rather than the many skimpy bikinis available on the high street. Some designs, such as vintage-inspired one-piece suits, offer a middle ground for women who may not be comfortable revealing their stomach and cleavage, but have no qualms about showing their arms and legs.

Albion Fit is based in the Mormon heartland of Salt Lake City, Utah. Some revealing elements, like lace-up backs and cut-outs, are incorporated into the label's swimwear designs, but on the whole they offer more coverage than the average two-piece suits on the market. Striped and floral patterns cover the brand's stylish one-piece swimsuits, some of which feature trendy off-the-shoulder necklines, and through e-commerce, Albion Fit ships internationally.

Cover is another American swimwear brand, based out of Dallas, Texas, that manufactures fashion-forward swimwear that's relatively modest, featuring long-sleeved one-pieces and swim shirts in addition to swim dresses. Religion is not listed as a part of the brand's ethos; rather, its website references the health-based need to protect wearers' skin from the sun. Nonetheless, the Texan label does offer a swimming head cover which is available by special order.

Had this sort of swimwear been available fifteen or twenty years ago, when I was growing up in the United States, my childhood might have been very different. I often dreaded attending pool parties or beach excursions with friends, wearing a plain black Speedo one-piece while they donned frilly, feminine two-pieces. I would have gladly traded in my uninteresting swimsuits for a patterned, surf-inspired design by Albion Fit or Cover. Trips to the Santa Cruz beach boardwalk and local waterpark would have been far more enjoyable if I had felt confident and comfortable in what I was wearing, and these new swimwear brands offer options for modest consumers like me, who seek a balance between the extremes of the bikini and the burkini.

There's also Israeli Jewish entrepreneur Nava Brief-Fried, who launched ModLi.co in 2015 and stocks a range of Israeli and American modest wear brands. Swimwear offered by ModLi.co is available in a variety of silhouettes, including swim dresses, skirted knee-length shorts paired with surf-inspired rash guards, and long tunic-and-leggings sets, modeled after the notorious burkini.

In the realm of modest athletic wear, while Nike may be the best-known retailer of the sports hijab, Muslim innovators have long been coming up with their own solutions to reconcile faith with sports. "Here's to a new generation of Muslim athletes" is the mission statement by American brand Asiya, named after a historical Islamic female icon and founded by Minnesota resident Fatimah Hussain who wanted to provide Muslim girls and women with basketball uniforms that would comply with their personal dress codes. Fatimah launched a Kickstarter campaign in 2016 – a year before Nike announced its own hijab design – to raise funds for the brand. On its e-shop today, Asiya sells a variety of athletic veil styles, all produced within the United States and priced at US $35. There's also a section dubbed Asiya Gear, which sells items like backpacks, headbands and long-sleeved performance T-shirts for both men and women. The website states that 50 percent of Asiya Gear profits go towards donating a sports veil and suit from the brand to a Muslim athlete in need.

Under-Râpt is another contemporary Muslim-owned brand specializing in modest activewear, and its founder, British-Egyptian designer Yasmin Sobeih, started conceptualizing a sports hijab in 2015 – a whole two years before the Nike Pro Hijab announcement. It was part of her label's initial business plan, which she created while studying at the London College of Fashion. "As a gym enthusiast, I noticed that many friends and family who preferred to cover when working out had the struggle of their hijabs falling off, plus being uncomfortably hot," she tells me when I interview her for the *National*. Her range offers a separate sports hijab as well as what she calls a "hooded base layer top", which is essentially a long-sleeved sports shirt with a face-framing hood attached to it. "The fitted design allows full coverage and keeps hair up tight during performance," says Yasmin. In addition, she offers "skights" – two-in-one sports skirts attached to tights – along with leggings, polo shirts, jumpsuits, hoodies, harem pants and hooded windbreakers. Not solely practical options for athletics, designs by Under-Râpt are fashion-forward and versatile, such as a long pink sweatshirt with printed sleeves, crafted from organic modal cotton. The designer says that international labels such as Vetements, Fenty and Yeezy have influenced her aesthetic. "They champion oversized and relaxed silhouettes," she says. "Gender fluidity has been conveyed through fashion, and now we see that the guidelines to dress modestly mean that over-sized forms are no longer regarded as unfeminine or deemed unfashionable."[15]

Yasmin markets Under-Râpt as an athleisure brand, rather than simply an activewear one, thus appealing to a wider consumer base. Although Under-Râpt is a UK-based business, Yasmin says that most of her orders come from the Middle East. She hopes to further expand the brand's presence in countries like Turkey, Iran and Saudi Arabia, in addition to Southeast Asia, where she says options in fashionable Islamic sports clothing are seriously lacking. Under-Râpt was among the global modest wear brands highlighted at the Contemporary Muslim Fashions exhibition in San Francisco in 2018, and she was overjoyed to see one of her brand's jackets worn by Halima Aden for the exhibition's campaign imagery. "It's very strange how I was inspired by seeing Halima Aden walk the Yeezy runway at New York Fashion Week, and now such an influential role model for both the Muslim community and in fashion is wearing pieces from my collection," she says.[16]

Eastern brands reinvent the abaya

In Asia, up-and-coming local designers dealing in modest wear have yet to go global with their labels, probably because of the predominance of more traditional clothing, be it shalwar kameez styles in South Asia or kimonos in Southeast Asia. As for the younger generation of consumers who eschew traditional garb, they prefer donning attire bought from regular Western high-street stores for their daily wear. The modest wear market in Indonesia, however, is ripe with talent, with Dian Pelangi (also featured at the Contemporary Muslim Fashions exhibition in San Francisco) at the forefront. Deemed a "tour de force in the global Muslim fashion scene" by the *Business of Fashion*, Dian showed her first collection at Jakarta Fashion Week at the age of eighteen. According to fashion historian Daniel James Cole, Jakarta is one of the main global centers for Muslim fashion, and Dian, who studied fashion in Paris and London, is leading the pack. The *Jakarta Post* credits the designer's popularity to "her precociousness regarding the tastes of her market balanced with fearless self-styling in her ability to transform an abaya using look-at-me colors, subtly-shimmering brocades and rhinestone detail while preserving the modest cut."[17]

With 5 million followers on Instagram, Dian is a celebrity in the modest fashion world, and with logomania (a brand's use of its own logo to create a print) being an undeniable luxury trend, she is probably one of the only modest wear designers who could get away with putting her own name – literally – on her garments. These paraded down the catwalk in front of me at Modanisa Istanbul Modest Fashion Week in April 2019, when I first saw her designs in real life. Dian's first and last name appeared on sporty, utilitarian belts (much like the cult belts created by streetwear brand Off-White), as well as on silk hijabs.

"There's a lot of typography, inspired by the captions on Instagram," Dian tells me after the show. After a decade of creating trend-setting, fashion-forward attire for hijab-wearing millennials, Dian switched things up – her digitally-attuned clientele themselves were the muses for this season. "This collection is inspired by social love, and by the energy and euphoria in social media. It's also inspired by the styles that modest fashion bloggers share on Instagram," says the designer. One of her looks features a sporty Adidas bum bag worn diagonally across the torso of a kaftan – an edgy, urban style that's become popular among streetwear enthusiasts on Instagram. An earthy palette of khakis, olive greens and sand tones were elevated with her print-on-print styling. "In Indonesia they normally mix colors and patterns – they love to mix everything," she says. "As the country with the biggest Muslim population in the world, I think Indonesia has a big role in the growth of modest fashion, because we are the producers of modest fashion and we are also the consumers."

Muslim fashion designers in the East often have very different agendas from those living in the West. Fighting Islamophobia is not high on their priorities, especially if they're based in Muslim-majority countries, and modest fashion is already readily available. Rather, their defining feature has been their tendency to modernize traditional silhouettes, like the abaya, with elements trending in Western fashion.

Take Kuwaiti fashion brand Riva, for instance, which has stores in the UAE, Saudi Arabia, Qatar, Bahrain and Oman, in addition to Kuwait. Founded in 1997, the label has managed to stay afloat in a competitive retail market because its design team has its finger on the pulse of fashion styles that are internationally trending. These are then incorporated into modest silhouettes native to the Middle Eastern region. In October 2018, the label's autumn/winter collection included garments like oversized woolly cardigans embellished with pearls, or completed with sporty striped trims, while longer versions were clearly abaya-inspired. Leopard print tunics, textured velvet palazzo pants, quilted robe-like blanket coats and drop-waist dresses in plaids and tartans were recreated in the same colors as those shown by international fashion houses on the runway, with slightly longer hemlines and an added dose of sparkle for the brand's quintessentially Middle Eastern client. Bum bags embellished with bee motifs were clearly Gucci-inspired, while micro-mini studded purses mirrored those by Valentino, and chunky cuff bracelets appeared to be a nod to Hermès.

Independent Middle Eastern modest wear labels tend to cater to the acutely fashion-conscious client, recognizing that Arab women in particular are especially attuned to international runway trends, and often try to incorporate them into their own wardrobes. The past five years have witnessed many new Arab fashion brands emerging on the market, just as some Middle Eastern countries are becoming more lenient with their dress codes. While the abaya may constitute official national dress in many Arab countries, traditional abayas are no longer strictly enforced in Saudi Arabia, for example, which is often seen as the leading Islamic nation in the East, to which other neighboring Arab countries look for inspiration and guidance on policy.

While the abaya seems to be on a path to becoming an optional outerwear garment in GCC countries (namely Saudi Arabia, Kuwait, the United Arab Emirates, Qatar, Bahrain, and Oman) as opposed to its former status as a strictly enforced piece of clothing, International Fashion and Design Council (IFDC) chairwoman Alia Khan is of the belief that it will retain its importance among Arab women. "I don't think the abaya will ever go away," she tells me. "It's such a comfortable and convenient outer garment. And it allows a woman to express herself, because abayas are getting more and more creative, elegant and well-designed."[18] The brewing culture of reform among the Arab world has made room for its designers to experiment with the shape and form of the abaya to give it a sleek, tailored look that mimics the appearance of a long trench coat, rather than a weighted-down overcoat with superfluous fabric. Many contemporary abayas are worn open, without buttons or other closures, allowing the wearers' stylish outfits underneath to remain visible. Some designers have experimented with panels of fabrics that are sheer, embroidered or lace, and many have done away with the classic black color altogether, instead opting for grays, neutrals, pastels, jewel tones and even whites.

"Generally speaking, Islamic fashion is moving away from the sobriety of black and leaning toward colorful choices," notes Faegheh Shirazi. "Indeed, the commodification of fashionable Islamic dress has proven so successful that innovative styles continually emerge to satisfy the trendy Muslim consumer."[19] Some Arab women, who are keen on retaining the silhouette of the abaya but are not satisfied with locally available offerings, take to wearing long cardigans and kimonos from Western labels instead, like Saudi Arabian fashion editor Marriam Mossalli, who says, "I've always worn funky abayas and I don't buy them from abaya brands, I buy Emilio Pucci robes and Chanel robes and wear them as abayas, with jeans."

"With abayas becoming optional, we're going to see a fashion revolution in Saudi," continues Marriam, who has witnessed the transformation of the fashion industry in Saudi Arabia over the past decade, and in 2018 was even featured on the *Business of Fashion* 500 list along with The Modist's Ghizlan Guenez. "We've already evolved the abaya, we have the ones that look like lab coats, and the tailored ones, and in 2016 we had this whole revolution with sporty abayas, and I think now that you have women entering the workforce, we're going to see what's going to be the new power suit," she says.

Saudi designer Arwa Al Banawi was born in Jeddah and lived in Switzerland and Dubai before launching her eponymous clothing label, which is centered on power suits, in 2015. "I come from a country [Saudi Arabia] where I have to dress in a certain [modest] way and I have to [incorporate] that for every woman," says the designer, who balances modesty with international appeal in her designs. Her first collection, dubbed "The Suitable Woman", showcased a range of patterned suits without a single abaya in sight. The tapered pants and matching blazers featured bold, retro prints, and some of the looks even featured Bermuda-style shorts in place of pants. While suits, by nature, are generally modest in that they cover the arms and legs, Arwa styled some of hers with crop tops to show their versatility across all cultures and fashion preferences. For her following collections, the designer started introducing blouses, dresses, vests and jackets into her range, while always including a few of her statement suits. In a local collaboration with Adidas Originals, Arwa debuted streetwear-inspired ensembles with oversized silhouettes, sassy Arabic slogans and slouchy, sporty maxi dresses.

While she launched her brand with power suits, today many of Arwa's long blazers, maxi jackets and shirt-dresses that feature feminist Arabic slogans along the lapels of collars are odes to the abaya. "It has been a huge inspiration in my designs as I took it as a challenge to modernize it for everyone and make it cool and easy to wear even for non-Khaleeji [non-Gulf Arab] women. I have clients from Europe who wear my abayas because my designs are modern, and they also can be worn as coats outside the region," she tells me. And although the abaya may no longer be a requirement in Saudi Arabia, it's a silhouette that designers like Arwa are not prepared to part with entirely. "To me, the abaya is what the kimono is to Japan – it's part of the culture and it has beautiful history," she says.[20] While Arwa's label attracts Middle Eastern customers as well as international clients, neither the words "Islam", "Muslim" nor "modest fashion" are used in the brand's marketing or PR campaigns, indicative of her desire to appeal to a much broader, international consumer base.

Some Middle Eastern designers, on the other hand, are content with serving a specific, localized market. Emirati graphic designer Fatma Al Mulla designed tech accessories (like the aforementioned colorful niqab-shaped silicone phone cases) and stationery under her namesake label, FMM by Fatma Al Mulla, before delving into the realm of ready-to-wear in 2014. During Ramadan of that year, she launched her debut collection of dresses, featuring bold and peppy Arabic pop culture-inspired prints. While the range of patterned A-line long dresses shared an identical cut, they were a hit, and immediately sold out, prompting Fatma to create seasonal renditions of these loosely fitting designs.

The short-sleeved kaftan-inspired dresses included orange designs with watermelon slice-shaped pockets, bubblegum-pink versions dotted with evil-eye emblems, turquoise styles decorated with palm leaves, fuchsia pieces flaunting traditional Arabic teapots and mustard versions featuring an assortment of Arabic oud (oil-based fragrance) and Vimto (a sweet drink that's popular during Ramadan) bottles. With these garments, Fatma wasn't really targeting a diverse or international clientele; rather, she focused on the wardrobe needs and aesthetics of Arab women in the Gulf countries. According-ing to the designer, approximately 75 percent of her clients live in the Middle East, and of those, 50 percent live within the United Arab Emirates. "I have that insight as an Emirati, and I have to think about what will be most worn by Emirati women," she tells me. "In the UAE, believe it or not, even though the Emirati population is very small, they are the highest spenders in retail."

While Fatma's dresses may be best-sellers among her Emirati clientele, the garments are not often spotted on the streets (or within the luxurious air-conditioned shopping malls) of Dubai. That's because, Fatma says, they're intended to be worn indoors, at ladies-only social gatherings. "The dresses that we do that are very loud, we've done them with the purpose of women wearing them in the house, or under the abaya when going outside. They wouldn't necessarily wear them to dress up and go somewhere," she explains. While this may sound like an unusual sales pitch coming from a fashion designer, the Islamic concept of haya, or modesty, has influenced the segregation of genders in Arab cultures, meaning women will actually often shop for fashion statements to wear indoors at women-only gatherings.

Another label that launched to respond to the needs of modest fashion followers living in the East is Dulce by Safiya. Libyan-Mexican Safiya Abdallah lived in Orange County, California for more than twenty years before moving to Dubai, and then launching her label in 2015. Her aim was to provide women in the city with glamorous alternatives to the traditional abaya. "I noticed in Dubai there are so many events all the time, and there was this need for something in between – women who don't necessarily want to wear a dress can wear this literally glam tracksuit to a party and still feel dressed up," she tells me. Luxe, oversized blazers, gold sequin-covered trenches, glimmering hoodie-and-gown hybrids and glittering metallic corsets (layered over turtlenecks to retain the modesty factor) are some of the garments the designer has created, but perhaps one of her most popular inventions thus far has been a statement beanie, designed as an alternative to the traditional hijab. Available in gold, rose-gold and chrome-color stretchy fabrics, the beanies are practical investments, she says, rather than mere style splurges. They're also reflective of a middle ground when it comes to covering your hair, much like the popular turban style.

"As hijabis, the hardest thing is, you don't want to look like a cone-head with a jersey scarf, and if you have kids and you're chasing them you don't want to always have a turban that you have to keep tightening. And this material is just amazing, it's non-slip, it grips your hair and you don't have to pin anything. You just put your hair into a bun, throw it on and it stays on all

"For Faiza, launching her brand was not any sort of religious mission. Rather, she felt fulfilled by the social drive to help women who follow conservative dress codes fit in and feel comfortable, in garments that were modern yet still followed cultural guidelines."

day," says Safiya, who started wearing the hijab herself in 2011, and found it difficult to feel confident in the boring, drab and bag-like garments that the modest fashion market was limited to at the time:

> I started with making hoods and beanies - because I felt that a hood was a way to inconspicuously cover your hair for people who live in Western countries. I guess I've walked across this bridge, where I'm bordered by both worlds, all my life, and I kind of wanted to create things for people in the middle who don't have a place.[21]

Much like Abaya Addict and Haute Hijab, the majority of Dulce by Safiya's clients live in the United States; however, unlike the former labels, Safiya has chosen to remain based in the UAE. She attributes her popularity among American modest wear consumers to her tendency to work with US-based celebrities and fashion influencers – one of her jackets has even been worn by Gwen Stefani. But it's California-based hijabi rapper Neelam Hakeem who is one of Safiya's most loyal supporters, often posting images of herself on Instagram dressed in Dulce by Safiya designs. For her 2018 music video "I'll Be the King" that also starred American singer Erykah Badu, Neelam wore three different looks by the brand. Safiya says the rapper had caught her attention early on, when she released one of her very first rap videos that went viral after it got reposted by the likes of P. Diddy and Will Smith. "She wasn't just a pretty face posting in her hijab. Even though she has that influencer side, she also spreads awareness and talks about real things that matter," says Safiya.[22]

Having a celebrity endorse your designs is a thrilling career high for any fashion designer – just ask Faiza Bouguessa, whose garments have been worn by Beyoncé. The designer launched her namesake modest wear label, Bouguessa, in 2014, after working for six years as a flight attendant for

Emirates Airlines. Sleek, modern and culturally relevant are the best words to describe her creations, and Faiza herself effortlessly embodies these characteristics. When we meet for the first time, she's dressed in an all-black ensemble, consisting of a fitted T-shirt and tailored ankle-length skirt, accessorized with minimalist gold jewelry that offsets the designer's short blonde bob, chopped just above her chin. Her artfully decorated showroom located in Dubai's Design District is an impressive space for a brand that has only been in existence for five years. Modular black rails hang from the ceilings, displaying Bouguessa's latest collection in a room that's large enough to host a runway show. The designer's specialty is contemporary abayas, though the word abaya doesn't quite do justice to the label's signature tailored overcoats, which are fashion-forward and versatile. Faiza, who is French-Algerian, says that her father was the one who gave her the business idea of revolutionizing the abaya.

"Looking around, I realized women in the Middle East were very into fashion but there was not a lot of difference between their outerwear designs," she says in her soft French accent. "So, I started looking into it, and I was trying to find my place in this, which was difficult because it's not my culture. I was born and raised in France, so even though I was born Muslim, I didn't really recognize myself in this garment. But then I thought, why not bridge the cultures and try to do something for both worlds?"

Faiza's garments are marked by a clean and polished aesthetic that is European-inspired, with subtle hints of Eastern-influenced elements, such as the occasional inclusion of a North African kaftan neckline or antique-gold striped pattern. Trench-like coats in hues like mustard, powder blue, olive green, khaki, gray, black and white are some of the label's abaya alternatives, while a luminous silver metallic version offers coverage with a glamorous punch. Suit-inspired separates, tailored dresses with voluminous skirts and

ankle-length shirt-dresses are wearable for women who follow diverse interpretations of modesty. "When you look at my designs, it's not obvious that
they're modest and that's what I'm trying to do," says the designer, who has
plans to expand globally and doesn't want to be pigeonholed into the realm
of modest wear, even though most of her clients are Muslim and based in
the Middle East.

For Faiza, launching her brand was not any sort of religious mission.
Rather, she felt fulfilled by the social drive to help women who follow
conservative dress codes fit in and feel comfortable, in garments that were
modern yet still followed cultural guidelines. Her plan was to focus first
on cementing a strong presence in the Middle East, before exploring international ambitions, but her first collection caught the eye of *Vogue Italia*
scouts, and she was invited to present at the *Vogue* Fashion Dubai Experience in 2014. The following year, she was invited to Milan Fashion Week.
"It was huge for me, for my second season to actually go and fly to Italy
and present my collection there, and then following that, things just kept
happening," she says. Beyoncé wore the designer's creations not once but
twice, first opting for a geometric abaya but wearing it open, exposing the
singer's legs, and second, for a velvet green robe, which she wore over a
red bodycon dress – both times showcasing the versatility of the garments,
which may be categorized as modest wear but don't necessarily need to be
worn to cover the wearer's body. Bollywood star Sonam Kapoor has been
spotted in a pink suit and matching coat by the label, and both Czech
model Karolina Kurkova and Saudi princess Deena Aljuhani Abdulaziz
have worn Bouguessa's blue, belted cotton dress.

The designer makes it clear that she doesn't spend any money on PR
– celebrity stylists approach her directly for their clients, which has helped
spread global awareness for the brand. Faiza was invited to showcase at the

2018 Contemporary Muslim Fashions exhibition in San Francisco by post (a rarity in the UAE, where communication tends to be electronic) a whole two years before the exhibition took place. She says that the main thing that she's noticed over the past two years, with the international modest fashion movement peaking, is that more customers are embracing her brand's mission and story. "[With non-Muslims in the West], I had this experience a few times initially, they would be interested in the clothes, but when I was speaking about [modest fashion] out loud, they would take a step back," she says. "But today it's different, and I know it has a lot to do with Halima Aden and the diversity in the industry." Though she has focused thus far on cementing her brand's presence within the Middle East, Faiza's expansion plans include partnering with high-end stockists in Europe and North America.

It's not only social-media-savvy customers whom these brands are attracting over apps like Instagram – they're catching the eyes of major retailers from internationally renowned multi-brand department stores and boutiques too. In 2010, Emirati abaya brand DAS, founded by sisters Reem and Hind Beljafla, landed at Harrods in London. In 2015, Madiyah Al Sharqi, the namesake label founded by a princess from the UAE Emirate of Fujairah, launched at upscale New York boutique Fivestory, and in 2018, Lebanese designer Zayan Ghandour of the eponymous brand Zayan The Label partnered with American fashion e-commerce site Shopbop. New York-based Moda Operandi, a luxury e-commerce website that allows customers to pre-order designer collections a season in advance, has also supported many Middle Eastern brands in its various online trunk shows, including Vanina, Anatomi, Bambah, Bthaina and Bouguessa. And in 2018, The Modist teamed up with UK-based online retail site Farfetch to offer modest wear designs from its in-house label, Layeur, on a global platform.

The past decade has seen the spread of Middle Eastern fashion brands to all corners of the world, and Marcela Danielova at Fashion Forward Dubai (FFWD), a platform that supports Middle Eastern designers, attributes this to both the Arab Spring and the newfound modest fashion awareness in the West. She also points out that designers from the East are now offering a wider variety. "I think Middle Eastern designers have always been known for couture in the past – like Elie Saab and Zuhair Murad. But in the past six years, many ready-to-wear brands have successfully popped up and penetrated the Middle East's borders," she tells me.[23] She notes that new-generation designers are experimenting with alternative silhouettes and textiles, and that streetwear seems to have become the new luxury. Marcela believes it's a combination of these design elements, the brands' exotic appeal and successful social media marketing strategies that impress buyers abroad.

But Saudi fashion editor Marriam Mossalli is more cynical, confident that international retailers are recruiting brands from the Middle East only to bring along the designers' wealthy associates and followers to their stores and e-commerce platforms. "You're not going to like my answer – it's just because they want the Arab VIPs," she says. "Every time I have a brand I want to sell to a store like Bergdorf's, if it has [the word] 'Ameera' or 'princess' attached to it, I know that it's going to get in."

Non-Muslim designers dedicated to modesty

Though Muslim and Arab designers, hand in hand with their loyal and evidently wealthy social circles, may be feeding the international modest wear market now, conservative fashion labels launched by creatives of other religions have long been attempting to sell modesty in the West. It's important to note, however, that these Western modest wear brands are dramatically different in terms of design aesthetics from Middle Eastern fashion labels, which are typically more embellished, bold and froufrou, with elaborate ruffles and layers, and add-ons like beading and embroidery. Modest wear labels founded in North America, on the other hand, are less avant-garde, perhaps inspired by religious commandments rooted in traditions that urge women to appear inconspicuous, or perhaps to serve a different, more practical Western lifestyle, one in which maids, cooks, nannies and drivers are not typical of middle-class living, and where over-the-top embellishments have little place.

One of the most decadent and deliberately modest labels that you'll currently find in mainstream American fashion is Batsheva. Available on luxury e-tail sites like MatchesFashion.com, the brand specializes in the production of vintage-inspired prairie dresses. It was founded in 2016 somewhat by accident by Batsheva Hay, a half-Israeli New Yorker, former lawyer and practicing Jew. Looking to mend one of her old Laura Ashley dresses, Batsheva decided to revamp the design with a higher neck and some ruffles on the sleeves and had some similar designs tailor-made in second-hand fabrics that she bought online. After receiving compliments, she decided to start selling the old-fashioned yet clearly in-demand dresses in both women's and children's sizes.

The designer's signature silhouette features elbow-length bell-sleeves, a frilled hem reaching the ankle, and a high, ruffled neckline. Fabrics are typically cotton, with vintage-inspired prints. Batsheva's aesthetic is quirky and borderline kitsch, and she happily refers to her designs, which she shows at New York Fashion Week, as frumpy. Though her approach to design may be heavily influenced by her own religious dress codes, there's nothing uniform or plain-Jane about Batsheva dresses. And while they may at first appear to be imported from a past era, they've become highly covetable fashion investments, endorsed by celebrities like Natalie Portman, Lena Dunham and Erykah Badu, as well as by numerous fashion editors and influencers. "Batsheva's skyrocketing success signals the way in which modest fashion – once a niche market – has entered mainstream consciousness," writes Pip Usher for *Vogue*. "No longer dismissed as the dowdy domain of religious folk, this multibillion-dollar industry is being driven by a young and cosmopolitan consumer who demands coverage in accordance with her faith but refuses to skimp on style."[24]

The Frock NYC is another New York-based fashion label, founded in 2010 by Orthodox Jewish Australian sisters Chaya Chanin and Simi Polonsky. While their designs mostly cover models' bodies up to the knees and elbows, they are still feminine and fashion-forward. Wrap dresses, slip skirts, pinstripe shirts and accessories like belts and bandanas fit in with mainstream, high-street style trends, and are priced competitively too.

Mimu Maxi is yet another New York-based fashion label, founded by a duo of Orthodox Jewish sisters-in-law, Mimi Hecht and Mushky Notik, in 2012. Tunics and skirts with cascading hemlines, asymmetric jersey dresses, turtleneck dresses and dresses with batwing sleeves are the modest-yet-stylish solutions offered by the label. The brand is particularly known in the community for its "skirt leggings", which are fitted knee- or ankle-length skirts crafted from stretch fabrics similar to those used to manufacture leggings, since many Jews believe that the wearing of pants (and by extension, leggings) for women is prohibited.

In 2014, Muslim fashion blogger Summer Albarcha (@summeralbarcha on Instagram) posted an outfit image on Instagram featuring a green skirt from Mimu Maxi. When the brand reposted the image on its own Instagram account, it was met with heated backlash from many Jewish followers, who found the endorsement of a Muslim blogger offensive in light of the Israel–Palestine conflict, but the brand stood by its decision to feature Summer's outfit image. "I find it very satisfying that beautiful, feminine Muslim women are inspired by and representing our Jewish brand," Mimi told the *Times of Israel*. "The fact that our brand has somehow been able to bridge gaps with other religions and celebrate the beauty of modesty beyond Judaism is a very, very good thing."[25]

Designs by Utah-based, Mormon-owned fashion e-commerce site Mikarose also marry modesty with practicality. Founded by Michaella Lawson in 2006, the brand sought to fill the gap in the market between church dresses and evening wear gowns, after Michaella struggled to find modest party dresses that were suitable for dinners or trips to the theater. Her resulting dresses under the Mikarose label appear similar to those found in many high-street stores like New Look or Forever 21, but their hemlines reach the knees or below, and sleeves cover the shoulders. Wrap dresses, lace dresses, velvet dresses and floral dresses from the brand are created to suit a variety of occasions, while skirts and tops offer a feminine, moderately modest approach to style without appearing aged or matronly. The brand was even stocked at select locations of popular membership-only warehouse store Costco between 2014 and 2016.

While modest fashion brands founded by Muslims in the Eastern part of the world tend to place more emphasis on unique, statement-making designs, the strength of these Western brands founded by women of other faiths are that their garments are easy to wear, versatile and long-lasting, as they aren't tied to fleeting trends. With the exception of Batsheva, whose eye-catching party dresses have been placed on red carpets and best-dressed pages, Jewish and Christian labels tend to create clothing with the everyday woman in mind – not the gala-hopping socialite who swears never to repeat an outfit.

CHAPTER 6

MARKETING MODESTY

It's the peak of the scorching summer season in the UAE, and I'm the stylist on set for a fashion shoot for *Luxury* magazine, a monthly lifestyle publication that comes out with Abu Dhabi's leading English-language newspaper, the *National*. The crew is situated on the balcony of a luxurious penthouse located on the famous man-made island, The Palm Jumeirah, in Dubai. Temperatures exceed 40 degrees Celsius. Although there is a rooftop swimming pool on the property that we plan on incorporating into one shot, there'll be no swimwear or scantily clad model in this fashion shoot. Pieces from the spring/summer collections that we've called in from Milan and Paris, along with designs supplied by regional Middle Eastern designers, include a strappy yellow gown by Gucci and a cobalt-blue mini dress by Lanvin, but I'm mindful of our conservative Abu Dhabi readership and publishing guidelines, and get started on putting together layered looks that are both stylish and, in my opinion, moderately modest.

After around half an hour of maneuvering the hangers housing designer clothes around on the rail with the team's fashion editor, my looks for the shoot are complete. The Gucci gown, which will later be shot on the model while she's in the pool, will be worn with a salmon-pink, fitted, glittered top underneath, and the shot with the Lanvin dress will be cropped at the thigh, thus disguising its actual length. A sleeveless Missoni dress will be topped

135

with a metallic Gucci bomber jacket, and a low-cut pink sequined dress by Dubai-based designer Dima Ayad will be completed with an off-white turtle-neck underneath. Without shelter from the sunlight, our model Celine is uncomfortable to say the least, but by the end of the day we're able to achieve what we set out to produce: a glamorous fashion shoot featuring high-end fashion labels in outfits that would resonate with the modesty-conscious consumers of the UAE.

But what constitutes modest dress is subjective, and many Muslims, particularly those entrenched in ultra-conservative schools of thought, would refute my depiction of modest fashion. Some would argue that, since a model was still used, and some skin was still shown, this shoot could not be suitable for Muslim women at all. Over the past decade this type of mindset has slowly shifted to embrace a more mainstream, Western-influenced view.

In Islam, idolatry is forbidden in the Quran, which is why Muslims do not condone the production and publication of images of the Prophet Muhammad, or God for that matter. Many Muslims extend this belief to all depictions of the human form – some very traditional Muslim homes are even devoid of family photographs.

Reina Lewis has noted that during the early-to-mid 2000s, Muslim fashion and lifestyle magazines struggled to depict women in a way that would make sense editorially while appeasing conservative readers. The dilemmas are not only rooted in the types of clothing these publications showcased, but also how that clothing would be featured on bodies, and how those bodies would be presented. Founded in 2003, *Emel* was the United Kingdom's first Muslim lifestyle magazine, headed by Catholic convert to Islam Sarah Joseph, and for the first seven years of the publication's existence, faces were not printed on the fashion pages except for when they accompanied real people being shot as part of a street style feature. Sarah was against the use of fashion models since she believed that they objectified women. The magazine made conscious efforts to connect its fashion features with Islam: some of its first stories, centered on textiles like cotton and silk, were accompanied by detailed explanations of the fabrics' foundations in Islamic history.

Some early Muslim women's magazines made it clear that revealing garments were to be worn at home, under outerwear or in segregated environments – a 2007 fashion feature in UK-based publication *Sisters* was accompanied with the disclaimer, "P.S.: All fashion ideas on these pages are intended for hijab-free environments. Please use them responsibly!"[1] At this time, fashion magazines in the Arab world looked very similar to their Western counterparts, though, contrary to up-and-coming Western titles like *Emel* and *Sisters*, faith and religion were hardly explored at all. Rather, the aims of magazines like *Elle Arabia*, *Grazia Middle East* and *Harper's Bazaar Arabia* were to spread awareness about international fashion trends, while also highlighting local entrepreneurs and personalities within the Arab fashion world.

In Indonesia, women's lifestyle magazine *Noor* launched in 2003, covering everything from Quranic interpretations to travel and reports on mainstream fashion shows. While it was intended to exist as a general lifestyle magazine for the Indonesian woman, its founders discovered that both readers and advertisers were most attracted to its fashion content. *Noor* featured ordinary women rather than professional models on its covers, which, according to Reina, conveyed that you could be an attractive, professional working woman while still covering your body for religious reasons.

Over the years, publications have become more flexible in their policies when it comes to depicting fashion visuals. When UK-based modest fashion magazine *Maysaa* launched in 2010, it styled models with less reservation – such as pairing a maxi skirt with a sleeveless, cleavage-baring top. "It would have been inconceivable even five years previous for a modest brand to risk this near naked body," claims Reina.[2]

In 2018, at the height of the global modest fashion boom, emerged a magazine dedicated wholly to this style movement. Editor-in-chief Sahinat Erkilic (@shahhatun on Instagram) co-founded *Hijab In Style* in the United States and the publication, available both in print and online, has featured famous modest fashion personalities including Mariah Idrissi, Lisa Vogl and Basma Kahie on its covers.

While it focuses primarily on head-covering women, *Hijab In Style* incorporates articles from a mix of hijabi and non-hijabi contributors and features a diverse range of Muslim women, from models and fashion bloggers to life coaches, personal trainers and cancer survivors. Like other fashion publications, the magazine opens with a range of runway reports, but with a modest edit – like a roundup of one hundred ways to wear stripes, showcased on hijab-friendly outfits from recent catwalks. Stories in the magazine include profiles on prominent modest fashion designers and entrepreneurs, as well as topics like outfit ideas for mothers, kid-friendly travel destinations, easy breakfast recipes, essential items to pack in your beach bag and tips to stay cool while covered up in the summer heat. Beauty features include seasonal makeup trends, and often highlight cosmetics that Westerners may not think hijabi women require, such as tanning products. This diversity in topics makes the magazine relatable to all female readers, not just Muslim, hijab-wearing ones – Sahinat has stated that *Hijab In Style* is "made by women, for all women."[3]

Muslim cover girls and image makers

Even if a model is covered from head to toe, traditionalists will still contest the modesty of her overall appearance. When Halima Aden starred on the cover of

Vogue Arabia in June 2017 for instance, the image, while celebrated by many, was not welcomed by the entire Muslim community. The cover shows Halima perched on a stool, her torso bent forward and back slightly arched, while a male makeup artist applies a touch of eye makeup to the model, marking another point of contention as Muslim women traditionally are not supposed to have any physical contact with males who aren't of close kin. Halima is dressed in a form-fitting black gown, layered over a turtleneck, and her head is wrapped in a matching black and gray headscarf, tied like a turban. Both her posture, and the inclusion of a male makeup artist, were seen to be controversial by critics.

When I meet Halima in Istanbul, at the first-floor restaurant of The Stay, a hotel off the coast of the Bosporus River, I'm curious as to how she'll defend the concept of modest fashion. Her opinion holds great importance, as she was one of the first global faces of modest fashion, yet she hasn't spoken much to the press about the controversies the field presents. She wears a royal blue and emerald green Arabian gown with a silk patterned turban, and her demeanor is lively and cheerful. I wonder if she'll shy away from the tough questions that I leave for the end of our thirty-minute interview, or if she'll be ill-equipped to answer them confidently, but I'm quickly proven wrong. When I ask the model if she sees any clash between her faith and working with male makeup artists, stylists and photographers in the industry, she brings up a valid point. "That's part of being in today's society, women and men work alongside each other, and even if I was a teacher, or a university student, those [men] would be my peers and my colleagues," she says.[4]

Nonetheless, organizations are forming to make Muslim models more comfortable in their work spaces, and this often involves catering to their requests for privacy or all-female teams. Way before Halima was signed by IMG Models, Muslims had been exploring the potential for modesty-conscious modeling work in the industry. In 2012, Brooklyn-based American-Muslim

"Nonetheless, organizations are forming to make Muslim models more comfortable in their work spaces, and this often involves catering to their requests for privacy or all-female teams."

Nailah Lymus launched a modeling agency dedicated to supporting modest models. Called Underwraps, the agency represents a range of women, from Muslim women who wear hijab to non-Muslim women who adhere to modest dress codes, and it helps its models come up with tailored guidelines for the shoots and projects they book. Nailah will recruit models through social media, and sometimes even approaches women on the street if she thinks they have potential to turn modeling into a career. "These girls have everything – the height, the look. And it's like a dream deferred because they dress a certain way," said Nailah to ABC News in 2013. "Muslim women are fashion-forward. We embrace everything that other women do, but we just have certain stipulations."[5] Azizah Hosein is one of the Muslim models who has been represented by Underwraps and her custom contracts forbid men on set to have physical contact with her, or see her with her hair uncovered.[6]

While Underwraps serves the American modeling industry, Umma Models, founded in 2017, is based in London and caters to the international industry. For the second season of Haute Elan's London Modest Fashion Week, Umma provided models for the weekend's runway shows. One of the agency's key aims, according to its website, is to "improve the pornographic stigma associated with modeling and give modest women an opportunity to work within the industry and with a company that adheres to the ways of a modest lifestyle".[7] On its website, Umma Models implies that if Muslim fashion brands hire mainstream models who don't follow modest dress codes in their personal lives, this could misrepresent their brand – especially if these same models are seen in "immodest" clothing for other shoots.

The website's layout mirrors that of other modeling agencies; interested brands and clients can search through the different models available, browse their portfolios and also view their body measurements, dress and shoe sizes. Models' descriptions will also state "hijab only" if they wear the hijab full-time and thus won't take it off for any shoot. Most of the women signed by Umma Models do wear the hijab, though there are some who don't cover their hair at all. In 2018, one year after the agency was founded, its website features a diverse array of faces: there's Haneen from Jordan, Nadia from Berlin, Sheng from Sydney and Afra from Abu Dhabi, to name just a few.

Halima's inclusion in the mainstream fashion industry has no doubt led to the rise of this new group of modest fashion models, many of whom wear the hijab and have no qualms about posing creatively for the camera or fronting print publications. The portfolio of New York-based Guyanese Muslim model Wafeeqa Azeem, for instance, includes an image of her submerged in a bathtub filled with flowers. She wears a black abaya from Deanna Khalil's Abaya Addict label with a black turban scarf, and the only skin visible is her face, hands and feet. Other images from Wafeeqa's portfolio include her dressed in a pink floral dress lounging on a bed, seated at a gold dressing table robed in an elegant bridal gown and matching headwrap, and sitting on a log in a forest while wearing a maroon dress and white lace hijab. Wafeeqa models part-time and didn't have any formal training in modeling.

"I would sometimes practice in front of a mirror as well as watch the occasional YouTube video," she tells me. She's worked with modest fashion labels like Hijabican and has been featured in various community start-up publications in the US, as well as in Caribbean lifestyle magazine *Adornami* and in a local Guyanese newspaper. "My first feature in Guyana received mixed reviews," says Wafeeqa. "I received a lot of positive feedback from strangers, but negative feedback from family and friends of the local conservative Muslim community. This put a dampener on what I thought was a beautiful picture. At the end of the day we all have our own individual journeys and we all have to make our own choices. I wish the Muslim community would embrace the right to choose over the right to criticize."

In 2018, Wafeeqa signed with Umma Models. "I knew I wouldn't have to explain my stance on modesty and my religious beliefs. It just seemed right that the first company that I would sign with would be a modest agency," says Wafeeqa, whose personal work stipulations include not allowing men on set to have any physical contact with her, and making sure the clothing she's styled in covers her entire body except her face, hands and feet.

While some mainstream models like Halima are happy to work with male photographers and makeup artists, some Muslim models prefer working with all-female teams, though this can be a challenge, as the realm of professional fashion photography is still mainly inhabited by men. New York-based fashion photographer Nicole Najmah Abraham specializes in capturing modest fashion and is the photographer behind the image of Wafeeqa Azeem wearing the black Abaya Addict design in the flower-filled bathtub. Nicole, who has experience in fashion design and graphic design, worked for American labels like Guess and Gap before turning to photography and seeing her images published in titles like the *Huffington Post*, *Newsweek Middle East*, *Vogue Arabia* and *Gaya Magazine*. Contributing to the modest fashion industry, she says, was a personal goal for her ever since attaining her degree in fashion design. "As a woman who adheres to the Islamic dress code of modesty, modest fashion is a major part of my everyday lifestyle," she tells me. Her foray into fashion photography was a natural extension of her designing career, as she had to teach herself how to take effective images of her own designs. This opened the door to opportunities to shoot look books, campaigns, portraits and street style for other brands and clients:

I knew immediately that I would document modest fashion because I understand it. Who better to provide this service than a woman [who dresses modestly]? Many companies hire males because photography is a male-dominated field, but a lot of models say it's uncomfortable to adjust garments or interact with male photographers, so hiring a woman creates a comfortable environment for models worried about their modesty [boundaries] being violated. I wanted to provide this alternative to this industry.

Nicole says that approximately 40 percent of the jobs she books fall under the category of modest fashion, and that her approach to photographing modest models deviates slightly from the usual approach. "Today's fashion [photography] tends to accentuate and focus on a woman's sex appeal, whereas modest fashion focuses on the woman herself. What else is there to see of her? Modest fashion answers that question. Without her displayed body parts, she can still look feminine and exude a powerful energy, and this is beautiful," she explains. At times bold and striking, and at others romantic and whimsical, Nicole's photography captures attitude, character and motion. An image shot of hijab-wearing interior designer Saudah Saleem shows her blush-colored headscarf fluttering in the wind, having its own Marilyn Monroe moment, while a photo of stylist Janna Rae during New York Fashion Week is the epitome of stellar street style composition, with Rae's all-red outfit providing a stark contrast to the yellow taxicab and street lines of the city backdrop.

Nicole believes that modest fashion photography is necessary for providing an alternative narrative to the mainstream, sexually driven nature of the fashion industry:

A woman isn't the plague, to be locked in the basement never to be seen or heard. Modesty is seen in how a woman leaves her home and interacts with society. She still contributes to society as a mother, teacher, entrepreneur or student. Imagine if we didn't document this, and the only images that remained were inaccurate images put out by extremists. I think there is a benefit to seeing modest women function with dignity and go against the whole "sex sells" agenda of most fashion companies. These images are a silent protest to that.

The rise of new media covering fashion and lifestyle

The past decade has been nothing short of transformative for publications founded by Muslim entrepreneurs in the West, or millennials in Asia and the Arab world. The traditional print magazine is slowly giving way to the rise of the e-zine, in addition to a multitude of Muslim-centric blogs and social media pages. Many online portals have been launched over the past few years by Muslim women looking to counter mainstream, patriarchal stereotypes of the religion, and quite a few of these websites have extensive fashion sections.

Amani Al-Khatahtbeh (@amani on Instagram) is a prime example of a Generation M personality – the Muslim entrepreneur's decision to launch the website MuslimGirl.com in 2009 was her direct response to the wave of Islamophobia in the United States after the September 11 terrorist attacks. In 2016, Amani was featured in the annual *Forbes* 30 Under 30 list in the media category, marking the first time a Muslim had made the prestigious roundup. That year, she also published her memoir *Muslim Girl: A Coming of Age*. Her website is a predominantly politically fueled online platform shedding light on current events in relation to Islam and women. When Amani was first building the site in 2009, she was faced with a design dilemma and her decision would set the tone for MuslimGirl.com for years to come. She wanted to start with an image illustrating the opening line of the Quran, and had two choices: a geometric calligraphy design, or an unusual, graffiti-esque pink Arabic script. "I went the unconventional route," she writes. "It was important to me that every detail about Muslim Girl was unconventional; that it was unique and accessible to young girls and showed that Islam was cool and interesting. It had to be anything other than usual."[8]

In its early days, the website's first few posts, which were published by moderators until the platform accumulated more members and contributors, were centered around lifestyle topics including different hijab styles. While some of its regular article topics range from American foreign policy and international humanitarian crises to mental health issues and educational initiatives, it also posts fashion and beauty articles with titles like "10 stores for your summer hijab needs", "5 spring fashion trends for Ramadan" and "Tips for a dope Eid makeup look from Sahur Saleim, an award-winning celebrity makeup artist". The latter article featured an interview with a popular Singapore-based Pakistani-Muslim makeup artist, and the accompanying imagery showed a bare-necked photograph of Rihanna, with bold red lipstick, gold eyeshadow and her collarbone tattoo on display.

There's also Amaliah.com, a UK-based lifestyle website that publishes the stories of over 200 contributors, who write about everything from news and current affairs to dodgy first dates. "We believe that a media company that centers the voices of Muslim women is a powerful tool for cultural change," reads the mission statement of the website, which was founded in 2016 with the initial aim of helping women source modest fashion options, before it broadened its scope to become a full-fledged lifestyle portal with thought-provoking articles that would get featured in publications like *Forbes*, the *Guardian*, the *Telegraph* and CNN. The website's co-founder and CEO, Nafisa Bakkar, does not cover her head, nor does the website dictate or prescribe any set definition of what Muslim women should look like, though it does focus on those who wear some form of the hijab and many stories in its fashion section highlight hijab-wearing influencers and personalities. "We do feel like we have to highlight covering women to add balance to the spectrum at large, however we try to include a range," says Nafisa. General modest fashion role models and Muslim bloggers who don't wear headscarves, like New York-based Egyptian influencer Nadia Azmy (@nadiaazmy on Instagram), are also featured within Amaliah.com's "style crush" category. When it comes to depicting fashion imagery, trend report roundups on various topics, from oversized knitwear and checked pants to sustainable fashion, are featured alongside galleries of photos from fashion-week runways and regular look book images from various high-street retailers, complete with mainstream models and their uncovered hair.

"I don't believe an item of clothing is inherently modest, it is more about how you style it," Nafisa tells me, though she admits that fashion features that don't require additional layering tend to get the most hits on the site. Amaliah.com also has a beauty section bursting with stories about new cosmetic brand launches, makeup trends, beauty tutorials and industry analyses, many of which target its Muslim readership with headlines like "Solutions for those Ramadan eyebags" and deeper stories exploring mainstream beauty ideals, like "Hijab is only acceptable when co-opted by a very Western notion of femininity". Other stories on the website explore topics with a feminist angle on Islam, from niqab bans and celebrities converting to Islam to writing your own marriage contracts and even getting tested for STDs.

While MuslimGirl.com and Amaliah.com are based in the West, there is also a movement underway in the Middle East to shatter stereotypes. *Jdeed* is one such publication, which was founded in Beirut, Lebanon, in 2017. Though holding no religious ties, the magazine, according to its founder and editor-in-chief Cynthia Jreige, was created in order to give emerging Middle Eastern designers, specifically Lebanese ones, a platform. "My aim was to diversify the offerings of the magazine sector in the Middle East, which was basically international titles like *Elle Arabia*, kind of adapted to the region, but not really," she says. "I felt they didn't truly cater to women in the Middle East." Cynthia's magazine is pointedly edgy, and deviates dramatically from other lifestyle titles in the region. Some stories in the publication address sexuality, which may be openly discussed in the cosmopolitan city of Beirut but is more taboo in other cities of Lebanon and the Middle East. "We shipped it to Jordan and the magazine didn't pass the postal control, we never really knew why, they never gave us a reason, but our second issue included an interview with the founder of a magazine that defends LGBT rights, so that might have been it," says Cynthia.

The magazine founder also has a knack for styling, and is the art director behind most of the magazine's fashion shoots, which are unconventional. Models' past makeup looks have included a psychedelic take on Cleopatra eye makeup, complete with glitter-dusted eyebrows, and featured props once included a pearl and crystal-studded Starbucks coffee cup. A bathtub full of mermaid Barbie dolls has been the setting for one shoot, while a life-size Burger King sign has provided the backdrop of another. Edgy, abstract and artistic, these fashion shoots are not strict about covering skin, and feature hardy leathers, sequin-emblazoned jackets, optical patterns and whatever else Lebanese designers are serving up for the season. Poses and styling are sometimes avant-garde and provocative, and the overall effect is a clear departure from the billowing, romantic gowns shot among desert dunes typical of the fashion shoots found in mainstream Arabian titles.

Modest fashion, while headlining stand-alone stories and shoots in other Middle Eastern publications, is not a concept Cynthia has explored much in *Jdeed*, because, she explains, there's simply not much demand for it in Beirut. "Aside from conservative Muslim mothers, you don't really see young people wear the abaya, they're mostly trying to follow the latest [international] trends. The demand for modest fashion in Beirut is probably the lowest in the region," she says.

Modest fashion meets the catwalk

The first official New York Fashion Week was held in 1943, with the first couture show taking place in Paris in 1945. Milan followed with its own fashion week in 1958, and London in 1984. These cities are known as the "Big Four" in fashion. Given the cultural taboos regarding the photography and publication of female models according to traditional Muslim schools of thought, the prospect of putting Muslim fashions on public runways can be controversial, even if the clothing covers the wearer's skin. As early as 1992, Turkish modest wear brand Tekbir (whose name means "God is the greatest") tested the waters, seeking a popular, mainstream method for publicizing its tesettür (modest dress) designs. "The initiative by Tekbir in 1992 to hold a catwalk show was seen as nothing less than revolutionary, meriting heated responses from secularists who derided the clothing as failed fashion and from religionists who deplored the use of non-religious models and the display of female bodies," notes Reina Lewis.[9]

Conservative religious organizations' lectures on the topic can be found online on various religious forums where users may seek advice about balancing faith with modernity. In 2005, South Africa-based religious website, *Voice of Islam* posted an online question-and-answer feature which included the topic of a fashion show being organized by an all-girls school in South Africa. A religious scholar from a branch of the Darul Uloom Deoband school deemed the event to be an "evil fashion parade" that was "in total conflict and negation of the Islamic concept of hijab with its emphasis on female concealment", and he wasn't happy that the event was taking place on the Muslim holy day of Friday.[10]

Such authoritative responses can be made regardless of the user's supposed Islamic training or expertise. A user's 2015 post on Muslim e-forum Ummah.com mentioned that she was considering volunteering for a charity photoshoot that was looking for ethnic minorities. The question she posed was, "Halal/Islamic modeling – is there such a thing?" One user's response read, "Halal modeling; sounds like an oxymoron to me. Best to stay away from it", and another said, "Women wear hijab to conceal their beauty. Not to flaunt it where men can see." One user even compared the term "halal modeling" to "halal alcohol", while another simply stated, "not allowed."[11] If a well-intentioned attempt to volunteer for charity photos can incite such ardent resistance, one can only imagine how some critics would react to Halima Aden donning her hijab and starring on magazine covers or stomping down international runways for all the world to see.

When I meet Halima in Turkey, I bring up this point of controversy within the Muslim community, but she is adamant that by modeling, she isn't going against her faith in any way. "I'm not Rapunzel stuck in a castle," she tells me, pointing out that some traditionalists have double standards when it comes to Muslim women. "In today's society you're out and about, and you're visible, no matter what. So why is it okay for me to be visible in the classrooms, why is it okay to be out in the malls, or just outside, but I can't be seen in a magazine?"[12]

British hijabi model Mariah Idrissi believes there's a middle ground when it comes to finding a balance between religious ideals and fashion industry norms. While she models in photoshoots that accompany interviews and stories that include her quotes on topics like diversity and humanitarianism, she avoids runway jobs. "I feel I can't justify being a hijabi on a runway – for me, I've just stayed away from that, it couldn't make sense in my head," she tells me. "I've always had a voice attached to every shoot I've done – whereas being on a runway you are literally there just to be seen, not heard."[13]

Nonetheless, contemporary modest fashion businesses, on the whole, are embracing the runways, while forming their own guidelines about how to portray modesty on them. Romanna Bint-Abubaker of Haute Elan London Modest Fashion Week, for instance, sees no contradiction, because her fashion shows weren't produced with an intention to "entertain" an audience:

> The reason you can tell the difference between us and our intentions and purposes [as opposed to many mainstream runway productions], is if you look at our front rows, they are 99.9 percent women, there aren't really any men that come sit in the front row, besides the odd one or two. They're allowed, they're permitted, but it's not an entertainment base, it's just a commercially driven event to showcase fashion, so that is your key indicator that it's not for the intention of any entertainment.

Haute Elan London Fashion Week partnered with The Cactus Agency to manage the production of its runway shows. The agency was founded by British-Pakistani Zaf Shabir, who studied fashion design and worked as a fashion buyer and male model prior to offering creative fashion branding packages. "The services we offer include fashion show direction, production, choreography, model management, styling, hair and makeup, execution, management and consultation – basically A to Z," he tells me. Zaf started working with Romanna for her Haute Elan fashion shows in 2013, and with Muslim Lifestyle Expo in 2015. He says:

Having worked in the mainstream bridal, commercial, lifestyle and beauty sectors for so many years, modest fashion was new, booming and exciting, however it was vital that the delivery was correct. There are regulations that need to be adhered to compared to other areas we work in, such as no excessive skin show, the use of clothing that doesn't expose any undergarments or body shapes and silhouettes, no cleavage and nothing sensual. When the models wear hijabs, we have to prioritize covering the hair, unless the client in particular wants to follow the trend of showing some hair at the front.

Though these modesty guidelines may sound off-putting for many fashion industry creatives, who often thrive on freedom and flamboyance while styling runway shows, Zaf works within the prescribed parameters to create end results that strike a balance between modesty and mainstream industry trends. In October 2018, the Muslim Lifestyle Expo took place in Manchester in the United Kingdom, bringing together a host of different brands and businesses covering everything from food to fashion. Modest fashion was a key focus of the expo, with runway segments highlighting modest wear brands from the Middle East, Malaysia, Italy and the UK. Zaf's knack for high-fashion styling came into play at the Luya Moda runway show, where models were draped in body-covering ensembles and headscarves but would have looked just as easily at home on an Italian runway. "Reflect your soul in your image" is the motto of Luya Moda, which is based in the UK but produces its garments in Italy. Models walking the runway robed in the brand's designs looked ethereal and stylish, exuding glamor in their pastel and metallic garments, completed with a range of different headscarf styles along with statement accessories like reflective sunglasses, crystal-studded head jewels and oversized hoop earrings. The overall modest-yet-attractive appearances of these models may distract from the fact that they're just playing dress-up, as audience members may have assumed that these women wear the hijab off the runways in real life too. But like any other fashion booking, these models were simply donning a costume for the occasion – upon closer inspection it's clear that many of the models from the show, like Alice Cocconi, whose modeling portfolio includes lingerie shoots, are neither Muslim nor hijab-wearing. But thanks to Zaf's styling, they sure look the part of the glamorous, modesty-conscious Eastern woman.

As Carla Jones notes, "It is not uncommon to see models in tank tops and short denim skirts weave their way through a crowd of well-to-do, piously dressed women as they exit a five-star hotel lobby after working an Islamic fashion show."[14] But some hijab-wearing models, like New York-based Wafeeqa Azeem, believe that Muslim brands that promote the wearing of hijab should only use models who cover their heads in real life too. She says that Muslim and modest wear brands have a moral obligation to hire models whose lifestyles align with those of their own brands, yet they tend to hire mainstream, non-covering models instead, presumably because there are more of them and they are simply more accessible. "If these companies are unwilling to hire Muslim models how do we expect the mainstream industry to hire us?" questions Wafeeqa. "The mainstream fashion industry has accepted modest fashion, but they have not accepted our religious beliefs in a sense. The hijab has become a fashion accessory thrown on any model booked for the gig, regardless of their understanding of what the hijab really is and what it represents."

Though Zaf agrees with Wafeeqa in theory, he says that from a producer's perspective, this is difficult to consistently implement when organizing runway shows. "The majority of the models we use are general, non-hijab wearing models," he says. "With a hijabi model it makes sense for them to

"The concept of the hijabi model is still relatively new – it has only been a couple of years since Halima emerged on the mainstream scene, and there are still only a handful of mainstream hijabi runway models in the world. The greater this niche grows, the more likely it is that the industry will have to take steps to accommodate the requirements of hijabis, such as providing private changing rooms and female stylists to assist with changing between looks."

participate in niche projects as such, but the backstage environment does not always have the capacity to accommodate a private changing area, which defeats the purpose of the hijab. If a designer has a hijab-wearing model for their segment only, which means that they do not have to change their clothes, then that makes it easier."

The behind-the-scenes factors that Zaf points out are all normal occurrences at fashion shows, where models usually have to undress completely and quickly, often in full view of the entire backstage crew, before embarking onto the catwalk in their next looks. However, the concept of the hijabi model is still relatively new – it has only been a couple of years since Halima emerged on the mainstream scene, and there are still only a handful of mainstream hijabi runway models in the world. The greater this niche grows, the more likely it is that the industry will have to take steps to accommodate the requirements of hijabis, such as providing private changing rooms and female stylists to assist with changing between looks.

While producers like Zaf may face some challenges in creating hijabi-friendly environments backstage, setting up a runway production in the UK is still a relatively easy feat, especially when compared to the restrictions in some countries in the Middle East. In Iran and Saudi Arabia, for instance, runway shows still remain the subject of controversy, while in more westernized, tourism-driven countries like the UAE, catwalk productions occur frequently, often with hardly any censorship. In cities like Dubai, even designs created by Muslim or Eastern designers can come across as risqué, yet are still paraded down runways in mixed-gender settings.

When Pakistani designer Faraz Manan showcased his 2015 Imperial Collection at The Four Seasons Resort in Jumeirah, for instance, the glamorous gowns and fusion wear shown were a far cry from traditional South Asian attire. Some of the couture pieces featured necklines reaching almost to models' navels, and with slits so high that their underwear was visible while they strode down the stately runway, facing a front row that seated both men and women, some even robed in traditional abayas and kandooras. While the collection may have been deemed scandalous by some, the designer's target market was not those seeking modest fashion – rather, it was the Middle Eastern woman who wears dazzling evening wear at special ladies-only occasions like weddings.

By contrast, the country of Iran may play host to runway shows, but they won't be held in mainstream five-star hotels or advertised to the general public. Iran has a tumultuous history in terms of women's dress codes. Nonetheless, the nation has a very lucrative fashion industry, though it operates in secret, since many of the designs displayed through the nation's various makeshift, invite-only runway shows are not in accordance with the government-mandated dress code. "This underground fashion scene, thriving mostly in large urban areas, is held in secret locations and attended by elite, trusted clientele… Locations are publicized only by word of mouth, and until the very last minute, few know the exact location. There is always the threat of being discovered," writes Faegheh Shirazi.[15]

During summer 2018, a video taken at a fashion show at a luxury hotel in Saudi Arabia went viral. It was no ordinary runway presentation, as it lacked a major criterion of a fashion show: models. Instead of humans modeling the garments, drones attached to hangers clipped to T-shirts and dresses flew down the makeshift catwalk in the center of the room. "This was not really something I would encourage or would like to see again," said the IFDC's Alia Khan to CNN. "When you see empty clothes flying in the air, it's just unappealing and not mesmerizing or beautiful."[16] This bizarre spectacle took place only months after the Kingdom hosted its first fashion week in Riyadh – dubbed Arab Fashion Week, where cameras were not permitted inside the venues and the audience was all female. For while runway shows are common in the nation, they are all private affairs and strictly women-only.

Fashion editor Marriam Mossalli says that fashion shows are nothing new in Saudi Arabia, and that through her agency, Niche Arabia, she has been producing them for the past decade. She foresees changes over the next few years, as the country's policies become increasingly moderate. However, she points out that if runway shows are opened up to the public, it may prove challenging for the designers. "Modest fashion does not yet exist in Saudi Arabia in the way that we think of it in the [international] industry," she explains to me over the phone. "We wear the abaya and underneath it we have our regular ready-to-wear. When I came into the office today, I was wearing my abaya, and underneath it right now, I'm in an Enza Costa dress."

Because the abaya has been a mandatory requirement for so many years, Saudi women have become accustomed to wearing it in public, over clothing that may not be typically modest. Marriam recalls taking one Saudi fashion designer to a modest fashion week organized abroad: the designer had brought along an elbow-length kaftan, but because it did not cover the arms up to the hands, organizers insisted it be worn with a long-sleeved shirt under it, much to the designer's despair. "That's Saudi fashion for you," says Marriam. "It doesn't fit the parameters of international modest wear, or what an Indonesian woman wearing the hijab might wear, because in Saudi, it's worn under the abaya."

Marriam adds that she does see potential for Saudi fashion shows to begin allowing photography in the near future – mainly because it's been prohibited for so long in order to respect the privacy of VIPs in the crowd, but with the rise of social media, says Marriam, this reluctance to be photographed is quickly waning. In 2018, she published the first volume of *Under the Abaya*, a coffee-table book showcasing street style from the Kingdom. Though she had been toying with the idea of this book for a couple of years, she says that it wasn't really possible to publish it even two years prior, since women generally were not comfortable showing their faces on a public platform. But when the fashion editor announced she was looking for photo submissions in January 2018, she received more than one thousand images. Still, she expected she would need to crop or block out subjects' faces due to cultural sensitivities, and she stated her intention to do so on the release form sent to the women whose photos were selected for the book. "I would say 99.9 percent came back in the comments section saying, 'can you please put my Instagram name on it, and not crop my face'," reveals Marriam. "So, it went from one extreme to the other."

She explains that this reflects a larger shift in thinking that has spread across Arab countries. "It's no longer taboo to show your identity," she says. "Now you have prominent Arab women like Princess Deena Aljuhani Abdulaziz [the former editor of *Vogue Arabia*] showing their faces in photographs and magazines, and it's had a trickle-down effect. This happened from the top – you see these women showing their faces and all of a sudden girls are like, 'we can show ours too'. It's now okay to show ourselves [on social media] and have our names attached to things. It's really changed the mentality."

CHAPTER 7

MODEST FASHION BLOGGERS

Today, the way in which clothing brands portray their modest wear designs on catwalks or magazine covers no longer takes center stage. A new media has been born: Instagram has given rise to hordes of young fashion bloggers (those who typically post regular content on their own websites) and influencers (those who may not link back to blogs but use social media apps like Instagram to post images and connect with their followers), of whom many are Muslim or proud adherents of other faiths, who use the platform to promote a modest fashion lifestyle. "The millennial God squad" is how a 2016 article in *Marie Claire* refers to these women who use their public platforms to marry faith with fashion,[1] while the headline of a 2019 *Forbes* article admits, "It's Time We Stop Ignoring Modest Fashion Influencers". The feature explains that in the past five years, the modest fashion niche has grown tremendously on social media, with more than 1.3 million posts on Instagram alone tagged with #modestfashion when the article was published.[2]

The past few years' international runway trends depicting loose silhouettes, layered garments, floor-sweeping hemlines and high-collared necklines did not merely materialize as a result of some creative nostalgia for Victorian fashions of eras past. High-fashion houses like Gucci pioneered the modesty movement on European catwalks, probably to target Middle Eastern spending power, but the increased tendency to cover up was also a calculated response to the emergence of the trend-setting and modestly dressed consumer on social media. Speaking to *Middle East Eye*, British modest fashion blogger Zaynah Ahmed stated, "Social media and the rise of modest fashion bloggers has shown the industry how much influence we have, hence they now collaborate with us to reach the Muslim market. If it wasn't for the bloggers and social media, I don't think we would have that many modest options to choose from in shops. They now cater for us."[3]

Romanna Bint-Abubaker unquestionably attributes the success of Haute Elan and London Modest Fashion Week to the crop of modest fashion bloggers who rose to fame in the UK. "The influencers played a huge role in getting the word out in the market and getting the mainstream to take notice of them. Had it not been for them, they would not have seen it; it would not have been visible," she tells me. Even the curators of the Contemporary Muslim Fashions exhibition in San Francisco admitted that Instagram was a primary source in scouting modest fashion brands and influencers for the showcase.

The fashion-blogging phenomenon that slowly started engulfing the digital realm in 2010 was not tied to a specific race, ethnicity, faith or class of people. Anyone with a laptop, tablet or smartphone could access what was first called a weblog, before the word was shortened to "blog", or create a social media profile – and hand in hand with the rise of fashion bloggers came style-conscious, digitally-aware Muslim women aspiring to share their own personal styles in the same way as their non-Muslim peers. They too wanted to display their knack for styling mainstream fashion trends; the only difference was that some of them wore hijab, and had a preference for clothing that was markedly modest. "In the virgin territory of the internet, new celebrities have been born," explains author Shelina Janmohamed. "They aim to satisfy the hunger of everything to do with building a Muslim lifestyle, whether it be hijab tutorials, poking fun at their own lives or creating rap music."[4]

The emergence of these hip, stylish Muslims was no overnight occurrence. Sudanese graphic designer Rihab Nubi (@riinubi on Instagram), who lives in the Emirate of Sharjah in the UAE, tells me that hijab-wearing, fashion-loving women have long existed, and are only now gaining exposure, thanks to advancements in technology:

> I like to believe that there have always been really dope hijabi and modest sisters out there in the world even before the social media age, however maybe it just wasn't popular until social media made it accessible for people to see alternative fashion styles from all over the world, which in turn eventually gave birth to today's diverse modest fashion scene. Seeing someone who looks like you, dress in a way you never thought you could dress, encourages and inspires you to start thinking outside the box that society has forced modesty into.

The vast majority of Muslim fashion bloggers who have gained fame within this niche blogging realm tend to wear some form of the headscarf. Speaking at a panel discussion at London College of Fashion in 2011, Muslim fashion blogger Jana Kossaibati of Hijabstyle.co.uk explained that since many media outlets portrayed the hijab as oppressive, forced upon women and even ban-worthy, blogs offered Muslim women a medium through which they could own the narrative surrounding the hijab and modest fashion. While modest fashion bloggers are a dime a dozen today, there are a few pioneers in the field who started their blogs early on. Two notable young women spearheaded the modest fashion blogging trend, becoming global faces of the movement: UK-based Dina Torkia (@dinatokio on Instagram) in the West, and Kuwait-based Ascia Al Faraj (@ascia on Instagram) in the East.

"Here are some facts everyone should know about hijab. It's a personal commitment to God; a beautiful tradition that encourages you to focus on your character rather than your looks; and, sometimes, it's a bloody fashion nightmare," wrote Egyptian-English Dina Torkia for *Vogue* in 2018.[5] Often referred to by her social media name, Dina Tokio, she started blogging in 2011 while living in Cardiff, Wales, and took to Facebook and YouTube to post styling tips and hijab-tying tutorials for fellow Muslim women struggling to tie in fashion with faith in the UK. Within a decade, she rose to become the most famous hijab-wearing personality in the country, working with brands like Liberty London, H&M and Tom Ford in addition to launching her own clothing line and writing a book, *Modestly*, which was published by Penguin Random House in 2018. Dina's outfit posts range from slouchy athleisure wear to more experimental ensembles with bold beauty looks. She often wears her hijab in a turban style, and frequently accessorizes with over-sized earrings. Today, her husband runs her business with her, and her two children occasionally make appearances in her social media posts as well. At the end of 2018, Dina began posting images without covering her hair, telling her followers that modest fashion and the hijab are ever-evolving, personal journeys.

Undoubtedly the most popular fashion blogger from the Middle East, Kuwaiti-American Ascia Al Faraj has evolved significantly since she first started blogging in 2012, categorizing herself as a hijab-wearing fashion blogger (though she gradually took steps to distance herself from the title "hijabi", before discarding the headscarf entirely in September 2019). While she would cover her head with loose beanie caps and turban-style wraps, the married mother of two was not strict about covering every strand of hair, her forearms are dotted with tattoos (like one that reads "do no harm take no shit") and she often sports a septum nose piercing. Some days opting for loose, minimal kaftans, and other days donning pearl-adorned denim jackets, chunky chokers or fishnet sleeves, Ascia's finger is constantly on the pulse of what's trending in fashion. She is known for her cool, streetwear approach to style, and her modern approach to covering up has caught the eyes of international fashion brands worldwide, with collaborations with high-end labels like Christian Dior, Tory Burch, Aigner and Kenzo under her belt. She is also constantly sought out for fashion and beauty campaigns by top global retailers and brands.

The original trailblazers of the modest fashion blogging movement, Dina and Ascia are seen to be celebrities in their own right and are often stopped in public for photos by their fans. Inspired by their drive, confidence and unique approaches to dressing modestly, other Muslim fashion bloggers began appearing in all parts of the world, from the United States and Canada to Europe, Asia, Africa and Australia, helping to influence more women to pursue their individual style preferences while maintaining a modest appearance.

Imane Asry (@fashionwithfaith on Instagram), for instance, is a Stockholm-based modest influencer whose personal style can be described as minimalist-chic. Her Instagram page shows a stream of Scandi style in a palette of neutrals. Khaki pants and trenches, matching suit ensembles and midi dresses and wrap skirts worn over jeans are paired with utilitarian belts, basket bags, sleek sunglasses and a hijab worn fitted around the head and draped elegantly over one shoulder. Imane began blogging when she was a teenager, after putting on the hijab, and her sartorial styling choices have even won her recognition in *Vogue*.

California-based "muse and tastemaker", according to her Instagram bio, Marwa Biltagi (@mademoisellememe on Instagram) is another hijab-wearing blogger in the limelight. The Irish-Palestinian influencer is a regular attendee of New York Fashion Week, where her bold-yet-demure style attracts the lenses of street style photographers and lands her on best-dressed web pages worldwide. With a penchant for layering, Marwa will pair a sleeveless plaid dress with a white blouse and classic Chanel bag, or a jacquard abaya-style coat with an acrylic clutch and red pearl-adorned Gucci heels. Designer brands are tastefully woven in with emerging Middle Eastern labels throughout her posts, which also feature stunning locations and her handsome golden retrievers.

Then there's Belgium-based fashion blogger Samia (@sauf.etc on Instagram), whose effortless tomboy style reflects that of many Muslim millennials, who opt for university sweatshirts and Vans trainers as go-to daywear outfits in the name of athleisure. A simple photo of the blogger in a light gray tracksuit, peach-colored hijab and white trainers will win her over 35,000 likes on Instagram. When she's not wearing baggy T-shirts, sweatshirts and jeans, she's dressed in printed maxi skirts paired with baggy knits and chunky trainers, topped off with layered necklaces and a loosely draped hijab.

London-based Somali blogger Basma Kahie (@basma_k on Instagram), on the other hand, mixes high fashion with a quintessential English touch in her Instagram photos. Her images include a gingham skirt outfit with a vintage bicycle in a field, a pastel floral dress bordered with colorful blooms taken on a sidewalk and a floor-length polka-dot dress in front of a large white door.

In the Middle East, an equally enviable army of fashion bloggers has been gaining momentum online. Edgy and borderline avant-garde, Dubai-based Palestinian-Canadian Leena Al Ghouti (@leenalghouti on Instagram) has emerged as a Middle Eastern street style star in the short two-year span that she's been posting her outfits on Instagram. Void of any froufrou, feminine dresses, Leena's sartorial choices consist of baggy jeans, twill pants, loose graphic T-shirts and structured blazers and jackets, with designer bags and shoes. Plaids, stripes and occasional animal prints are more prevalent than florals on Leena's feed, and her images usually feature her trademark miniature sunglasses and black headscarf.

Also based in Dubai is American-Moroccan modest fashion blogger Saufeeya Goodson (@saufeeya on Instagram), who was named by *Refinery29* as one of the top influencers to follow in the Middle East in 2017, and by *Vogue* as one of the women redefining modest dressing in the Middle East. Starting out on Instagram, Saufeeya's good looks and striking sense of style quickly put her in the spotlight, earning her fashion campaign opportunities with the likes of Fendi, and being flown out to Milan to enjoy a front-row ticket to the Aigner Munich show. Her personal style is a reflection of her diverse background – at times she'll be decked out in brightly patterned headscarves, glamorous kaftans and chunky jewelry, or she'll keep her looks simple and sleek, opting for denims, turtlenecks and tailored suits.

Kuwaiti Dalal Aldoub (@dalalid on Instagram), meanwhile, combines her distinctive Arabic style with high-fashion brands and trends, completed with her white or light-colored tightly wrapped hijab, which covers her neck and all of her hair. Ruffled abayas, tiered maxi dresses and long, loose tunics feature aplenty in her wardrobe and are complemented with Christian Dior trainers, Manolo Blahnik heels, Balenciaga totes and Saint Laurent crossbody bags. Jo Malone perfumes and Fenty by Rihanna cosmetics are also highlighted by the blogger, who posts her various beauty looks just as often as her outfit photographs. Her penchant for makeup was noticed by *Vogue Arabia*, who published a beauty interview with her in 2017.

Some popular modest fashion bloggers in the Middle East have no Arab heritage and are converts to Islam, yet their knack for infusing traditional Arabic styles with fashion-forward trends, and of course excellent photography, has earned them hundreds of thousands of followers. Based in Qatar, Estonian convert to Islam Eileen Lahi (@eslimah on Instagram) is one such blogger, whose Instagram feed is a fairy-tale depiction of modest fashion. Massive ferris wheels, swings situated in the middle of the sea, views of majestic mosques and awe-inspiring rocky mountains from her various travels have been some of the backdrops of Eileen's images, where she is pictured in a range of outfits – sometimes romantic and whimsical, and other times basic and casual.

A few Instagram personalities in the Gulf region prefer not to show their faces at all on social media, instead creatively cropping images from the neck down. Although this is hard to achieve while still portraying an aesthetically pleasing photography feed, Emirati Maith (@al.maiiith on Instagram) has been successful in doing so. She retains her distinctive Khaleeji (Gulf Arab) style while traveling to Europe, often showcasing striped linen travel sets and abaya-inspired overcoats, with Gucci, Dior and Celine bags in hand, on the streets of Knightsbridge in London. Embroidered kaftans and bedazzled high heels make regular appearances in her photos, which often also feature Arabic tea sets, macarons and designer perfumes.

While hijab styling has become one of the main features of modest fashion blogging, there are many modest fashion bloggers who choose not to wear a headscarf. Dubai-based Sameera Hussain (@missmulberry on Instagram) started blogging in 2014 while living in Glasgow, Scotland. "It wasn't really that I was trying to inspire other Muslim girls or anything like that. It's really none of my business whether people are covering up or not, it just so happened that I was a Muslim girl who put together outfits that were kind of modest," she tells me. Sameera self-identifies as a modest blogger, as she adheres to conventional modesty guidelines when it comes to covering her body. "I do post outfits that are modest within my own boundaries, and I know that there are a lot of other girls who probably do have the same boundaries as me, for example not showing [bare] legs. If I'm wearing short dresses I will wear tights, I try not to wear clothing that's tight and shows the outline of my body, and I try not to wear sleeveless tops," she says. "Those are my sort of guidelines – I would never put a picture up of me in a bikini or showing too much skin."

Loose T-shirts tucked into plissé maxi skirts, printed above-the-knee dresses coupled with leggings or skinny jeans and smart blazer-and-pants pairings make frequent appearances on Sameera's feed. She says that her followers are supportive and encouraging, and have never refuted her interpretation of modesty just because she doesn't cover her hair. Rather, they follow her approach to styling and layering using garments from the high street. "In mainstream shops today, you will find more covered up options, but a few years ago you wouldn't, and I had to be really savvy with how to put together options which covered my shoulders and legs. So, I would put together outfits on a budget, and that's really how it started, people would always ask, 'Where did you get this?' or 'Where did you get that?'" Occasionally, when Sameera posts images from mosques or during Ramadan prayers, she'll be wearing a loose headscarf to accompany her modest outfits.

Muslim social media influencers cash in on beauty blogging

While not all modest fashion bloggers cover their hair, hijabi women are nonetheless the faces of the style movement on social media, and one of the first major blogging trends that young Muslim women spearheaded was the concept of the hijab tutorial, which quickly became a worldwide phenomenon among Muslim millennials. Following in the steps of Ascia and Dina, bloggers used YouTube to post their tips and tricks of the hijab- and turban-tying trade, before moving to platforms like Instagram to share these tutorials.

Afghan-Dutch blogger Ruba Zai (@hijabhills on Instagram) posted a range of hijab tutorials on YouTube early on in her blogging career, before gaining hundreds of thousands of followers online and being recruited to star in luxury brand campaigns. She was a face for Dolce & Gabbana's abaya line in 2017. That same year, she starred in a Yves Saint Laurent Beauty campaign and has collaborated with makeup brands like Jo Malone, Beauty Bakerie and Tarte Cosmetics.

Also in 2017, Malaysian television actress Neelofa was signed by French cosmetics company Lancôme as its first hijab-wearing ambassador, and Muslim YouTube beauty vlogger (video blogger) Nura Afia (@nuralailalov on Instagram) became the first hijab-wearing ambassador for American makeup brand CoverGirl. The partnership with CoverGirl put an unprecedented beauty-themed spotlight on the hijabi Muslim woman in America – Nura's face was plastered all over the brand's television campaigns for its So Lashy mascara, as well as on a billboard at Times Square in New York City.

"These appointments are part of a growing recognition that the female Muslim community has a significant role in the development of this market, and that consumers increasingly want to see their versions of themselves and their lifestyles reflected back to them by the beauty industry," Shelina Janmohamed told the *New York Times*.[6]

But even a realm as fickle as beauty doesn't come without politics, especially when visibly Muslim figures are involved. In 2018, hijab-wearing British influencer Amena Khan (@amenakhan on Instagram) was hired by L'Oréal Paris for a haircare campaign. "They're literally putting a girl in a headscarf – whose hair you can't see – in a hair campaign. Because what they're really valuing through the campaign is the voices that we have," said Amena to *Vogue*.[7] The move was seen as ground-breaking for the beauty industry. However, shortly after it was announced, Amena was dropped from the campaign when controversy arose following pro-Palestine tweets that she had written in 2014.

Amani Al-Khatahtbeh, the founder of MuslimGirl.com, was the hijabi public figure of choice for American beauty brand Revlon, who awarded her with its Changemaker Award in 2018. However, the author and entrepreneur publicly declined the award due to the cosmetics company's association with Israeli Wonder Woman actress Gal Gadot, who had tweeted in support of the Israeli army, in which she once served. Amani viewed this to be in conflict with her pro-Palestine stance – articles and poems featured on MuslimGirl.com often advocate for the Palestinian cause.

Modest fashion bloggers as ambassadors of Islam

"The connectivity of the ummah [the global Muslim community] has been one of the most powerful effects of the internet," states Shelina Janmohamed. "Affordable, accessible and democratic, the internet, mobile and social media are tools for Generation M to achieve their aspirations and become part of a worldwide network of peers who share their values."[8]

Because their adherence to the hijab is made so visible in their online platforms, fashion bloggers who cover their hair become global representatives of the Muslim community. Sabrina Salhi, founder of Unveiled, a female-only ladies' night entertainment concept, tells me how she believes Muslim bloggers' efforts have helped humanize the Muslim woman in the media:

The hijab was so elusive and referred to as the veil, and now, with the rise of social media, never has there been a time where people have been confronted with the image of the modern Muslim woman so much – I think we've hit a new milestone. I think it has been accepted, it's mainstream now, it's okay. I remember when Dina Torkia first started on Facebook and Instagram, and the whole social media scene was still beginning, just to see someone wearing the hijab on the platform was like "wow", it was so new. But now with thousands and thousands of influencers, I think it has become normalized. Dina achieved what she set out to do - to take the hijab and make it mainstream.

In her autobiography, Dina writes, "My wearing of the hijab was like shouting out to the world, 'I am a Muslim and a proud one, too!' We were very much unapologetically Muslim back then."[9]

While levels of modest dress differ among practicing Muslims, the headscarf is seen to be "the single most obvious marker of faith – even more unambiguous than a beard or turban."[10] Muslim modest fashion bloggers who wear some form of the headscarf and are thus visibly Muslim have become a new breed of ambassadors for Islam, particularly in the West. When MuslimGirl.com's Amani Al-Khatahtbeh decided to start covering her hair, she recognized the headscarf's symbol as "a public marker that I belonged to this people", explaining, "I wanted it to be so that before people even knew my name, the first thing that they would know about me is that I am a Muslim." She self-describes her wearing of the hijab as an "outward rebellion" against Islamophobia and was proud to wear it "on my head like an issue for public debate". Amani recalls being a teenager in America, when a classmate asked what religion she followed. "I didn't wear the headscarf at the time, so I had the chance to hide behind being uncovered," she writes.[11]

Modest fashion photographer Nicole Najmah Abraham says that Muslim women who cover their hair and post images of themselves on public platforms like Instagram are naturally going to be perceived as representatives of the religion, and with this pedestal, she says, comes certain obligations. "I do believe that Muslim women that follow the command to wear the hijab and dress modestly become, by default, the poster children of what a Muslim is or isn't because they visibly show their faith. So knowing that, they have a duty to make their faith look good and carry themselves accordingly," she explains.

Haute Hijab's Melanie Elturk believes that whether a Muslim woman is a blogger or not, acting as an ambassador for Islam is a fundamental purpose of wearing the hijab, and says that when she leaves her house every day, she is like a walking, talking advertisement for the religion. "The act of wearing the hijab itself means you're consciously making an effort to be recognized as a Muslim woman," she tells me. "If you're wearing a hijab, inherent within that is this notion that you are an ambassador. You're putting yourself out there as this religious woman who adheres to Islam so, whether you like it or not, you're an ambassador of Islam."

Still, while some hijab-wearing, Muslim modest fashion bloggers may have become icons for modern Islam in the West, others are not motivated by any altruistic desire to change the face of Islam in the media, and would rather be known for their fashionable flair. Even some hijabi models like Shahira Yusuf, who is signed with Storm Models, are uncomfortable with being put on a pedestal as a model Muslim woman. "I'm interested in talking about being Muslim, but I'm not interested in being a role model. I feel that's too much responsibility to put on a person," she told the *Guardian* in 2018.[12] Similar feelings have been expressed by the leaders of the modest fashion blogging movement, Dina and Ascia, who, as the years have passed, have taken to less-rigid styles of covering their heads, gradually revealing more of their hair, before discarding hijabs completely. Their decisions to de-veil were highly controversial within the Muslim social media community. In Instagram comments, users were quick to unfairly judge Dina and Ascia for being hypocritical, saying that they were distancing themselves from the one symbol that they had each built their platforms on, and consequently earned fame and money from.[13]

Negative reactions from followers tend to push these modest fashion bloggers further away from associating with the hijab. In October 2018, Dina posted a message on her Instagram stories comparing the community of hijabi women on social media to a "toxic cult" that she no longer wanted to be a part of. Ascia made a statement on YouTube in 2018 clarifying that she would rather not be referred to as a "hijabi", saying, "I am not meant to be your Muslim role model, that was not what I set out to be, ever." In the fifteen-minute video, she revealed, "I do not consider myself to be a hijabi because I don't feel that it is in line with the viewpoint that I have now approaching thirty... I consider myself in the modest fashion space."[14]

Some followers are choosing to unfollow modest fashion bloggers whom they once viewed as role models. One Amaliah.com writer, a British convert to Islam who posts under the name ModestlyWrapped, claims that she'd rather unfollow these women to avoid seeing their images on her social media feed, to minimize the risk of getting influenced by their increasingly lax approaches to wearing the hijab.

British-Muslim model Mariah Idrissi points out that some ex-hijabi fashion bloggers may have stopped covering their hair because they had been forced to cover it in the first place by family members, and their rejection of the hijab is simply their way of finally making their own decisions about how to dress. "Some of them, from what I've heard, have similar stories where they have strict dads who made them wear it, and I feel bad that they've had that, but at the same time, you can't live a lie," Mariah tells me. She believes that by essentially gaining fame from showing off a lifestyle they didn't believe in wholeheartedly, these bloggers were not completely truthful with their followers. "It's like hating a brand but then promoting it," she explains.

Dubai-based Zahra Valji, founder of the home decor brand Ayah Home, which infuses traditional Arabic calligraphy with contemporary woodwork design, started wearing the hijab when she was fourteen years old and living in Britain, and says that both Dina and Ascia provided her with invaluable styling inspiration. She gives me some insight as to why devoted followers of formerly hijabi bloggers may feel somewhat betrayed by them:

> It was so inspiring to see girls the same age as me paving the way for modest fashion with such confidence and style. Growing up in Essex, my sister and I were the only Muslim Asian girls in the school and I was the only hijabi. Although I still witnessed a fair share of Islamophobia, having influencers representing us in fashion magazines and on social media normalized and stylized the hijab and made me feel less like the odd one out. Far-right political groups are pushing out their accusatory propaganda that Muslim women who wear hijab are oppressed and have no rights. I felt a sense of pride seeing influencers representing us hijabis as positive promoters who were raising awareness and challenging these ridiculous assumptions.

Zahra says she understands that a public platform can expose these bloggers to modest fashion policing, and she condemns social media users who leave disrespectful comments. Nonetheless, she feels "let down" by the influencers' remarks about not wanting be categorized as hijabi women. "Denying the fact that they wear the hijab and saying they are just 'modest fashion bloggers' is a disappointment to all of the hijabis who have followed their journey from the beginning, where their follower base initially came from," she explains.

Still, Zahra recognizes that committing to the hijab presents an individual struggle unique to each wearer. Tying themselves to this symbol of Islam may have brought about an immense amount of pressure for public personalities like Dina and Ascia, who were not prepared to take on the responsibility of becoming a voice for all Muslim women. Fashion, rather than faith, seems to be the primary message they want to spread through their social media platforms, regardless of whether or not they cover their hair.

I had been following modest fashion blogger Saira Arshad for five years on Instagram before finally meeting her face to face in Dubai. Canadian by nationality and East African by background, Saira was born and raised in Toronto before moving to Kuwait, and then relocating to the UAE, before moving back to Toronto. She works as a teacher by day, and modest fashion and travel blogger by night, and while she covers her head in the trendy turban style of hijab, she's also wary of being labeled. "I'm not going out there trying to be a poster child of Islam," says Saira light-heartedly when we meet. "You become responsible for an entire population when you're just trying to live your life and wear nice clothes."

Saira (@shazaira on Instagram) started her blog when she first moved from Toronto to Kuwait, as a way of staying in touch with her friends and family. "I would just sit there and write, nothing was edited, it would be like, 'today I saw a cheetah in someone's car'," she says of her first days of blogging. "When I moved to Kuwait that's when I really started to wear my hijab as a turban because it was really hot." Saira says she was inspired by fellow modest fashion bloggers like Ascia and Dina, who pioneered the turban-tying style of the hijab. "It was just a different way to wear your hijab, which traditionally, growing up in Islamic school, had to have everything covered, tight, right up under your chin," says Saira. "And I just wanted to do something different. I've always loved clothes, I've always loved styling different things together and the turban just added like an accessory piece to that – I was still wearing my hijab while expressing my style."

It's this expression of style that motivates Saira to keep up her blogging and social media activities, rather than any political or religious incentive. "It just happens that I'm Muslim and it just happens that I wear a headscarf. I would never go out of my way to make a point about the hijab, my faith is my personal choice," she explains. "I'm struggling just as much as the next Muslim, whether or not I show that on social media, which I don't." While many assume that fashion bloggers are only in the business for the fame and recognition they can earn on Instagram, the idea of being heralded as some sort of icon representing Muslim women worldwide is not an idea that appeals to Saira at all. "That's like putting the weight of the whole religion on my shoulders and I'd rather not have that. I'm just here to say, 'Hey, I'm just having fun, and just because you are a Muslim or a modest fashion dresser or wear the hijab doesn't restrict you from doing whatever you want to do. Want to travel solo? Go do it, go live your best life and dress however you want to.'"

Cyber bullying through modest fashion policing

When fashion bloggers become famous, their followers can feel invested in their personal journeys. This celebrity status can attract stalker-like behavior from strangers, who develop obsessive ideals about their role models and feel entitled to judge everything from their appearance to the lifestyle that they portray on social media.

"A lot of modest fashion bloggers get a lot of hate," says Saira, who recalls a time when two men sent her a message on Instagram claiming she was a bad influence on their daughters. "They sent me a whole essay," she says. "I genuinely think if anything, I would be taken as a good influence – I'm not representing anything bad on Instagram." Saira admits this experience may be a trifle compared to the vicious personal attacks that other modest fashion personalities fall victim to on social media. "Other massive bloggers who wear the hijab are scrutinized for every little thing – like their hair, or wrists – just let them live," she exclaims.

"Bloggers, like brands and print media, face vociferous criticism if their visuals transgress presumed community codes of dress and visual representation," writes Reina Lewis, who also notes that these critics often differentiate between legitimate hijab and non-legitimate hijab.[15] Some Muslims believe that if a hijabi woman's ankles are showing, or parts of her neck and hair are visible, then she is not covering properly. Some would even argue that form-fitting silhouettes, distressed denims and eye-catching colors worn by hijabi women fail to constitute modesty. While opinions vary, traditionalist definitions of covering your head as a Muslim require that the neck and all hair be concealed, which wouldn't include a turban (unless it's worn with a turtleneck) or a loosely tied headscarf.

"Rather than hosting their own sites, many seek to police the new practices of modest fashion through sustained attacks on the comments function of others' sites. These commenters do not patrol mainstream media to police female modesty: the modest fashion field is their chosen battleground," writes Reina.[16]

Dina, along with many other Muslim fashion bloggers, uses the term "haram police" to refer to cyber bullies who condemn and chastise Muslim fashion bloggers in social media comments. One fashion blogger who has been on the receiving end of hostility on Instagram is UK-based British-Pakistani Seima Rahman (@seimarahman on Instagram). Though Seima covers her head with a headscarf, she often posts images of herself in loose short-sleeved T-shirts, or pants cropped above the ankles. Layering pieces bought off the high street, Seima sometimes pairs a blouse and pants with a cropped top or bralette on top. Off-the-shoulder shirts, leather leggings and fishnet stockings are also components of her wardrobe, which reflects seasonal trends but fails to appease some of her religiously driven followers. It takes thick skin to be a modest fashion blogger, and Seima says that she is now used to the fashion policing and nit picking. "It's so common now. I do read the comments and I have learned to ignore them. I think criticism will always be there, especially for Muslim fashion bloggers. I deal with it by completely ignoring it and by being confident in what I do and what I wear," she tells me.[17]

This sort of policing behavior is not a phenomenon linked solely to fashion. For instance, Nura Afia, who became an ambassador for CoverGirl, was called hypocritical for wearing the hijab to cover her hair while also wearing makeup that would attract attention to herself. And bloggers aren't the only ones dodging the haram police – they also deterred Dubai-based designer Safiya Abdallah from branding her fashion label as a modest wear brand, let alone an Islamic one, even though covered-up garments are her forte:

> That was never my goal because I was always worried if I didn't fulfill the requirements of this person or that person, I would be judged for that, and that I would be called a "fraud" or something. People can be crazy. And because people on social media can be anonymous, they can say what they want and tear you down, and I never wanted to be part of the negativity. It's not right, I feel like these people just drive people further away from Islam actually than bring them closer.[18]

It seems the haram police are less zealous in the United States. "I don't get a lot of hate on social," says Haute Hijab's Melanie Elturk, adding that the rare aggressive messages that she does get are usually from outside of the country. "People interpret [modesty] through the culture that they live in, so the negative comments usually come from people who are outside of the American culture, don't understand the way that we dress, and think that it's haram," she says. While she tells me that she'll block and delete comments to keep her profile clear of negative energy, she doesn't feel any animosity towards these followers, and understands that modesty is subjective depending on your culture:

> The way that people dress and interpret the hijab differs greatly if you're in America, versus in the Middle East, versus in Russia, versus in Africa, versus in Malaysia. I mean it's so different, so when they see something that's outside of their norm and outside of their paradigm, it's difficult for them to accept. As an American here, wearing jeans and a sweater doesn't make you stick out; it's considered modest within the American landscape, but of course the guidelines still need to apply that it's not tight, it's not revealing and it's not see-through.

When I ask Halima Aden whether she has had online encounters with the haram police, she says that they leave spiteful comments under her Instagram photos regularly, but that her followers are quick to stand up for her. But while she keeps her cool online, she can't help but feel disheartened by the negativity. "It is hard. I went from being really liked within my little community, to people leaving these comments," she says, adding that most of the time, the commenters turn out to be two-faced since they don't practice what they preach. "This actually does bother me, because people will say modeling is haram, but then they're the ones commenting on my photos on Instagram and they themselves have photos on public platforms – it's just the hypocrisy of it all. I'm really learning now you have to live for you, and that's the advice I give to girls, because if you listen to every single person who has an opinion, you're going to be stuck not living at all," she says.[19]

To avoid controversy entirely, some modest fashion Instagrammers, bloggers and brands post disclaimers on their websites, thus hoping to ward off potential trolls. "Hijabtrendz is not a religious or political website, nor does it seek to promote any such causes. This site is merely for informational and entertainment purposes," was the disclaimer stated at one point on the blog Hijabtrendz.com, for instance.[20]

Such caution is understandable when in extreme cases, the battleground becomes the streets: in September 2018, Iraqi fashion and beauty influencer Tara Fares was shot three times while driving her car, the victim of a targeted murder. Some speculated that her westernized lifestyle, promoted via her Instagram account through various fashion, beauty and travel posts, did not adhere to traditional Iraqi societal expectations.

A word about modest fashion bloggers from other faiths

While a search of the hashtag #modestfashion on Instagram will bring up numerous images of women wearing the hijab, Muslim women don't hold a monopoly over the modest fashion blogging niche. Emily Smith (@modestgoddess_ on Instagram), for instance, is a Mormon-American fashion blogger based in Utah. Her daily dress code includes covering the shoulders and knees, and with swimwear, covering the majority of her torso. So, while her usual attire ranges from striped midi dresses to jeans with cap-sleeved, short-sleeved or long-sleeved tops, she may bare some more skin if she's at a beach or a pool party, where she'll be in a swimsuit from her own label, Tanlines Swim. Emily's aim with her blog was to increase the circulation of images promoting modest fashion through third-party platforms like Pinterest and Instagram, to help inspire other women to put together stylish yet conservative outfits. There's also an interfaith element to her approach to fashion – in 2018, she traveled to Toronto for the International Modest Fashion and Design Festival, a predominantly Muslim initiative, with a focus on hijab-appropriate brands.

Rachelle Yadegar (@rachelleyadegar on Instagram), is an Iranian-American Jewish fashion blogger and co-founder of the clothing label Raju. Born in New York and raised in Los Angeles, her feed features garments like shirt dresses, blazers and denim skirts, and these always cover her shoulders and knees. Like other modest fashion bloggers, Rachelle wears trendy slip dresses and strappy tops by layering them over long-sleeved blouses and turtlenecks. And while one may assume that non-Muslim fashion bloggers might feel that the hijab overshadows other elements of modest fashion, Rachelle has welcomed the hijab's move into the mainstream. "Especially being an Orthodox Jew, head covering is a huge thing when you get married. So I love seeing the hijabs all over the fashion industry," she tells me.

Rachelle credits her faith and desire to express her Jewish values through style as a motivator for starting her fashion blog, NotWithoutMyHeels.com. "Faith was and is a huge part of my lifestyle. I wanted to inspire women and girls around the world, to show that you don't need to dress provocatively to look beautiful," she says. When it comes to fashion policing on social media, it isn't only activist Muslims pointing out skin and putting down fashion bloggers; Rachelle says that she deals with her fair share of negativity too: "Haters are going to hate, and I have come to ignore these comments."

CHAPTER 8

THE GREAT DEBATE – IS MODEST FASHION A CONTRADICTION?

Attacks from social media stalkers who surf modest fashion bloggers' Instagram posts and point out their apparent lack of modesty are just one type of critical voice amid the swirl of controversies surrounding the concept of modest fashion. Others challenge the colors and cuts of garments, the wearers' intentions, whether expensive luxury labels are compatible with the humble ideals of modesty and whether taking selfies can ever be classified as an act of modesty.

There have even been "fatwas" (Islamic legal rulings) deeming designer abayas to be un-Islamic entirely, or worse, sinful.[1] However, it isn't only religious Muslim voices who have been critical. Gucci's lavish gowns, for example, ushered in a new era of fashion on the runways that was heralded as modest, but some question how bright colors, metallic textiles and elaborate brooches can fit into this category. "While some of these clothes are 'modest' in hue as well as length and cut, there may be pieces that would look at home on an exhibitionist. Covered in embellishments and constructed in bold, look-at-me colors and prints, these are clothes for women who want to dress up, not down. You could argue that, in a way, there's nothing modest about them," states Connie Wang, senior fashion features writer at *Refinery29*.[2]

Using fashion to stand out rather than blend in

"Modest fashion might come across as a humblebrag: you have to be a pretty stylish, pretty good-looking woman to claim ownership of such radical dowdiness," writes Naomi Fry for the *New York Times*.[3] She adds that, ironically, it's a younger age group of women in their twenties and thirties who are buying into this way of dressing, despite the conventional societal belief that these are the times when women are of child-bearing age and should thus show off their bodies before they grow old and unattractive. But the modest designs trending worldwide are not for wallflowers – they're for women who may not want to flaunt their bodies, but are flaunting fashion just the same.

Fashion historian Daniel James Cole, who organized a symposium on "Meeting Through Modesty" at New York University in 2016, believes that while the overall tradition of modesty is similar across the three Abrahamic faiths (Judaism, Christianity and Islam), the customary guidelines for covering Muslim women's bodies are stricter than those followed by Jews, who have long been appropriating Western attire to cover to the knees. Glamorous, floor-length designs, Daniel believes, are directed at Muslim consumers who are often expected to cover to their feet. But even then, this type of clothing can be at odds with the Muslim ideal of modesty. "Many people argue that the idea of 'fashionability', or clothing that is beautiful, goes against Islamic ideas of modesty," he tells me over the phone. "So, if you're wearing something pretty or fabulous, it might be haram."

But many Muslim women argue that regardless of what fabrics are used, as long as garments cover their skin, modesty is kept intact. "When we first started Abaya Addict, we got a lot of heat from within the global Muslim community for being too colorful or using prints that drew attention," says Deanna Khalil. "But we believe that [it's okay] so long as women are covering what needs to be covered." Color is one detail that critics of mainstream modest fashion often focus on, as some colors are seen to be more controversial than others. A 2010 focus group study showed that some Turkish women consider the color red to be incompatible with tesettür. "Ideally a woman who is covered should not draw attention, but the color red clearly attracts the eye," noted researchers.[4] This echoes the beliefs of some Orthodox Jews.

Modest fashion photographer Nicole Najmah Abraham explains that these beliefs differ depending on a person's background and heritage. "Color and pattern are associated with regions and cultures," she says. "You go to West Africa, for example, and modest women have on bold prints and colors. The whole area consists of women dressed modestly in this way. So if a woman wore all black in this region, she would be bold, standing out more than a woman in bright African prints." Furthermore, many Arab women who do dress in black abayas still appear striking and glamorous, depending on how they've accessorized the garment and styled their makeup, and, sometimes, their hair. "I can point you to many gorgeous women who can stand out in all-black abayas," says modest fashion model Wafeeqa Azeem. "I would not associate wearing bright colors with being non-discreet versus wearing muted colors with being discreet. I can guarantee you it is possible to wear bright colors and not stand out – many of us [in America] stand out when we wear muted colors."

Fashion designer Safiya Abdallah, on the other hand, sees no conflict between dressing conservatively and standing out. Fashion, for her, is a creative outlet through which you can express yourself, while at the same time covering your skin:

I believe that expressing yourself shows your character, and it's really important because it's a part of your identity. I feel like if you take that away from somebody they almost become anonymous, you know, like forgotten. Nobody wants to be labeled or put in a box and be considered the same as everybody else. So some people started tying their hijabs differently, trying to set themselves apart [from other Muslim women] - accepted by Westerners, but still staying strong in their belief of God and what they're covering for.

Others staunchly disagree. "Hijab is something meant to conceal and cover up, while fashion is meant to be shown, to be noticed by people. It even feels strange when you say the phrase 'hijab fashion'. Many would question whether it is even allowed in Islam for women to have fashion," claims Muslim marriage coach Irfan Ullah Khan in a critical analysis of the Muslim fashion market for the blog HappyMuslimFamily.org. His review proceeds to deconstruct the ways in which Turkish modest fashion retailer Modanisa depicts its fashion imagery, and concludes that overall, it is un-Islamic since portions of models' necks are shown, and since top-and-pants outfits without any outer garments, he believes, are unsuitable to be worn in public spaces.[5]

Many critics of the modest fashion movement object to modeling, displaying fashion on female figures, posting public images on social media and sharing images of makeup-laden faces. The whole point of the concepts of haya, tzniut and modesty is to encourage a sense of humility, as well as privacy between the genders, and this, they believe, conflicts with the inherent purposes of modeling, blogging and social media, which encourage the worldwide circulation of images.

In 2013, then-blogger Rania Iswarani of FashFaith.com told the *Huffington Post* that there's no clash between the concepts of modesty and fashion in the realm of blogging, since it's the garments, and not the wearers' bodies, that are attracting the eyes of onlookers. "People perhaps do pay attention to them, but not to their skin. The body is covered. So these people are attracted to the clothes Muslim women are wearing," she stated.[6]

When it comes to modeling for high-profile publications with motives that may not be compatible with those of modesty, the argument may change. In May 2019, Halima Aden made global headlines again, this time for being the first hijabi model featured in the annual swimwear issue of *Sports Illustrated*. Halima is featured among barely covered women, but she wears swimwear that is hijab-appropriate. In one image shot in the water, she dons a green turban with a cobalt blue turtleneck and leggings, underneath a printed kaftan that's pulled up to her thigh, exposing the outline of her hips and legs. Halima proudly posted images from the shoot on her Instagram, with a caption about conquering odds and celebrating diversity. While many applauded the Muslim model for shattering glass ceilings, others questioned the compatibility between a Muslim face of modest fashion and a magazine that prides itself on its titillating imagery. The *Guardian*'s Marina Hyde notes that sex, not beauty, has historically been the selling point of the *Sports Illustrated* swimwear issue, which in 2004 featured a topless model on its cover. "It would be insulting Halima's intelligence to pretend that the photo that they've styled her with her kaftan hitched right up to her backside so we can see plenty of tightly spandexed leg is anything particularly to do with their alleged commitment to 'modesty'," she writes.[7]

Many news outlets described Halima's *Sports Illustrated* feature as historic, and rightfully so. From burkinis being banned in European nations to being embraced on the pages of the prominent swimwear magazine – it's a feat you can't take lightly. And while Marina implies that modesty is inherently at odds with *Sports Illustrated*, I find that the circumstances aren't all that different on

"From burkinis being banned in European nations to being embraced on the pages of the prominent swimwear magazine – it's a feat you can't take lightly."

social media. Many men use Instagram to troll attractive women, searching for revealing images and posting lewd comments, but in spite of this, modest fashion bloggers are thriving on Instagram, where they are attracting a public audience. So, is modest fashion forever in conflict with social media, one of the main modes that helped catapult it to the mainstream? Egyptian fashion magazine publisher Susan Sabet told *Vogue* in 2018, "The Quran states that [believers] should lower their gaze and be modest. When you have a lot of social media influencers who are basically posing on social media with millions of followers, and are not lowering their gaze, a lot of people see this as a bit controversial. This has people saying, 'Is this right? Is this really a modest person at the end of the day?'"[8]

It's an inner dilemma I'm constantly faced with – especially when I'm all dressed up in an exciting new outfit, have had a decent blow-dry at the hairdresser's and am tempted to post my own photo on Instagram. I'm a Muslim millennial too – a member of Generation M – and finding a balance between traditional interpretations of our faith and contemporary trends is an ongoing challenge. Personally, I've come to terms with putting images of my personal style on Instagram. For me, occasional sharing on social media can still be in line with the principle of inner modesty, as long as the images I post aren't superfluous selfies or near-naked images from beaches and yacht parties.

The role of intent

What first started out as a movement to share, inspire and inform readers, through descriptive written posts online or thoughtfully produced video tutorials, has become, in some cases, a race to post selfies on social media. Many modest fashion influencers no longer link their Instagram photos back to a comprehensive online blog; rather, their only mode of sharing is through Instagram, where they merely post photos of themselves and their material goods, often with little text. Some bloggers are driven by collecting more likes and followers and, essentially, gaining fame, and this conflicts with the Muslim concept of inner modesty. "I think most people start out with the right intentions but it can turn into something else," says Safiya Abdallah.

On the other hand, some Muslim fashion personalities claim that wearing, making and endorsing clothing that is both stylish and conservative can be an act of "dawah", or the Islamic act of inviting others to the religion, as it can make Islam look more inviting or approachable. "Hijab is walking dawah," says Deanna Khalil of Abaya Addict. "It tells everyone around us, 'she's Muslim'. And what we want is for people to not just see us and think of our religious differences, but to see us as they would see other productive members of society – we too can be well dressed and leading colorful and fulfilling lives deserving of respect."

Wafeeqa Azeem, the Muslim fashion model based in New York and signed to Umma Models, sees her role as a way to help improve the reputation of Muslims in the United States' mainstream media:

I feel like the media has dragged us through the mud and back as a religion. They have made us seem barbaric, unapproachable and unrelatable. With the emergence of modest fashion I feel we are able to put forward a different narrative, one of being relatable to every other female out there. It has made both men and women see the beauty in the hijab and Muslim women. I can't tell you the amount of times I have done photoshoots [in modest dress, with my head covered] and had many non-Muslims come up to me telling me how beautiful I looked, and taking pictures of me. This brings such great joy to me, as Muslims are often synonymous with terrorists, thanks to the media.

Maha Gorton, a Dubai-based childrenswear designer and luxury brand ambassador, tells me, "I understand how posting pictures of oneself can be considered narcissistic and contradictory to the concept of modesty to some extent, but there's a right way to do it and it really can inspire more people to realize how nice they can look without baring all."

Consumerism versus a modest lifestyle

On social media, users can feel obliged to constantly showcase new clothing and accessories, and many fashion bloggers are hesitant to post images of the same garment more than once. "Our economy is built on a linear economic model – one fueled by the consumption of goods made, used and discarded, only to be replaced by newer, better goods. No industry is based more on this fast-consumptive model than fashion, with its ever-changing styles and new trends," writes Sass Brown, Dean of the Dubai Institute of Design and Innovation.[9] In 2018, the *Independent* reported that many shoppers were in the habit of purchasing clothes online, wearing them once for social media with the tags still on, only to return them afterwards.

Dubai-based modest fashion blogger Sameera Hussain admits there is a great deal of pressure among fashion bloggers, including those who categorize themselves as modest, to keep up constantly trendy appearances. "There is that pressure of needing new things, and there are definitely Instagram trends some people feel like they have to follow, like 'I better go get one of those Gucci belts because everyone has a Gucci belt'," she says. But Sameera, who focuses more on high-street shopping, says she doesn't let the pressure get to her, and will continue wearing and posting images of items that may be five or more years old, updated with current styles.

I've fallen prey to the influence of bloggers who promote consumerism myself, particularly when it comes to the Gucci belt that Sameera mentions. For a while in 2018, these were a staple part of fashion bloggers' outfits – even modest ones. Their ankle-length dresses and jeans-and-blouse ensembles were finished off with leather belts flaunting the double-G logo of the brand, and I admit, I too went and bought myself one emblazoned with pearls. I may style my splurge with relatively skin-covering garments, but the fact remains that spending £350 (US $425) on a belt is not an instance of modest spending.

"Today's fashion industry is about consumerism and objectification – buy, buy, buy and be judged by what you wear," stated Shelina Janmohamed to the *Telegraph*. "Muslim fashion is teetering between asserting a Muslim woman's right to be beautiful and well-turned-out, and buying more stuff than you need, and being judged by your clothes – both of which are the opposite of Islamic values."[10] The group she fondly calls Generation M, however, are some of the main businesses who are targeting Muslims and their money.

Some labels recognize the dichotomy at stake, and take steps to overcome it. When retailers worldwide were offering massive discounts in stores and on websites in winter 2018, London-based modest wear brand Till We Cover posted an image reading "Anti Black Friday" on Instagram, giving the explanation that over-consumption leads to clothing waste and that they would like their customers to "buy less but better". In 2019, at Modanisa Istanbul Modest Fashion Week, the brand debuted its first recycled garments on the runway, and the designer, Ruby Aslam, has aims to become more sustainable to be in line with the deeper ideals behind modesty. "I want to be in a position where customers may have had Till We Cover for maybe a year or so, and they come back, and for a nominal amount we buy back and recreate that stock. We then upcycle that garment – we call it closing the loop," she tells me.[11]

Many Muslim women took to dressing more conservatively during the Islamic Revolution in Iran as a way of protesting consumerist ideals imported from the West. But on the whole, the current revival of modest fashion, through social media, seasonal runway trends and fast fashion, advocates the very concept of consumerism that these women fought to eradicate from their society.

The donning of the hijab, in its traditional sense, is often seen to be at odds with the pressure and fast pace of the modern fashion and beauty businesses. "At times, when I'm flipping through *Cosmo* at the doctor's office, I feel again that surge of pure delight that I've managed to find the single most effective figurative flip-off to the [Western] beauty industry," says Pamela K. Taylor, who has adopted conservative dress and the hijab since her conversion to Islam in 1986.[12] But Elizabeth Bucar points out that even if Muslim women cover their hair to dress modestly, if they accumulate a huge collection of various headscarves, in a range of colors, patterns and textiles, that all have to be washed, ironed and folded, their habit of hoarding may go against religious principles. "Islamic economic theory favors sustenance over capitalist production, which is why waste (or 'israf') is considered a problem."[13]

Early Muslim lifestyle magazines in the West, struggling with how to depict fashion in a way that would both appeal to their readers and appease their religious beliefs, also faced ethical dilemmas. *Emel's* editor-in-chief Sarah Joseph stated, "Because fashion can be ridiculously expensive… I ask people to be realistic and to be ethical about it and we have had massive debates in this office on whether it's ethical to, you know, profile a £3,000 (US $3,640) pair of shoes." Though the magazine would go on to feature a range of price points, from high-street to high-end, in making the decision to avoid luxury labels it would miss out on lucrative advertising deals with these brands, choosing instead to follow the path they found to be more in line with Islamic ideals.[14]

American author Lauren Shields likens consumerism to a religion in itself, followed subconsciously by most people who ascribe to the belief that we must be constantly dressed in the trendiest of clothing, and that the more options we have, the more likely we are to be deemed fashionable. Inspired by hijab-wearing Muslim women whom she encountered in America, Lauren experimented with dressing more modestly and wrote a book about her experience – *The Beauty Suit: How My Year of Religious Modesty Made Me a Better Feminist*. Lauren refers to "the beauty suit" as the appearance that society pressures women to adopt:

> Uncovered, stylish, "done" hair; makeup that's expensive and time-consuming but considered tasteless when there's "too much"; clothing that hugs our bodies and exposes our arms, legs, and sometimes stomachs and backs; shoes that are agonizing to wear and expensive to own but are somehow near mandatory for professional wear; these are the components of the beauty suit.[15]

Conforming to these ideals of beauty, according to Lauren, "has become a prerequisite for empowerment" and is seen as imperative for a "liberated" woman. "This is nothing more than misogyny, disguised as feminist rhetoric," she claims.[16] For her, dressing modestly meant ridding her wardrobe of clothes she would no longer wear, rather than going out to purchase a new collection of conservative clothing.

London modest fashion blogger Zinah Nur Sharif (@thezirkus on Instagram) believes that while dressing modestly can be both fun and fulfilling, overdressing can make a person look shallow. "Imagine turning up with a dress, high heels and a perfectly done manicure to play golf? Now that is when you have crossed the line and being stylish has become your primary motivation and way of life. Style should be a secondary concern and should not take over your life," she says.[17]

While some might argue that luxury fashion is inherently at odds with modest spending, Halima Aden, who tells me that she purchased her first pair of designer shoes in 2017, from Alberta Ferretti, points out that the money spent on seasonal, cheap, fast fashion could add up to more than that spent on a few luxury items:

> I could go and spend, in the course of years, so much money on shoes that fall apart and that aren't made from good materials, or I could invest one time on something I can keep forever. But I also think that today you have to be careful with policing how people spend their money, because that's their hard-earned money; if somebody wants to go splurge, let them splurge, we can't police people's wallets, and I think the best way to be modest is to think about what's healthy for the environment, and what's sustainable – and some of those things are expensive.

Producing garments that are eco-friendly and sustainable

I'm seated at Modanisa's Istanbul Modest Fashion Week in April 2019, and the runway presentation by Dubai-based designer Rabia Z, who has collaborated with Modanisa on this collection, is about to begin. When it does, it's immediately clear that this is no ordinary runway show, where the clothes alone are the primary focus. The garments paraded down the catwalk are great, but there's another statement that the designer is trying to make. "Green is the new black" and "Ethical is the new normal" are typed across placards held by the models, who sport luxe coat-and-pants power suits and asymmetrical monochrome tunics crafted from eco-friendly textiles. With modesty already covered, sustainability is the cause this collaboration champions – and it's an approach that has not yet been implemented by the majority of modest fashion brands.

"I think the modest fashion scene lacks an ethical lens and a holistic approach," says Amaliah.com's Nafisa Bakkar. "We need to start moving towards a conversation around ethics." Whether consumers choose to conceal or reveal, when they are caught up in an endless cycle of trends propagated by the fast-fashion industry, they often find themselves needing to get rid of old clothing to make space for new spends. In America alone, according to the Environmental Protection Agency, citizens generated more than 16 million tons of textile waste in 2014. Less than 20 percent of this was recycled, and approximately 60 percent ended up in landfills.[18]

There has been an increasing spotlight on transparency in the fashion industry – that is, in regards to the ways a brand sources its textiles and produces its garments. As modest fashion finds its way into the mainstream, there will be an increased demand for sustainable fashion – the production of designs that are long-lasting and recyclable, require minimal energy to produce and are made under humane working conditions.

In 2013, more than 1,000 were killed and over 2,000 injured when Rana Plaza, an eight-story building housing various garment factories (that produced clothing for Walmart, Primark and Mango among other brands) collapsed in Bangladesh due to poor construction, the illegal building of three additional floors, and a lack of adherence to safety protocols. While problems in the structure of the building had been previously flagged by engineers, these were ignored by owners who insisted their employees continue working in order to keep up with the bulk clothing orders from international brands. This tragic event caused an international outcry and fueled the argument for safe, responsible workplaces and production lines.[19]

"Fashion retailers have been exposed surrounding their corporate responsibility in ethical laboring and manufacturing, and as a result of such controversies, customers are no longer just impulse buyers but consider where and how the product is made," says Yasmin Sobeih, the founder of London-based Under-Râpt. Sustainability is key to the DNA of Yasmin's business: "I'm extremely passionate about upholding a fully transparent supply chain," she tells me. "I believe that if Under-Râpt is to inspire and encourage personal health then this must start at the very core of our supply chain and at the very core of our product. By contributing to our environment and global welfare we are ensuring that we are conforming to our consumer's social, ethical and personal values."[20] The designer works only with fabrics that are organic, eco-friendly, sweat-resistant and anti-bacterial, and keeps close tabs on her manufacturers to ensure her garments are being made humanely.

While basic human rights violations often take place when clothing is created in bulk quantities, in unmonitored workshops and factories, a hallmark of home-grown fashion labels – especially if their garments are produced in the Middle East – is their reluctance to mass-produce their designs. Firstly, they often simply don't have the demand for the thousands of pieces that are required for bulk orders at factories, as they sell privately online or through a handful of stockists, and secondly, tailoring costs are relatively inexpensive in the region – many designers strike deals with neighborhood tailoring shops to help bring their designs to life.

Though Haute Hijab is based in New York, Melanie Elturk says she keeps close tabs on her production facility in the Emirate of Ajman, which has been making her scarves for the past seven years. The manufacturer who she is partnered with produces exclusively for Haute Hijab, and Melanie is working on raising funds to buy him out, so that she owns the entirety of her supply chain. She tells me that ethical production and sustainability are fundamentally ingrained in her brand, as opposed to being buzzwords or trends to cater to. "It's so part and parcel of our values as Muslims, that it should be a given with any Muslim-owned company," she explains. "When it comes to labour, wages, fair trade, sustainability, all those things are Islamic principles that we should all be adhering to. As Muslims we want to be part of the solution and not the problem. We're custodians of this earth and we're going to have to answer for everything we did here."

Likewise, Romanna Bint-Abubaker says that launching a fashion business is not entirely fulfilling on a spiritual level, and believes that initiatives founded on Islamic principles, such as modesty, should also give back to the community in some way. In 2016, she founded the We Are One foundation to empower single mothers in India by training them in the basic skills of garment production. These women were compensated for their work, and helped produce the designs for Romanna's in-house clothing line, Rad Label.

Non-profit organization Fashion Revolution, which campaigns for a reform of the fashion industry and increased focus on transparency, released its 2018 Fashion Transparency Index that studied the production policies of 150 well-known retail brands. It found that the average score (ranked out of a possible 100 percent for how much they disclosed) was only 21 percent, and no brands scored above 60 percent.[21] "Having access to this information is changing the purchasing habits of customers," says Yasmin, who references a 2018 report by *Business of Fashion*, which found that millennials in particular are driving the demand for sustainable solutions to fashion, and that 66 percent of global millennials are willing to spend more money on clothing that's sustainable.[22]

In 2019, Melanie created a new role at Haute Hijab, titled director of design and innovation, and hired an expert in the field of sustainability, who had consulted with American fashion designer Eileen Fisher on her "Green Eileen" initiative. She says that Haute Hijab is now looking into ways to create hijabs from sustainable materials like rose petals, mushrooms and coffee grounds. However, not all modest fashion brands share the eco-friendly priorities of designers like Rabia, Yasmin, Romanna and Melanie, as creating sustainable clothing generally costs more and takes longer to produce than most fast-fashion alternatives. But if millennials are pushing for transparency and sustainability, and they are the target group with purchasing power, then brands, even modest wear ones, will have to start reforming themselves.

CHAPTER 9

IS MODEST FASHION HERE TO STAY?

In regions of the world where there are large pockets of Muslim communities, there's no doubt that up-and-coming modest wear designers will flourish both year-round and during peak shopping periods like Ramadan.

However, style trends usually tend to follow a standard timeline, and the concept of modesty, showcased on the catwalks of international fashion capitals and stocked on the shelves of high-street stores, appears to have peaked, becoming an over-used buzzword by the press and by key players in the industry. It's also been employed as part of a marketing gimmick to attract consumers. Take Marks & Spencer's modesty pants, for instance, which are essentially plain cotton pants with an elastic waistband. Or Tide's specialty laundry detergent for black abayas, which, it seems to me, could be just as efficiently washed with any run of the mill laundry soap. There are also the numerous hijab-wearing dolls that have entered the toy market, manufactured by Barbie and Middle Eastern brand Fulla. Barbie's version is modeled after Muslim Olympic fencer Ibtihaj Muhammad, while Fulla dolls are available with a variety of outfits and headscarves. But while modesty may be the buzzword of the moment behind these innovations, the future remains uncertain for modest fashion as a permanent retail category, even among industry experts.

Some, like the *Telegraph*'s Lisa Armstrong, believe it's only a matter of time before the runways grow tired of concealing models' bodies and return to revealing them as they used to. "The debate then is not whether fashion will eventually swing away from modesty back to minis and cleavage. It will. Because fashion is about reacting against the status quo," she writes.[1] American fashion historian Daniel James Cole, on the other hand, is on the fence about the lasting potential of modest fashion in the mainstream. "I think that it is a trend, at this time," he tells me. "But it's not necessarily a passing one. It's trending but at the same time I think it's establishing a market that can sustain itself."

Creating a space for home-grown modest fashion brands

Sunset Mall, located on Jumeirah Beach Road in Dubai, does not share the hustle and bustle of its neighboring boutiques, restaurants and cafés: on a normal day, the two-story shopping center is relatively empty. But on a Thursday night in the middle of the holy month of Ramadan, the case is quite the opposite – a line of cars spills out of the mall's parking lot and onto the main road, as eager shoppers anticipate entry to the annual Eventra Ramadan exhibition. Upon disembarking the escalator and arriving on the first floor, visitors choose to head left or right to begin their round of the exhibition. The outer walkways of the mall are lined with stalls displaying the wares of local and regional fashion designers, along with a handful of homeware and beauty brands. If you've decided to visit the exhibition at its peak period, between the sunset prayer and night-time Ramadan prayers, you'll be swept up in a throng of abayas, with women snatching last-piece kaftans from racks and haggling loudly with staff for special discounts.

The market for emerging designers in the UAE is quite prosperous, and Ramadan is the best time of the year to make sales. Women seek stylish modest wear in the form of kaftans, dresses and capes for their sheesha nights (nights spent smoking hookah pipes) and suhoors (pre-dawn meals), plus more formal attire for the three days of Eid that wrap up the holy month. Many of the designers present here are purely Instagram brands – meaning they have Instagram profiles where they take orders from clients, but they don't physically stock their products in any stores. Exhibitions like these, although accompanied with astronomical rent charges averaging around £600 (US $728) per day, provide emerging designers with opportunities to make direct sales to customers and spread the word about their home-grown labels.

Emerging brands have also benefited greatly from similar pop-up setups at the UK's Muslim Lifestyle Expo, Australia's Mod Markit and Canada's International Modest Fashion and Design Festival, but these provide neither permanent nor stable business models. Social media too is a difficult platform to sustain a business on, if a brand doesn't have its own established e-commerce portal. Instagram, for instance, has been a significant avenue through which home-grown, start-up labels can build brand awareness. However, its algorithm changed in 2016, no longer organizing users' feeds in chronological order but making its own decisions about what type of content users see. Many smaller brands that had previously enjoyed sufficient exposure on the platform became virtually invisible to many of their followers, and their businesses suffered as a result.

Zeruj Port, a fashion mall established in Istanbul in 2018, has been designed to give local modest wear labels a more stable platform where they can sell their wares. The shops within the mall house labels that built their following on Instagram, where they would post images of their designs and coordinate sales with potential customers, before finally investing in physical retail spaces.

Home-grown fashion brands, however, are not powerful enough to sustain the growth of modest fashion; the effort will have to be made from

"The demand for inclusivity doesn't end at body sizes and skin tones – at Dubai Modest Fashion Week in 2019, Abu Dhabi-based designer Asiya Rafiq showcased a collection of modest wear created especially for people of determination (a new term implemented in 2017 by the ruler of Dubai), who use wheelchairs or live with conditions that may inhibit their movement."

players in the mainstream industry. And although major retailers may be increasing their modest wear offerings – some, like Macy's, with committed collections year-round – it's hard to predict whether this will still be the case long term. As Haute Hijab's Melanie Elturk points out, "Modest fashion may be cute now, it may be a trend that some people are trying out, but you know, fashion is fickle, and while you can go to the mall and flip through fashion magazines and see Zara and all these stores with women wearing head coverings, that's probably not going to be the case two to three seasons from now."

So, where does the future of modest fashion lie? According to Lisa Vogl of Macy's Verona line, while the hype surrounding modest fashion may die down, the lasting appeal of modern modest attire will not. "I think sometime in the near future modest fashion in Western countries will no longer be 'newsworthy'; I believe it will become more and more the norm," she tells me.

British-Muslim fashion model Mariah Idrissi points out that some retailers are needlessly jumping onto the modesty bandwagon just to ride the hype. Stores like Marks & Spencer, she says, don't need to promote specialized modest wear collections, since they already offer more conservative styles in their regular lines. "I think the 'modest' thing only works when it's literally a brand that you know doesn't make modest clothes," she explains. And more effective than releasing time-sensitive capsule collections, says Mariah, is hiring relevant spokespeople to help promote a brand's designs to more diverse communities. "You just need a brand representative of the people you're trying to target," she says. "If anyone wants to target the modest consumer, do a social campaign – a style edit of modest girls who style the clothes."[2] It's also worth noting that some brands earn credit for supposedly ground-breaking garments that have in fact been around for some time. "A sports hijab is nothing I haven't seen before. I saw sportswear for Muslim women in Egyptian markets everywhere while growing up, but it's not 'cool' until it has a mainstream label on it," writes Dina Torkia. "It's the same when a big brand does a 'Ramadan Collection'. All they've really done is use existing products and stuck a Ramadan label on it to cash in. This is just lazy. Muslim women are wearing brands all year round, so if these companies really want to champion inclusion, don't turn us into a trend. We aren't just about Ramadan or Eid, or even merely a sports hijab."[3]

Zahra Aljabri, the co-founder of Mode-sty, an early modest fashion website aimed at women of all faiths, acknowledges that Western brands often accredit the Middle East market with the highest purchasing power. "Brands have relied mostly on limited market research which has led them to believe that Muslim spending is concentrated in the Middle East where Muslims spend their Ramadan evenings shopping in malls," explains Zahra. "What's puzzling is, why go after a foreign market with customers you don't understand and who have constant access to modest clothing, while ignoring the estimated US $100 billion market in the west – a market these brands are more familiar with who have very limited access to modest clothing?" She adds that the Middle East contains only around 20 percent of the global Muslim population, and even if these same garments were to become accessible to consumers in the West, the prices would need to be adjusted in order to be affordable for Westerners. "Most price points also cater to the 'oil rich' myth of high-spending Middle Easterners. Most people don't have lavish clothing budgets," she writes.[4] For modest fashion to truly thrive long-term, Zahra believes, brands must treat the retail category as they do other sub-categories of fashion, like those that cater to plus-sized or petite women.

Just as retailers like ASOS provide Petite, Tall and Maternity categories, modest fashion will be more successful if it is inclusive. Dubai-based designer Dima Ayad, for instance, whose designs are available online at The Modist, creates elegant ready-to-wear and occasion wear for women of all shapes and sizes. Many of her cuts include loose but glamorous kaftans, luxe belted robes and embellished, maxi-length kimonos.

Though the fashion industry has been notorious for promoting a limited, Western-influenced definition of beauty, multiculturalism is now being reflected on international runways, as models from all sorts of diverse heritages are increasingly earning spots at the big international fashion weeks. But showcasing a range of color isn't the only important change needed in the industry – body inclusivity needs to be addressed too. French-Algerian modest designer Faiza Bouguessa tells me that seeing diverse body shapes on international catwalks has changed her own approach in how she displays her creations. "When I'm looking for models for a fashion shoot now, I'm thinking, 'there's no way I'm going to take a model if she's too skinny'," she says. Seeing models that are not confined to the traditional size zero sizes has also had a personal effect on the designer. "Now I look at models in a different way, and at myself a different way," she says. "It's so crazy how the fashion industry has a power over how we see ourselves." Whereas the constant influx of ultra-skinny models as the faces of fashion brands can cause insecurities among regular women, even those as trim as Faiza, the sight of a range of body sizes in the limelight can normalize them. "It's great," says the designer. "It's a really nice time to be in fashion."

The demand for inclusivity doesn't end at body sizes and skin tones – at Dubai Modest Fashion Week in 2019, Abu Dhabi-based designer Asiya Rafiq showcased a collection of modest wear created especially for people of determination (a new term implemented in 2017 by the ruler of Dubai), who use wheelchairs or live with conditions that may inhibit their movement. Her practical, functioning garments incorporated zippers and Velcro for ease in dressing, and clothing fitted with magnetic buttons was designed for those who suffer from Parkinson's disease.

Cementing the demand for modest styles

A Bain & Company study found that modest fashion, or clothing that can be worn by Muslim women, made up approximately 40% of women's luxury ready-to-wear in 2018.[5] Modest fashion may always fulfill a need for women who seek high necklines, long sleeves and long hemlines, but it remains to be seen whether modesty will dip out of style like other buzzwords, or secure its place in the global fashion industry. Nicole Najmah Abraham, the modest fashion photographer who has worked with Wafeeqa Azeem, believes that there's long-term potential for the retail category so long as Muslim consumers continue to spend on fashion – "which will be forever," she says with a laugh.

Gender and women's studies professor Susan O. Michelman, who specializes in the history of dress, culture and textiles, published a research paper nearly two decades ago hypothesizing the growth of modest fashion in the American retail market:

> Despite highly media-hyped immodest style, often aimed directly at young women, an increasing number of modesty-seeking consumers, often linked by strong religious values, are having an influence on the consumption of fashion… If the consumer demand is there, designers, producers, and retailers of fashion will need to consider modest fashion as an important component of America's appearance and clothing choice.[6]

Religious values are not a prerequisite for following modest fashion and as the retail sector grows, becoming more integrated into mainstream fashion offerings, it may attract women who are not religious but find the prospect of covering more skin appealing.

The demand for accessible modest fashion is being met by retail markets across the globe, and the Islamic Fashion & Design Council (IFDC) has been working to implement modest wear as a normalized, universal retail category in department stores worldwide. Pret-A-Cover is the name of the program, neatly sidestepping the whole modest versus immodest terminology debate.

While chairwoman Alia Khan agrees that department stores like Harvey Nichols, Bloomingdale's, Nordstrom and Neiman Marcus offer garments that are suitable for modesty-conscious consumers, she believes that they are not displayed or promoted in an effective manner for the modest shopper. "We realized that a lot of the stores had a lot of offerings that people didn't really know about," she tells me. Alia points out that while retailers like Mango and DKNY have experimented with seasonal modest wear collections, there have been a mixture of hits and misses due to the fact that many brands don't understand the psychology and personal tastes of the modest wear consumer, and thus aren't able to win over their loyalty. Lucas Raven, a fashion and retail consultant who is part of the Pret-A-Cover team at IFDC, states:

> Only the customer knows how frustrating it is to find that perfect dress but then not have the sleeves long enough, or items that are too tight, etcetera. Having to layer one's outfit is time consuming and not ideal. The Pret-A-Cover department liberates the consumer from all of this. Now, all they have to do is walk into the Pret-A-Cover departments of participating stores and never feel frustrated again - they will find stylish clothes that meet their criteria by their favorite designers. Goodbye painstaking shopping experiences, hello finding something perfect every time.[7]

In 2015, the IFDC partnered with textile and manufacturing company Beximco, signing a deal that would introduce this new retail category to stores worldwide. While incorporating Pret-A-Cover as a permanent section in stores is a work in progress, the Pret-A-Cover Buyer's Lane initiative (a fashion-week-style platform that showcases brands' latest collections through creative videos rather than traditional runway shows) has introduced modest wear brands into multi-brand boutiques. In autumn 2018, for instance, senior buyers at Debenhams in Kuwait selected six designers represented by the IFDC, including Natasha Kamal, PhiCasa, ZAW Fashion and Talabaya, to sell their collections at a ten-day fashion event at the boutique. By the end of the event, Natasha Kamal and ZAW Fashion had nabbed ongoing placement deals with the department store.

Alia tells me that Pret-A-Cover should appeal to all consumers, regardless of their faith. "We believe that everyone at some time in their life has to refer their style to a modest level. Whether it's because they have to go to a big meeting that's going to be a little more conservative, or go see their grandparents and be more conservative, everyone's touched by that in some way or another," she says.[8]

Expanding the movement to cater to modesty-conscious men

When it comes to fashion, millennial Muslim men are big spenders too, and many of them seek to strike a balance between modesty and modern-day living. The IFDC has launched a subdivision in its organization called "Modest Man" and has begun consulting with brands about catering to modesty-conscious men.

It's also a niche that Romanna Bint-Abubaker is exploring. She says that one of the panel discussions at a previous London Modest Fashion Week was centered on how modesty affects and impacts men, and adds that men have been relatively underserved when it comes to modest fashion. "The reality is, there is a growing modesty market for men, with longer T-shirts and sweatshirts that cover their rear for instance, and there are more designers creating collections in that space because it's definitely an issue," she says. Perhaps the ongoing styles where young men wear their jeans so low that their undergarments are visible has become such a common sight that we've become desensitized to it, yet these would be classified as immodest approaches to dressing, claims New York-based American-Muslim writer Nuriddeen Knight. When she wrote a blog post titled "We have to talk about male modesty" in 2017, some of her readers criticized her, commenting that men simply don't have the same guidelines for modesty as women do in Islam, and that women "easily outclass men in numbers when it comes to continual immodest dressing".[9] But Nuriddeen, who has a master's degree in psychology and traveled to Jordan to study Islamic theology and spirituality, says that according to Islam, modesty is just as incumbent on Muslim men.

In 2018, she wrote a blog post about how one central male figure in Islamic history can be seen as a role model in empowering modern men to safeguard their sexual modesty. The story of Prophet Yusuf (or Joseph, as he's referred to in biblical history) is known by many: he was his father's favorite son, and as a result, his jealous brothers abandoned him in a well in the desert. He was found by a passing caravan and sold as a slave to a rich house-hold. Growing to be a handsome young man, Yusuf caught the attention of his master's wife, who tried to seduce him. Though he refused her advances and was deemed innocent, the wife's obsession with him grew, and Yusuf was then imprisoned for a period of time, believed to have prayed for prison as a refuge from the inappropriate attention that the master's wife and her friends were giving him. "He refused all these women because of his conviction and morality," says Nuriddeen. "We live in a time where people are expected to express themselves sexually, and promiscuity is okay, and that's even more true in society for men. We never really think of the pressures that men have to face if they are trying to be modest. We often think about the man who wants to take advantage of that kind of scenario with women, but what about the man who doesn't?" She explains that men who don't indulge in promiscuity in today's society are labeled as weak, or even gay, and that those who pass their twenties with their virginity still intact are often ridiculed.[10]

Plus, mainstream modes of dress for men, she says, are often far from modest. "Tight jeans are definitely not modest, along with sagging pants of course, as well as shirts that just hit the tops of their jeans, so when they bend over, their backs show. Muscle T-shirts that are meant to show off your muscles, and any T-shirts that have designs that are inappropriate, those are kind of the major things that would not be modest for men, as well as hairstyles that are meant to be flashy," she tells me. In terms of covering their bodies, she explains that, Islamically, it's only obligatory for men to cover the area between their navel and their knees. "But that isn't necessarily modest," she points out. "In a lot of traditional Muslim cultures, men cover their bodies just as much as women do, and some even cover their heads with turbans or kufis [caps popular among Muslim men in parts of Africa and South Asia]." In many Gulf countries, for instance, men's national dress consists of kandooras that are long-sleeved and ankle-length, and are often worn with ghutra or keffiyeh head coverings, which are square-shaped pieces of cloth held in place with black rope cords.

Texas-based male lifestyle blogger Subhi Taha (@subhi.taha on Instagram) is on a mission to destigmatize Muslim attire for men, often adopting an appearance that's visibly Muslim, or at least Eastern-inspired. Under his eponymous clothing brand, Subhi Taha Collective, he sells unisex modest wear.

Minimalist kandoora-inspired shirt dresses and tunics and abaya-influenced capes are available in neutral shades, and marketed to both men and women. Oftentimes, he models these himself on his Instagram page, where he'll pair crisp white kandooras with sporty bomber jackets, or throw a Palestinian keffiyeh scarf over a tracksuit set. Sometimes he wears heavy shawls draped over a shoulder, or tied like a sarong over his pants. When he wears regular Western attire, his outfits are often completed with long, cape-like cloaks in shades of brown, gray, khaki, olive or black.

Just as the fashion-blogging world has shed light on female Muslims aspiring to share their interpretations of modesty, this parallel men's movement is gaining momentum. Like Subhi Taha, London-based Zaahid Ahmed (@zaahidma on Instagram) chronicles his modest outfits on Instagram, and his attire also features a combination of Western street trends and traditional Eastern garments. He often pairs South Asian "kurtas", or long tunics, with cuffed jeans and a backwards baseball cap, or he'll wear joggers with a long thigh-length jumper. Sometimes, he'll even wear a white or black Arabian kandoora, styled with sporty trainers and a winter jacket. Zaahid says that his faith inspired him to begin sharing his outfit photos on Instagram in 2016. "I consider fashion and faith to go hand in hand, as Islam is a lifestyle and everything has to be observed," he tells me. He explains that he works as a stylist and personal shopper for Muslim men seeking to dress modestly in accordance with the traditions of the Prophet Muhammad, while also striking a balance with contemporary urban style trends. "Ninety-eight percent of my clients are Muslim, and they are mainly young men looking to express their style without compromising on their religion," he says.

Scrolling through Zaahid's broody Instagram feed, marked by his masculine style and urban poses amid architectural backdrops, it's clear that, like the female fashion influencers spearheading the modesty movement, he is a social media model. Modest modeling is an up-and-coming field for men – London-based agency Umma Models, for instance, represents a range of male models and male grooming brands in particular will seek out Eastern models for their campaigns for beard oils, balms and fragrances. Founder of The Cactus Agency Zaf Shabir is also a part-time model, having worked for brands like Toni & Guy, Vidal Sassoon and House 99 by David Beckham over the past ten years. "The majority of my work has been mainstream fashion and commercial. Only in the last few years I dabbled with the Asian and ethnic markets," says Zaf, whose own appearance – long black hair and a thick black beard – makes him an ideal candidate for shoots with briefs for Middle Eastern- or Asian-looking models.

At Haute Elan's London Modest Fashion Week in 2018, Zaf opened the runway show for Jubbas, a UK-based label that specializes in tailored 'jubbas' (the colloquial term for Arabian kandooras or thobes) for men. Founder Akil Desai launched Jubbas.com in 2012 to provide the UK menswear market with traditional Eastern silhouettes. While kandooras may look simple, there are many different variations, and Jubbas.com offers twenty-two different styles, including designs that are printed, pleated, button-down, zippered and collared, available in a range of fabrics and colors. There's even a style called "bling diamante jubba", which features a panel of crystals at the front neckline. While cuts are certainly traditional, Akil says that add-ons like these are what give his designs a contemporary appeal.

"We source the detailing on the garments, such as buttons, zips and metal cuffs, which adds a modern twist to the designs," he says. Although some Muslims in the West would only consider wearing jubbas on special occasions, Akil tells me that the silhouette is growing in popularity. "Our garments are worn for weddings, Eid, and family gatherings, but now people have started to wear them at work and as evening wear," he says. The brand has witnessed a steady increase in demand over the past few years – in 2016 it produced 12,000 units, and in 2019, 36,000 units.

Akil credits the brand's popularity to the fact that most of its designs are available in twenty-four different sizes, with a customized, tailored approach ensuring a variety of fits. After selecting a design, men choose from five to six different length options and four different chest sizes. "Our customer also loves the fact we tailor matching thobes for fathers and sons, starting from the age of one month onwards," adds Akil. Although his primary target market is undoubtedly Muslim men, the entrepreneur says that quite a few orders come from men outside the faith. "As a growing market, a lot of non-Muslim men who have worked, or are currently working in the Middle East, have started purchasing from us," he says.

In the West, it's still rare to see Muslim men adopt a cultural dress code, even though, as Nuriddeen points out, many Muslim women in the West adopt hijabs and abaya-inspired cloaks. Perhaps this is because many traditional religious scholars put the onus of modesty on Muslim women, rather than men, and this is the mindset that has trickled down for generations, along with cultural gender roles, which regard men as the breadwinners and women as mothers and housewives. Often this is intensified when families migrate to non-Muslim countries, as they feel they must take extra steps to hold onto their values, and avoid what they consider immodest about Western culture. While the men take up conventional Western clothing, dressing in a way that signals their religion and culture is a sure way for the women in conservative families to hold onto an outward appearance of being a Muslim, even if it means looking foreign or out of place.

CONCLUSION

Coming to terms with the phrase "modest is hottest"

My starting point for this book was my childhood Mormon friend Courtney, who gave me a T-shirt decorated with the words "Modest is Hottest". Wearing those words across my chest gave me confidence and a sense of reassurance as a young teen. The T-shirt validated my religious beliefs, but I hadn't purchased it from a mosque or Muslim brand. It was given to me by a schoolmate who looked nothing like me – she was white-skinned and had wavy, dirty-blonde hair and yet still had modest dressing engrained in her upbringing, just as I had. When I first came home with that T-shirt, my mother took one look at it and was overjoyed that I was so proudly presenting her with a message she had been instilling in me for years. When I wore it in public, strangers passing by would often give a half-smile once they read the slogan. However, there have been some wider criticisms about my T-shirt's mantra. Looking "hot" or even "sexy" is a motivator for many women when they get dressed in the morning, whether or not they comply with faith-based guidelines. But this concept presents a contradiction for many Muslims, or orthodox followers of Christianity or Judaism. Conservatives argue that women, if striving to be modest, should not be making efforts to look attractive to men in the first place. So, wanting to look hot may be at odds with one's religion.

I have one Pakistani-Muslim friend named Amna who doesn't wear the hijab but covers her body up to the elbows and ankles. When we're shopping, or getting ready to go out together, I may tell her that a garment with a lower neckline or a higher hem than she would usually wear looks "hot" on her. Very often she retorts, "It's hotter in hell," implying that she'd rather cover up her body than risk going to hell for showing it off. Though she says this somewhat jokingly, she'll nonetheless layer the garment in question to make it suit her personal standards of modesty. When she's finished getting ready, and most of her skin is covered, my initial assessment of her appearance hasn't changed – she still looks hot, in my opinion; the lack of a shadow of cleavage, or glimpse of an ankle, doesn't detract from her overall attractive look. So why must "hot" and "modest" be mutually exclusive descriptors in fashion?

Mormon writer Rebecca Moore penned a blog post in 2014 about how dressing modestly is often taught as the responsibility of women just so that men are not sexually tempted by them. One user commented, "I detest the phrase 'modest is hottest'. It implies that we women should be dressing for men, to look more appealing for them."[1] April Kelsey, who grew up in a fundamentalist, evangelical Christian community, writes, "'Modest is hottest' is a phrase that needs to disappear... because it plays right into the secular objectification and hyper-sexualization of women."[2]

When I was fourteen, however, oblivious to these various analyses and arguments, that gray T-shirt with those three words emblazoned on it felt like a godsend. It was an empowering statement and an encouraging interfaith symbol, reminding me that I wasn't alone. That dressing modestly was not just a decree for Muslims, but that young women of other faiths, like Courtney, followed certain dress codes too. Today, teens adhering to modest dressing don't need a slogan T-shirt in their wardrobe in order to fortify their faith-meets-fashion preferences; all they need to do is search the hashtag #modestfashion on Instagram to discover a treasure trove of inspirational images of women who showcase varying degrees of covering up while still looking fabulous. For Muslim women in particular, this new, and conveniently hip, retail category is driving a never-before-seen merging of fashion and feminism.

Fashion is political for Muslim women

This newfound celebration of modest fashion in the twenty-first century has generated a unique creative space for women of Muslim and other faiths. Clothing worn for faith-based purposes has long been considered drab and boring – certainly not in the realm of the fashion-forward, but the modest fashion movement has changed this. Some Muslim followers of modest fashion are using the style revolution as an opportunity to come out of their shells, which were built from layers of cultural traditions and community expectations that relegated women to the background, enshrouded and blending in with one another, without any recognition of their individuality.

On one hand, Muslim women are finding a sense of freedom with modest fashion. But on the other, they're still being ostracized for covering up. Amani Al-Khatahtbeh points out that when Angela Merkel, the Chancellor of Germany, visited Saudi Arabia in 2017 and refused to wear the legally required headscarf, she was touted as a feminist leader; however, six months prior, she had called for a ban on face veils in Germany, essentially working to take away women's privilege of choosing whether or not to veil.[3] While this could come across as hypocritical, recent violent attacks where men disguise themselves using niqabs have called into question the safety and security risks posed by the burka and niqab, which factors into many countries' opposition to it. And while France has been at the forefront of the burka debate, not all European nations are as staunchly opposed to face veils. Although the Netherlands banned the garment in public buildings and on public transportation in 2019, the *Independent* reported that many police officers and bus drivers weren't taking any steps to actually enforce the ban.[4]

Many modest fashion followers who cover up to conform to religious guidelines are adamant that their portrayal of modesty is inherently liberating, rather than oppressive, sometimes even in the wearing of the niqab, which is a contested practice even among Muslims. "Wearing niqab is not easily digested in the Muslim community," says American-Trinidadian niqabi photographer and henna artist Shagoofa Ali (@mamoii_ on Instagram). "Often women who decide to wear niqab are looked at as backwards, extreme, or uneducated by our peers."[5]

But words by Arab-American poet Mohja Kahf give a powerful reading to the concept of the veil: "I see without being fully seen; I know without being known. I shore up an advantage over what I survey. Like a goddess, like a queen of unquestioned sovereignty, I declare this my sanctuary."[6] Likewise, Pakistani writer Maliha Masood highlights the sense of power that can come with being fully veiled: "As a physical barrier, the veil denies men their usual privilege of discerning whomever they desire. By default, the women are in command. The female scrutinizes the male. Her gaze from behind the anonymity of her face veil or niqab is a kind of surveillance that casts her in the dominant position."[7]

Although the majority of bloggers at the crux of the modesty movement wear some sort of head covering, social media influencers who don niqabs are also on the rise. The idea of women shielding their face from the public yet sharing images of themselves on social media may seem paradoxical, but women like Shagoofa show that you can dress up in stylish streetwear, strike an edgy pose for the camera and post blogger-style images on Instagram, even with a veil covering the majority of your face. Canadian-Pakistani Aima Warriach (@niqabaechronicles on Instagram) is another niqabi gaining popularity on social media, not because she posts outfits of herself, but because she provides provocative commentary on current events, even when topics such as homosexuality, sexual education and mental health are considered taboo in the Muslim community. "I don't just destigmatize niqab but also introduce liberation that isn't rooted in my conformation to the status quo," Aima says.[8]

The reasons behind Pamela K. Taylor's taking up of modest dress, which, in her case, included the wearing of hijab soon after her conversion to Islam, certainly sound feminist: "I did not want to be judged by my body, my beauty, or the lack thereof, but as an individual, for my personality, my character and my accomplishments. It was, for me, an unambiguous rejection of the objectification of women by men, by advertisers, by the beauty and fashion industries, and Hollywood," she writes. "My choice to wear a headscarf was, essentially, the most dramatic, proactive, feminist statement that I could make in my personal life, an in-your-face rebellion against the feminine mystique."[9] Pamela has fronted the movement for a more feminist interpretation of Islam – in 2005, she became the first female Muslim in Canada to lead a congregational prayer and preach a religious sermon at a mosque, which are both roles that have historically been reserved for Muslim men only.

Haute Hijab's Melanie Elturk points out that while some feminist activists shed their clothes for their cause, Muslim activists who conversely cover up can certainly be regarded as feminists too. "I think that dressing modestly can be a form of feminism – for example in France when they banned the burkini just because it's an Islamic garment, I think that it can be a form of feminism if you're wearing it out of defiance to say, 'Hey, this is my right, just as you can take off all your clothes, I can put clothes back on'." Vela Scarves' Marwa Atik, however, is reluctant to link dressing modestly and covering your hair with political discussions and agendas. When asked if she believes that her headscarf business helps fight stereotypical images of Muslim women, she says, "I don't like the word 'fight'. It immediately makes it seem like Muslim women are expected to always engage in an argument [about being] oppressed. I don't have to answer or prove that to anyone. Hijab is a personal choice, not a political conversation."

Other Muslim women in the modest fashion industry are hesitant to use the word "feminist" to describe their business activities, finding it to be too often associated with stereotypes of "oppression" and also, too loaded of a word to associate with something as trivial as personal style. "I hate talking about feminism. Choosing to cover up is just that – a choice," says Deanna Khalil of Abaya Addict. "It's funny because some feminists think hijab is oppressive, but all of the women I know who wear it have found that the decision to cover is in fact liberating them from a hyper-sexualized society."

Dubai-based designer and brand ambassador Maha Gorton also says that adhering to a modest dress code can be liberating, more so even than the dress codes that men conform to. "It's funny how women not baring all is considered oppressive, but men having to wear a tie around their necks, making them all look the same, is considered normal," she points out.

Many women argue that the subject of female modesty is overly stressed in religious and community conversations. British-Muslim Rhianna Beaumont, noticing a lack of representation of Muslim women of African heritage on social media, launched a campaign called #AfroHijabi on Instagram to shed light on the diverse images of the modern Muslim woman. She started wearing the hijab when she first converted to Islam, but later stopped covering her hair, and she questions why this should make her any less of a Muslim in the eyes of the community when there are more pressing issues they should concern themselves with:

Why is so much emphasis placed upon the way a woman dresses? This is not to override the Quran and sunnah and the obligation for women to cover (which scholars already have a differing opinion on), but to ask why so much emphasis is placed upon this more so than being mentally stable, or being happy, or being dutiful to one's parents, or looking after the earth that Allah has given us, or being just and kind to one's own children.[10]

While supposedly feminist platforms and arguments so often focus on modes of dressing and whether or not certain garments are liberating or oppressive, author Lauren Shields points out that these approaches negate the very point of feminism. "An obsessive focus on dress as the only way to express modesty is not only unhelpful but also reductive. Modesty isn't just about the body and how much is revealed, but also about behavior and values," she explains, echoing the deeper-than-surface meanings of modesty that are promoted by religious perspectives too.[11]

The hijab in particular is a loaded political symbol. Some Muslim women believe that the hijab is mandatory and cover their hair, some believe that it may be mandatory but they're not yet prepared to start covering themselves, and others believe that it's not required at all. Some women go many years wearing the hijab and then decide to take it off, while others start wearing it at a later stage. Some prefer the protective nature of clothing that conceals their bodies, while others find it to be simply more comfortable than attire that shows more flesh.

But because there are so many conflicting opinions surrounding the obligatory or voluntary nature of the hijab, Muslim women as a community are unable to portray a united front. Instead, a simple piece of cloth has been the focus of much nit picking and public debate, even by the religion's young, educated and enlightened followers, as is made evident even through some modern-day Muslim social media users' tendencies to "police" modest fashion bloggers' approaches to modesty, going so far as to judge the "legitimacy" of their hijabs.

Rafia Zakaria recounts a time when she visited Egypt's Cairo University with a delegation of academics in 2009. She was the only Muslim woman present who was not wearing a headscarf, and was met with skepticism by the university's female Muslim faculty members who wore hijabs. "They asked me several times if I was Muslim and several times I said yes," writes Rafia. "They did not respond but they also did not engage; they seemed to imply that if I was Muslim, I should be dressed like they were, should choose to wear my Islam visibly... In choosing not to wear it, my allegiances were suspect; I had chosen a team and it was not their team."[12]

Many other Muslim women can share similar experiences, and some may sometimes even feel intimidated to visit certain mosques out of fear that their skinny jeans, T-shirts or nail polish (considered impermissible during prayer by many traditionalists, as it inhibits water from directly touching the fingernails, which is a part of the required ablution performed by Muslims before they pray) will incite other women in the mosque to rebuke them. This has happened to me a handful of times – my nails are usually painted a shade of bubblegum pink, and women wearing black abayas, sometimes complete with niqabs, have pointed to my hands with a "tsk tsk" right after prayer. And if I wear jeans or leggings with a shirt that reaches above the knees, I'll stick out like a sore thumb at any mosque in the Middle East, becoming the subject of exaggerated glares from other women. When I visit mosques now, I throw on an abaya over my outfit but leave my nails as they are, ignoring any lectures that may come my way.

While ultra-conservatives may sport niqabs on a day-to-day basis, others look for ways to balance their beliefs with the more liberal, contemporary cultures they've been raised in, although this sometimes alienates them from the orthodox Muslim community. Maliha Masood says that in the United States, "the emphasis on image is so strong, that if you don't look like a caricatured Muslim you simply cannot be one." A caricatured Muslim, she goes on to write, "is undoubtedly veiled."[13] But if Muslim feminism is about embracing equality, as well as differences in interpretations, then the community or sisterhood that exists among women who follow one mode of covering will have to be extended to all Muslim women, regardless of whether they cover their hair or not.

To raise awareness for tolerance and acceptance among Muslim women, Dubai-based Safiya Abdallah, who started wearing the hijab herself after having children, launched a campaign in partnership with *Vogue Arabia* in 2018. "What I tried to hone in on was the fact that the word modest has so many meanings," says Safiya. Under her Dulce by Safiya label, she created a simple T-shirt emblazoned with the text, "more than a hijabi, more than a non-jabi". "This was to promote women supporting women – it wasn't like, 'your hijab isn't hijab enough' or 'you took off your hijab, you're not one of us anymore'. In our culture sometimes we outcast people the second they're not following the book to our standards, and this campaign was just about saying, 'I stand with everybody',", she says.[14] Her video campaign stars UAE government council member H.E. Sara Al Madani, Los Angeles-based journalist Shyema Azam, Mariah Idrissi and Maria Al-Sadek, who each articulate their personal definitions of modesty. Safiya interviewed around 300 people for the project, and says that eight out of ten spoke about mannerisms and character, rather than physical appearance and clothing.

Although Muslim faces like Halima Aden, Mariah Idrissi and Dina Torkia, along with the multitude of modest fashion bloggers on social media, continue to front modesty campaigns, MuslimGirl.com's Amani Al-Khatahtbeh believes that the premises of the modest fashion movement are hypocritical, in that designers are obviously targeting Muslim women with their more covered-up designs but are failing to support them in other ways. Living in the US and having been quite regularly exposed to Islamophobic attacks, injustices and insults, Amani claims that brands and blogs riding the modest fashion hype and celebrating Muslim women on a fashion-themed platform are not really taking a genuine approach to helping correct stereotypes about the client the movement is catering to. "While the world scapegoats Islam, Muslim women quickly become the most vulnerable targets, and yet, the fashion industry and corporations are simultaneously eager to profit off of them," she writes.

She adds that hardly any of the big brands that have delved into modest wear for Muslim and Middle Eastern markets have actually hired designers, consultants or models who are from the target market they are catering to. "Nor have they championed causes that would benefit the women from whom they'd gain the profit," she explains. "Muslim women are hot right now. The thing is, we can't be cool with society vilifying our identities while at the same time trying to profit off them."[15]

Fashion as a personal outlet of self-expression, regardless of faith

The modern-day, modesty-conscious woman, regardless of her faith or lack of it, does not dress up for the opposite sex. Fashion is her favorite outlet of self-expression, and she enjoys styling her daily outfits, choosing accessories and trying out the latest makeup trends, be it a dramatic cat-eye or bold lip color. If she isn't motivated by religious or political reasons, her tendency to cover up may be no more than an expression of personal style.

There are a number of factors that could sway women into following a modest fashion lifestyle – and fashion, just as much as faith, can act as a motivator. I hadn't ever come close to donning the hijab (apart from during prayers or mosque events when they are required) until witnessing this onslaught of new turban hijabs, spearheaded by influencers like Ascia Al Faraj and designers like Safiya Abdallah. Though it may not be a hijab in the traditional sense, this cool new head covering that has been trending among Generation M is one of the sparkling gems of modest fashion – and I'm sold. If I were to start wearing a turban like this, I would likely be chastised by conservative members of my Muslim community, both for wearing a head covering haphazardly and not regularly, and for donning one that they may deem to be "illegitimate" hijab. But the point is, I wouldn't be wearing it with any religious intention to cover my hair at all; it would be purely a personal styling choice – my way of following a micro-trend presented by the modest fashion movement.

Fashion trends are in constant flux. But modesty is much more than a fleeting trend for those who believe that the way in which they dress reflects their inner ideals. And the demand for modest fashion is only growing, attracting women, high-profile Hollywood stars included, who find it appealing for the dignity it provides. Maybe society has progressed (or regressed, depending on how you see it) and is now referencing early theories of dress from the Victorian era, which regarded modesty to be the second most important function (the first was protection) of clothing.[16]

Whether they're young Muslims seeking to fight stereotypes or ordinary working women in the West who ascribe to no particular faith but are fed up with their bodies being sexualized, women of all types are reclaiming ownership of the fashion narrative. Perhaps the *Telegraph*'s Lisa Armstrong sums it up best in her article about how demure style became the biggest trend in

"Fashion trends are in constant flux. But modesty is much more than a fleeting trend for those who believe that the way in which they dress reflects their inner ideals."

fashion: "If burning bras and letting it all hang out were symbols of emancipation fifty years ago, taking back control of how we display our bodies is the new freedom."[17]

When online luxury shopping platform The Modist first went live in 2017, its agenda seemed to be purely about fashion. By the end of 2018, however, it launched its #ALaModist campaign, which took a strong feminist stance. This campaign was shared through newsletters emailed to customers, magazine ads and sponsored Instagram posts, featuring a diverse array of modestly dressed women of varying ages, ethnicities and approaches to covering up. The accompanying message was:

> It's never been a more extraordinary time to be a woman. The fight for equality is far from over, but change is happening. We're expressing our individuality and creativity on our terms. A more modest silhouette is becoming a positive fashion choice for women around the world. But let's clear the air; when we say modest we don't mean in spirit. It's what we choose to reveal. This is the à la Modist silhouette. These are our bodies. Our femininity. Our stories. We believe that fashion à la Modist is liberating. Chic. Confident. Inclusive of everyone. To the judgement of no one. This is us. These are our times.[18]

These words epitomize the pulsating energy that's central to the modest fashion movement. For the women leading this style revolution, questions about the permissibility of walking runways and posting selfies, and criticisms about visible necks and flashes of ankle, are no longer relevant. In the twenty-first century, it's the freedom of choice that's being claimed by women of all faiths or none, and in an ironic reversal of historical shifts, it's the right to cover up, rather than to expose skin, that's being championed.

THE BLACK BOOK OF MODEST FASHION
Key players in the industry

Afia Ahmed: a London-based writer and researcher who has covered current events in the field of modest fashion and contributed a chapter to the book *It's Not About the Burqa*

Aheda Zanetti: the Lebanese designer based in Australia who made the first burkini, which is trademarked to her brand but has become a popular term to refer to Muslim swimwear

Aima Warriach: a Canadian-Pakistani graphic designer based in Toronto who wears the niqab, posts politically fueled images and advocates for body positivity (@niqabaechronicles on Instagram)

Akil Desai: the founder of UK-based modest menswear label Jubbas, which recreates the traditional kandoora silhouette in a variety of designs (@jubbas.com_ on Instagram)

Alessandro Michele: the Italian fashion designer who, upon becoming the creative director of Gucci in 2015, introduced distinctively modest looks at the brand's seasonal runway shows (@gucci on Instagram)

Alexa Sue-Anne Dudley: an American Apostolic Christian fashion blogger and modest fashion enthusiast based in Tennessee (@1998miss on Instagram)

Alia Khan: the co-founder and chairwoman of the Islamic Fashion and Design Council (IFDC), listed as one of the fifty most influential women in the Arab World by *Arabian Business* (@ifdc_org on Instagram)

Amani Al-Khatahtbeh: a hijab-wearing Jordanian-American entrepreneur who launched online platform MuslimGirl.com at the age of 17 (@amani on Instagram)

Amena Khan: a British fashion and beauty influencer, who in 2018 became the first hijabi to star in a hair campaign by L'Oréal (@amenakhan on Instagram)

Annelies Moors: a professor of contemporary Muslim societies and co-author of *Islamic Fashion and Anti-fashion*

Anniesa Hasibuan: an Indonesian fashion designer who, in 2016, was the first to showcase a collection at New York Fashion Week that featured hijabs on all of the models

Arwa Al Banawi: a Saudi fashion designer based in Dubai, who specializes in abaya-inspired silhouettes and power suits (@arwaalbanawi on Instagram)

Ascia Al Faraj: a Kuwaiti-American modest fashion influencer who previously covered her hair with turbans and is considered one of the pioneers of the modest fashion blogging movement (@ascia on Instagram)

Asiya Rafiq: an Indian modest wear designer based in Abu Dhabi, who, in 2019, created a special collection for women with disabilities

Ayana Ife: a hijab-wearing fashion designer who, in 2017, became the first participant on American reality television series *Project Runway* to create modest wear for every challenge (@ayanaife on Instagram)

Basma Kahie: a London-based modest fashion influencer with Somali heritage who wears the hijab (@basma_k on Instagram)

Batsheva Hay: A Jewish fashion designer based in New York who is known for her ruffled vintage-inspired dresses with modest silhouettes (@batshevadress on Instagram)

Carla Jones: an anthropology professor who has studied the role of Muslim fashion in Indonesia

Chaya Chanin and Simi Polonsky: Orthodox Jewish sisters from Australia who launched their modest wear brand, The Frock NYC, in 2010 (@thefrocknyc on Instagram)

Daniel James Cole: a fashion historian who has studied religiously motivated dress, and in 2016, organized a symposium titled "Meeting Through Modesty" at New York University

Deanna Khalil: the Italian-Palestinian fashion designer behind modest wear brand Abaya Addict, which was founded in Dubai but is now based in Chicago (@abayaaddict on Instagram)

Dian Pelangi: a popular Indonesian modest fashion designer and influencer (@dianpelangi on Instagram)

Dima Ayad: a Dubai-based fashion designer who incorporates inclusive sizing in her business model (@dimaayad on Instagram)

Dina Torkia: a British-Egyptian modest fashion blogger known across the globe for the hijab-tying tutorials she posted online starting in 2010, and the author of her autobiography, *Modestly* (@dinatokio on Instagram)

Elizabeth Bucar: a religion and philosophy professor who authored *Pious Fashion: How Muslim Women Dress* and *The Islamic Veil: A Beginner's Guide*

Emily Smith: a Mormon modest fashion blogger, and founder of swimwear brand Tanlines and lingerie brand Unmentionables (@modestgoddess_ on Instagram)

Emma Tarlo: an anthropology professor, author of *Visibly Muslim: Fashion, Politics, Faith* and co-author of *Islamic Fashion and Anti-fashion*

Faegheh Shirazi: a Middle Eastern cultures professor and author of *Brand Islam: The Marketing and Commodification of Piety*, which touches on the commercialization of Muslim fashion

Faiza Bouguessa: a Dubai-based French-Algerian luxury modest fashion designer who has dressed Beyoncé and took part in the Contemporary Muslim Fashions exhibition at the de Young museum in San Francisco (@bouguessa on Instagram)

Fatma Al Mulla: an Emirati fashion designer who creates printed and embellished kaftan dresses in addition to stationery, home decor and tech accessories (@fmm.dubai on Instagram)

Fatuma Yusuf: an American hijabi who modeled for Banana Republic's first hijab collection (@thisgirlfatuma on Instagram)

Feriel Moulai: the first hijabi model to walk the runway at Paris Fashion Week, who also starred in a 2019 Farfetch campaign and 2019 modest swimwear shoot in *Vogue Arabia* (@realferiel on Instagram)

Franka Soeria: an Indonesian fashion journalist, entrepreneur and co-founder of Think Fashion – the organizer of the original Modest Fashion Weeks that take place in major cities worldwide (@modestfashionweeks on Instagram)

Halima Aden: a Somali immigrant to America and the world's first mainstream hijabi runway model (@halima on Instagram)

Ghizlan Guenez: the Algerian-born founder and chief executive of luxury e-commerce site The Modist (@ghizlan_guenez_ on Instagram)

Hana Tajima: a British-Japanese hijabi fashion blogger and designer who has collaborated on a recurring modest wear collection for Japanese clothing brand Uniqlo (@hntaj on Instagram)

Hanan Tehaili: a Canadian hijab-wearing fashion and beauty blogger and YouTuber (@hanan.tehaili on Instagram)

Hoda Katebi: an Iranian-American writer and author of *Tehran Street Style,* whose work explores the relationship between politics and modest fashion (@hodakatebi on Instagram)

Kerim Türe: the Turkish entrepreneur who co-founded modest fashion e-commerce platform Modanisa in 2011 (@modanisa on Instagram)

Langston Hues: a Detroit-based street style photographer who compiled images of diverse, modestly dressed women in his book, *Modest Street Fashion,* in 2014 (@langstonhues on Instagram)

Lisa Vogl: a hijab-wearing convert to Islam and the co-founder of modest fashion label Verona, which has been stocked at Macy's and ASOS (@veronacollection on Instagram)

Maha Gorton: a childrenswear designer and luxury modest fashion brand ambassador of mixed British and Egyptian heritage (@mahagorton on Instagram)

Maria Al-Sadek: a Palestinian-Puerto Rican modest fashion influencer who wears the hijab and is based in New York (@mariaalia on Instagram)

Mariah Idrissi: a British hijab-wearing model and activist with mixed Moroccan and Pakistani heritage, who rose to fame after debuting in a campaign for H&M in 2015 (@mariahidrissi on Instagram)

Marriam Mossalli: the Saudi fashion editor and founder of luxury consultancy firm Niche Arabia, who compiled the book *Under the Abaya: Street Style from Saudi Arabia* in 2018 (@marriam.mossalli on Instagram)

Marwa Atik: a Syrian modest fashion influencer and co-founder and designer of American hijab brand Vela (@velascarves on Instagram)

Melanie Elturk: a modest fashion blogger and founder of high-end headscarves brand Haute Hijab, which is based in the United States (@hautehijab on Instagram)

Michaella Lawson: a Utah-based Mormon designer who launched modest fashion brand and boutique Mikarose in 2006 (@mikaroseclothing on Instagram)

Mimi Hecht and Mushky Notik: Orthodox Jewish sisters-in-law who launched modest wear brand Mimu Maxi in New York in 2012 (@mimumaxi on Instagram)

Nabiila: a hijab-wearing modest fashion blogger and clothing designer based in the UK, with mixed Turkish, Algerian and Russian heritage (@nabiilabee on Instagram)

Nabilah Kariem: a South African fashion and travel blogger who wears a hijab, often topped off with hats or clips (@nabilahkariem on Instagram)

Nadia Azmy: an Egyptian New Yorker and fashion influencer who formerly wore the hijab and blogged under the name Winnie Detwa (@nadiaazmy on Instagram)

Nafisa Bakkar: the writer, co-founder and CEO behind online platform Amaliah, which publishes stories about Muslim women (@amaliah_com on Instagram)

Nailah Lymus: a New York-based clothing designer and founder of Underwraps, the first agency dedicated to representing Muslim and modest models (@amirah_creations on Instagram)

Neelam Hakeem: a hijab-wearing African-American poet and rapper who has received shout-outs from Will Smith and P. Diddy (@neelam_ on Instagram)

Nicole Najmah Abraham: a hijabi photographer based in Brooklyn who specializes in capturing images of modest fashion (@najmdesignsphotos on Instagram)

Nura Afia: a hijabi beauty blogger and YouTuber who, in 2017, was named a brand ambassador by American cosmetics company CoverGirl (@nuralailalov on Instagram)

Nuriddeen Knight: an author and public speaker who has written about women's roles in Islam and how commandments for modesty are applicable to Muslim men (@figandoliveblog on Instagram)

Ozlem Sahin: a Turkish entrepreneur and co-founder of Think Fashion – the organizer of the original Modest Fashion Weeks that take place in major cities worldwide (@modestfashionweeks on Instagram)

Rabia Z: A Dubai-based designer who, at Modanisa Istanbul Modest Fashion Week in 2019, collaborated with the e-commerce platform on a sustainable and eco-friendly modest wear collection (@rabiazofficial on Instagram)

Rachelle Yadegar: the Jewish modest fashion blogger behind NotWithout MyHeels.com and co-owner of fashion label Raju, based in Los Angeles (@rachelleyadegar on Instagram)

Reina Lewis: an art historian, culture studies professor and author of *Modest Fashion: Styling Bodies, Mediating Faith,* who has extensively studied the evolution of Muslim fashion in the West

Rhianna Beaumont: a former hijab-wearing Muslim in the UK who launched the hashtag #AfroHijabi to shed light on the representation of black women in the Muslim community (@rhianna.beau on Instagram)

Rihab Nubi: a Sudanese graphic designer and modest fashion influencer who wears the hijab and lives in the Emirate of Sharjah (@riinubi on Instagram)

Roksanda Ilinčić: a London-based Serbian designer who specializes in creating elegant modest wear in the mainstream luxury fashion industry (@roksandailincic on Instagram)

Romanna Bint-Abubakr: the London-based founder of modest wear platform Haute Elan and Haute Elan London Fashion Week (@hauteelan on Instagram)

Ruba Zai: the Afghan-Dutch hijabi fashion influencer who, in 2017, became a face of Dolce & Gabbana and starred in a Yves Saint Laurent Beauty campaign (@hijabhills on Instagram)

Ruby Aslam: the London-based founder of modest wear label Till We Cover (@tillwecover on Instagram)

Sabrina Salhi: the Dubai-based hijabi entrepreneur who launched Unveiled – a women's only nightlife concept that brings together music, dancing, food and fashion pop-ups (@unveileddxb on Instagram)

Safiya Abdallah: a Dubai-based, hijab-wearing Libyan-Mexican modest fashion designer who specializes in glamorous ready-to-wear and often dresses popular American rapper Neelam (@dulcebysafiya)

Sahinat Erkilic: also known as Shah, the co-founder and editor-in-chief of *Hijab In Style* magazine, which launched in the United States in 2018 (@shahhatun on Instagram)

Saima Chowdhury: a hijab-wearing modest fashion blogger and podcast host who is based in the UK (@saimasmileslike on Instagram)

Saira Arshad: a Toronto-based fashion and travel blogger who often wears her hijab tied like a turban, and has lived in Kuwait and Dubai (@shazaira on Instagram)

Sameera Hussain: a fashion, beauty and travel blogger living between Glasgow and Dubai, who dresses modestly without covering her hair (@missmulberry on Instagram)

Sarah Joseph: a Muslim convert who was the CEO and editor-in-chief of British Muslim lifestyle magazine *Emel*

Saufeeya Goodson: a Dubai-based Moroccan-American modest fashion blogger who covers her hair (@saufeeya on Instagram)

Seima Rahman: a hijabi fashion and beauty blogger based in Coventry (@seimarahman on Instagram)

Shagoofa Ali: a niqab-wearing photographer and henna artist based in Oklahoma (@shagoofali on Instagram)

Shahira Yusuf: a Somali-British hijabi model who is signed to Storm Models – the same agency that first recruited Kate Moss (@shvhira on Instagram)

Shelina Janmohamed: the author who uses the phrase "Generation M" to refer to the group of millennial Muslims who balance faith with modernity in all areas of life, including fashion (@loveinaheadscarf on Instagram)

Subhi Taha: a Dallas-based male fashion influencer of mixed Palestinian and Filipino heritage, and designer of unisex modest clothing (@subhi.taha on Instagram)

Summer Albaracha: an American fashion blogger who covers her hair and, in 2012, launched the platform Hipster Hijabis in St. Louis (@summeralbarcha on Instagram)

Wafeeqa Azeem: a Guyanese hijabi doctor and model based in New York and signed to Umma Models (@wafeeqaswardrobe on Instagram)

Yasmin Jay: a Sydney-based hijabi, fashion influencer and designer specializing in elegant, feminine modest wear (@yasssminjay on Instagram)

Yasmin Sobeih: the British-Egyptian designer behind sports and athleisure brand Under-Râpt, which is crafted using organic and sustainable textiles (@under_rapt on Instagram)

Zaahid Ahmed: a UK-based male modest fashion influencer and personal shopper (@zaahidma on Instagram)

Zaf Shabir: a British-Pakistani male model, and the founder and creative director of The Cactus Agency (@zafshabir on Instagram)

Zahra Aljabri: a New York-based spiritual mindset coach, writer and founder of early modest fashion website Mode-sty (@zforzahra on Instagram)

Zinah Nur Sharif: a Yemeni fashion blogger who wears the hijab and works in luxury fashion marketing (@thezirkus on Instagram)

GLOSSARY

Abaya – a long outer garment that covers the female body, traditionally black in color and part of the cultural dress for women in Arab countries

Allah – the Arabic word for "God"

Ameera – the Arabic word for "Princess"

Blogger – an individual who posts texts and/or photos on their own online website

Burka – a long outer garment that covers the female body, including the face, sometimes with a mesh veil across the eyes

Burkini – a one- or two-piece swimwear garment that covers the entire body from neck, to wrists and ankles, often times accompanied by a fitted hood to cover the hair

Busana Muslim – the term for "Muslim dress" in Indonesia

Dishdash – a colloquial term for the traditionally neutral-toned, long-sleeved, ankle-length garment worn by Arab males

Eid Al Fitr – the holiday celebrated by Muslims at the end of the month of Ramadan

GCC – an alliance of Arab countries known as the "Gulf Cooperation Council" including Saudi Arabia, Bahrain, Kuwait, Oman, Qatar and the UAE

Ghutra – (also called keffiyeh) the patterned headscarf, typically black and white or red and white, that's part of the cultural dress among men in many Arab countries

Hadith – a collection of the Sunnah, or words, sayings and traditions of the Prophet Muhammad, which along with the Quran, make up the foundational authoritative sources of Islam

Halal – an Arabic word meaning "permissible" according to the commandments of Islam

Haram – an Arabic word meaning "impermissible" according to the commandments of Islam

Haya – an Arabic word for "modesty," referring to both the inner embodiment and outer portrayal of it

Hijab – the headscarf worn by many Muslim women

Hijabi – a Muslim woman who covers her hair with a headscarf

IFDC – the abbreviation for the International Fashion and Design Council

Iftar – the meal eaten at sunset, marking the end of the fasting day for Muslims during the month of Ramadan

Influencer – a person who uses digital platforms like blogs and social media apps like Instagram to post photos and videos, oftentimes receiving money or free products from brands in exchange for promoting them to their many followers

Instagram – a social media app used to share photos and videos

Israf – an Arabic word signifying exaggerated, in excess of or wasteful

Jilbab – a word used to denote religious dress among Muslim women in Indonesia

Jubba – (also called thobe, kandoora or dishdash) a term used to signify the typically neutral-toned, long garment worn by Arab males

Jummah – the Arabic word for "Friday," on which Muslim men are required to join for a congregational prayer

Kaftan – a loose dress, often belted, worn by many Arab women

Kandoora – (also called thobe, kandoora or dishdash) a term used to signify the typically neutral-toned, long garment worn by Arab males

Keffiyeh – (also called ghutra) the patterned headscarf, typically black and white or red and white, that's part of the cultural dress among men in many Arab countries

Khaleeji – hailing from a Gulf Arab country

Kufi – a fitted cap worn by many Muslim men in Africa, South Asia and parts of the Arab world

Kurta – a long tunic, part of the cultural dress in South Asian countries

LDS – the abbreviation for the Church of the Latter-day Saints, or Mormon Church

Manteau – a long overcoat available in a variety of prints, fabrics and colors, worn by Muslim women in modern-day Iran

Niqab – a veil that covers a woman's hair and face, leaving only her eyes visible

Niqabi – a woman who wears a face veil, or niqab, along with a head covering

Prophet Muhammad – the messenger of Islam, believed to be the last and final prophet, whose actions and sayings Muslims strive to follow

Ramadan – the Islamic month when Muslims are required to fast daily

Shayla – a headscarf worn by Arab women with their abayas, often made to match the abaya

Sheesha – a tobacco pipe also known as hookah, which is a popular social pastime in Arab cultures

Skights – modest two-in-one athletic garments in which leggings are attached to skirts to offer more coverage

Souq – a traditional Arab bazaar or marketplace

Suhoor – the pre-dawn meal that Muslims eat before fasting, during the month of Ramadan

Sunnah – the words, actions and traditions of the Prophet Muhammad, which Muslims strive to emulate

Tesettür – a Turkish word for modest Muslim dress

Thobe (also called jubba, kandoora or dishdash) a term used to signify the typically neutral-toned, long garment worn by Arab males

Turban – an ornate way of tying a hijab with fancy knots and bows that has become popular among Muslim women

Tzniut – the Hebrew word for the trait "modesty," and the dress code guidelines of Jewish women

Veil – a word used to signify a type of head and/or face covering often worn by religious Muslim, Christian and Jewish women

Vlogger – a blogger who shares content through videos on platforms like YouTube and Instagram

Wahabi – the following of a strict, orthodox interpretation of Sunni Islam, propagated by Saudi Arabia

NOTES

Introduction

1 https://www.telegraph.co.uk/fashion/style did-demure-dressing-become-biggest-trend-fashion/

2 https://www.whowhatwear.com/modest-fashion

3 https://www.theguardian.com/fashion/2018/sep/25/end-cleavage-sexy-clothes-milan-fashion-week

4 Shelina Janmohamed, *Generation M: Young Muslims Changing the World.* London: I.B. Tauris, 2016, 151

5 https://www.forbes.com/sites/deborahweinswig/2017/03/31/is-modest-fashion-the-next-big-thing/#1c52883b9e97

6 https://www.questsearch.co.uk/2017/06/modest-fashion-booming-global-market/

7 https://www.bustle.com/p/why-muslim-jewish-modest-fashion-is-so-popular-but-christian-fashion-week-failed-2987672

8 https://www.independent.co.uk/life-style/fashion/modesty-fashion-shopping-covering-up-hijab-abaya-muslim-jewish-orthodox-christian-a8003726.html

9 https://www.amaliah.com/post/40756/turban-hijab-became-symbol-modern-muslim-woman

10 https://www.dawn.com/news/1435706

11 Reina Lewis, 'Marketing Muslim Lifestyle: A New Media Genre' in *Journal of Middle East Women's Studies.* November 2010; 6 (3): 75–76. doi: https://doi.org/10.2979/MEW.2010.6.3.58

12 https://www.dailymail.co.uk/femail/article-4648726/JULIE-BURCHILL-slams-new-modesty-dressing-fashion-trend.html

13 Maryam Namazi, 'Pret-a-patriarchy: On Modest Fashion' in *The New European.* United Kingdom: Archant, May 31, 2018, 36

14 Maryam Namazi, 'Pret-a-patriarchy: On Modest Fashion' in *The New European.* United Kingdom: Archant, May 31, 2018, 36

15 https://www.nytimes.com/2017/11/02/t-magazine/modest-fashion-clothes.html

Chapter 1

1   https://newrepublic.com/article/148995/feminist-future-modesty

2   https://www.c-span.org/video/?c4645885/rep-carolyn-maloney-wears-burka-house-floor

3   Rafia Zakaria, *Veil*. New York: Bloomsbury Academic, 2017, 80

4   https://www.mumsnet.com/Talk/am_i_being_unreasonable/3099758-To-be-surprised-that-M-S-has-a-section-on-their-website-for-Modest-Clothing

5   Dina Torkia, *Modestly*. London: Ebury Press, 2018, 138

6   Reza Aslan, *No God but God*. New York: Random House Inc, 2011, 73

7   Amani Al-Khatahtbeh, *Muslim Girl: A Coming of Age*. New York: Simon & Schuster Paperbacks, 2016, 20–21

8   Amani Al-Khatahtbeh, *Muslim Girl: A Coming of Age*. New York: Simon & Schuster Paperbacks, 2016, 36

9   https://www.popsugar.com/fashion/Modest-Celebrity-Fashion-36794409

10 https://www.nytimes.com/2017/11/02/t-magazine/modest-fashion-clothes.html

11 https://www.harpersbazaar.com.au/fashion/modesty-fashion-trend-2018-17172

12 https://www.harpersbazaar.com.au/fashion/modesty-fashion-trend-2018-17172

13 https://www.theguardian.com/fashion/2018/sep/25/end-cleavage-sexy-clothes-milan-fashion-week

14 https://www.newyorker.com/magazine/2018/09/10/batsheva-hay-rethinks-the-traditions-of-feminine-dress

15 https://www.elle.com/uk/fashion/a20509330/unpicking-sheer-layering-in-the-age-of-metoo/

16 https://religionnews.com/2018/01/08/mormons-miss-the-point-of-metoo-by-focusing-on-modest-gowns-at-golden-globes/

17 https://www.independent.co.uk/voices/modest-clothing-mayim-bialik-harvey-weinstein-sexual-harassment-muslim-women-a8004501.html

18 https://www.thenational.ae/lifestyle/comment/the-term-modestwear-fails-to-acknowledge-a-wider-movement-1.775062

19 https://www.racked.com/2018/6/4/17417386/political-candidates-women-female-dress-code

20 https://www.glamour.com/story/hoda-katebi-modest-fashion-double-standard

Chapter 2

1   https://www.marieclaire.co.uk/fashion/autumn-trends-2018-607628

2   https://www.thenational.ae/lifestyle/fashion/covering-the-body-feels-more-mysterious-and-appealing-roksanda-in-dubai-1.671528

3   https://www.refinery29.com/en-us/2017/01/134958/modest-clothing-fashion-trend

4   Faegheh Shirazi, *Brand Islam: The Marketing and Commodification of Piety*. Austin: The University of Texas Press, 2016, 162

5   Faegheh Shirazi, *Brand Islam: The Marketing and Commodification of Piety*. Austin: The University of Texas Press, 2016, 144

6 https://www.theguardian.com/fashion/2018/sep/25/end-cleavage-sexy-clothes-milan-fashion-week

7 https://en.vogue.me/archive/legacy/tommy-hilfiger-ramadan-2016-collection-middle-east-exclusive/

8 http://www.dazeddigital.com/fashion/article/30450/1/meet-the-designer-behind-uniqlo-s-first-uk-hijab-range

9 https://edition.cnn.com/style/article/muslim-fashion-industry/index.html

10 https://www.abc.net.au/news/2018-10-20/modest-muslim-fashion-at-adelaide-fashion-festival/10397248

11 https://www.thenational.ae/lifestyle/fashion/modest-fashion-takes-a-turn-on-italian-runways-1.409647

12 https://www.huffingtonpost.co.uk/entry/modest-fashion-week-london_uk_58aad7ffe4b037d17d29711b

13 https://www.telegraph.co.uk/women/life/london-modest-fashion-week-faith-can-fashionable/

14 http://www.arabnews.com/node/1253741/business-economy

15 https://www.businessinsider.sg/lindsay-lohan-shocks-with-hijab-at-london-modest-fashion-week/

16 https://www.thenational.ae/lifestyle/luxury/modestwear-gets-first-dedicated-exhibition-in-the-united-states-1.768444

17 https://www.hollywoodreporter.com/news/contemporary-muslim-fashion-exhibition-opens-san-francisco-1146713

18 https://www.thenational.ae/lifestyle/luxury/halima-aden-my-family-doesn-t-understand-modelling-is-a-real-job-1.874105

19 https://www.thenational.ae/lifestyle/luxury/halima-aden-my-family-doesn-t-understand-modelling-is-a-real-job-1.874105

20 https://www.thenational.ae/lifestyle/fashion/modestwear-pioneer-mariah-idrissi-talks-faith-and-fashion-1.833871

21 https://www.abouther.com/node/7611/fashion/fashion-news/there%E2%80%99s-new-hijabi-model-town-shahira-yusuf

22 https://www.theguardian.com/fashion/2018/sep/02/shahira-yusuf-i-have-always-felt-beautiful-

23 https://www.thenational.ae/lifestyle/luxury/halima-aden-my-family-doesn-t-understand-modelling-is-a-real-job-1.874105

Chapter 3

1 *The Quran*, 24:31 and 33:59 (Sahih International translation)

2 Fadwa El Guindi, *Veil: Modesty, Privacy and Resistance.* Oxford: Berg, 1999, 155

3 Reza Aslan, *No God but God.* New York: Random House Inc, 2011, 66

4 http://www.muslimink.com/faith/benefits-blog/122-haya-modesty-in-islam

5 Reina Lewis, *Muslim Fashion: Contemporary Style Cultures.* Durham: Duke University Press, 2015, 61

6   Fadwa El Guindi, *Veil: Modesty, Privacy and Resistance.* Oxford: Berg, 1999, 137

7   Fadwa El Guindi, *Veil: Modesty, Privacy and Resistance.* Oxford: Berg, 1999, 140

8   *The Bible,* 1 Timothy 2:9–10 (New Living Translation)

9   *The Bible,* 1 Peter 3:3–5 (New Living Translation)

10 *The Bible,* 1 Corinthians 11:4–6 (New Living Translation)

11 https://bible.org/article/what-head-covering-1-cor-112-16-and-does-it-apply-us-today

12 https://www.lds.org/topics/modesty?lang=eng#_

13 https://womensconference.byu.edu/sites/womensconference.ce.byu.edu/files/carolmcconkiemodesty.pdf

14 https://www.vogue.com/article/orthodox-judaism-fashion-laws-of-modesty

15 https://www.rabbinicalassembly.org/sites/default/files/Modesty%20Final.pdf

16 Barbara Goldman Carrel, *Shattered Vessels that Contain Divine Sparks: Unveiling Hasidic Women's Dress Code* in Jennifer Heath, *The Veil: Women writers on its history, lore, and politics.* Berkeley: University of California Press, 2008, 48

17 Barbara Goldman Carrel, *Shattered Vessels that Contain Divine Sparks: Unveiling Hasidic Women's Dress Code* in Jennifer Heath, *The Veil: Women writers on its history, lore, and politics.* Berkeley: University of California Press, 2008, 51

18 https://www.rabbinicalassembly.org/sites/default/files/Modesty%20Final.pdf

19 Barbara Goldman Carrel, *Shattered Vessels that Contain Divine Sparks: Unveiling Hasidic Women's Dress Code* in Jennifer Heath, *The Veil: Women writers on its history, lore, and politics.* Berkeley: University of California Press, 2008, 48

20 Gila Manolson, *Outside/Inside: A Fresh look at Tzniut.* Southfield: Targum Press, 1995, 43

21 Leila Ahmed, *A Quiet Revolution: The Veil's Resurgence, from the Middle East to America.* New Haven: Yale University Press, 2011, 43 and 46–47

22 Mohja Kahf, 'From Her Royal Body the Robe Was Removed: The Blessings of the Veil and the Trauma of Forced Unveilings in the Middle East' in Jennifer Heath, *The Veil: Women Writers on Its History, Lore, and Politics.* Berkeley: University of California Press, 2008, 33–35

23 Fadwa El Guindi, *Veil: Modesty, Privacy and Resistance.* Oxford: Berg, 1999, 134

24 Fadwa El Guindi, *Veil: Modesty, Privacy and Resistance.* Oxford: Berg, 1999, 161

25 Fadwa El Guindi, *Veil: Modesty, Privacy and Resistance.* Oxford: Berg, 1999, 168

26 https://www.thenational.ae/lifestyle/fashion/the-evolution-of-the-abaya-1.704710

27 https://www.thenational.ae/lifestyle/fashion/the-evolution-of-the-abaya-1.704710

28 Mohja Kahf, 'From Her Royal Body the Robe Was Removed: The Blessings of the Veil and the Trauma of Forced Unveilings in the Middle East' in Jennifer Heath, *The Veil: Women Writers on Its History, Lore, and Politics.* Berkeley: University of California Press, 2008, 36

29 Elizabeth Bucar, *Pious Fashion: How Muslim Women Dress.* Cambridge: Harvard University Press, 2017, 76

30 Carla Jones, 'Images of Desire: Creating Virtue and Value in an Indonesian Islamic Lifestyle Magazine' in *Journal of Middle East Women's Studies.* November 2010; 6 (3): 103. doi: https://doi.org/10.2979/MEW.2010.6.3.91

31 Elizabeth Bucar, *Pious Fashion: How Muslim Women Dress.* Cambridge: Harvard University Press, 2017, 20

32 Rafia Zakaria, *Veil.* New York: Bloomsbury Academic, 2017, 101

33 Amani Al-Khatahtbeh, *Muslim Girl: A Coming of Age.* New York: Simon & Schuster Paperbacks, 2016, 118

34 https://www.nytimes.com/2018/06/29/opinion/sunday/hoejabi-hijabi-muslim-culture. html

35 https://www.amaliah.com/post/40756/ turban-hijab-became-symbol-modern-muslim-woman

Chapter 4

1 https://www.thenational.ae/lifestyle/fashion/sauce-has-launched-the-region-s-first-online-made-to-measure-eveningwear-collection-1.683355

2 https://www.thenational.ae/arts-culture/modest-fashion-a-look-at-the-rising-popularity-and-why-labels-are-turning-to-the-middle-east-for-inspiration-1.10662

3 Emma Tarlo and Annelies Moors, *Islamic Fashion and Anti-fashion: New Perspectives from Europe and North America.* London: Bloomsbury Academic, 2013, 203

4 https://ceif.iba.edu.pk/pdf/ThomsonReuters-StateoftheGlobalIslamicEconomyRep ort201516.pdf, 136

5 https://www.telegraph.co.uk/news/2017/11/29/muslim-population-uk-could-triple-13m-following-record-influx/

6 https://www.vogue.com/article/modist-founder-ghizlan-guenez-interview-personal-style-modest-fashion

Chapter 5

1 Shelina Janmohamed, *Generation M: Young Muslims Changing the World.* London: I.B. Tauris, 2016, 12

2 Leila Ahmed, *A Quiet Revolution: The Veil's Resurgence, from the Middle East to America.* New Haven: Yale University Press, 2011, 196

3 Amani Al-Khatahtbeh, *Muslim Girl: A Coming of Age.* New York: Simon & Schuster Paperbacks, 2016, 2–3

4 Faegheh Shirazi, *Brand Islam: The Marketing and Commodification of Piety.* Austin: The University of Texas Press, 2016, 174

5 Shelina Janmohamed, *Generation M: Young Muslims Changing the World.* London: I.B. Tauris, 2016, 228

6 Leila Ahmed, *A Quiet Revolution: The Veil's Resurgence, from the Middle East to America.* New Haven: Yale University Press, 2011, 196

7 Shelina Janmohamed, *Generation M: Young Muslims Changing the World.* London: I.B. Tauris, 2016, 145

8 https://blackorchidshop.com/pages/about-us

9 https://www.launchgood.com/project/next_ummah_apparel#!/

10 Shelina Janmohamed, *Generation M: Young Muslims Changing the World*. London: I.B. Tauris, 2016, 32

11 https://www.theguardian.com/lifeandstyle/2011/apr/23/nigella-lawson-burkini-bikini-swimming

12 https://www.theguardian.com/fashion/2016/mar/30/fashion-mogul-pierre-berge-its-out-at-islamic-clothing

13 https://www.independent.co.uk/news/business/news/burkini-marks-and-spencer-sells-out-france-ban-muslim-islam-attire-a7205456.html

14 Faegheh Shirazi, *Brand Islam: The Marketing and Commodification of Piety*. Austin: The University of Texas Press, 2016, 185

15 https://www.thenational.ae/lifestyle/fashion/over-sized-and-on-trend-new-modest-styles-from-under-rapt-1.780304

16 https://www.thenational.ae/lifestyle/fashion/over-sized-and-on-trend-new-modest-styles-from-under-rapt-1.780304

17 http://www.thejakartapost.com/news/2013/07/21/dian-pelangi-young-designer-grand-ambitions.html

18 https://www.thenational.ae/lifestyle/fashion/the-evolution-of-the-abaya-1.704710

19 Faegheh Shirazi, *Brand Islam: The Marketing and Commodification of Piety*. Austin: The University of Texas Press, 2016, 154

20 https://www.thenational.ae/lifestyle/fashion/the-evolution-of-the-abaya-1.704710

21 https://www.thenational.ae/lifestyle/fashion/dulce-by-safiya-is-modesty-that-s-a-la-mode-1.773752

22 https://www.thenational.ae/lifestyle/fashion/dulce-by-safiya-is-modesty-that-s-a-la-mode-1.773752

23 Hafsa Lodi, 'In conversation with: the incubator and the innovator' in *Mojeh Magazine*. United Arab Emirates: HS Media Group FZ LLC, October 2018, 58

24 https://www.vogue.co.uk/article/the-multibillion-dollar-modest-fashion-industry-thats-gone-global

25 https://www.timesofisrael.com/no-skirting-the-issue/

Chapter 6

1 Reina Lewis, 'Marketing Muslim Lifestyle: A New Media Genre' in *Journal of Middle East Women's Studies*. November 2010; 6 (3): 83. doi: https://doi.org/10.2979/MEW.2010.6.3.58

2 Reina Lewis, 'Fashion Forward and Faith-tastic: Online Modest Fashion and the Development of Women as Religious Interpreters and Intermediaries' in Reina Lewis, *Modest Fashion: Styling Bodies, Mediating Faith*. New York: I.B. Tauris, 2013, 58

3 https://www.hijabinstyle.com/hijab-in-style-decemember

4 https://www.thenational.ae/lifestyle/luxury/halima-aden-my-family-doesn-t-understand-modelling-is-a-real-job-1.874105

5   https://abcnews.go.com/Entertainment/muslim-fashion-designer-nailah-lymus-pushes-modest-modeling/story?id=18433341

6   https://www.nbcnews.com/news/asian-america/underwraps-builds-first-agency-muslim-modest-fashion-models-n757616

7   https://www.ummamodels.com/about

8   Amani Al-Khatahtbeh, *Muslim Girl: A Coming of Age.* New York: Simon & Schuster Paperbacks, 2016, 71

9   Reina Lewis, *Muslim Fashion: Contemporary Style Cultures.* Durham: Duke University Press, 2015, 84

10 Faegheh Shirazi, *Brand Islam: The Marketing and Commodification of Piety.* Austin: The University of Texas Press, 2016, 185

11 https://www.ummah.com/forum/forum/family-lifestyle-community-culture/marriage/438941-halal-islamic-modelling-is-there-such-a-thing

12 https://www.thenational.ae/lifestyle/luxury/halima-aden-my-family-doesn-t-understand-modelling-is-a-real-job-1.874105

13 https://www.thenational.ae/lifestyle/fashion/modestwear-pioneer-mariah-idrissi-talks-faith-and-fashion-1.833871

14 Carla Jones, 'Images of Desire: Creating Virtue and Value in an Indonesian Islamic Lifestyle Magazine' in *Journal of Middle East Women's Studies.* November 2010; 6 (3): 107. doi: https://doi.org/10.2979/MEW.2010.6.3.91

15 Faegheh Shirazi, *Brand Islam: The Marketing and Commodification of Piety.* Austin: The University of Texas Press, 2016, 165

16 https://edition.cnn.com/videos/world/2018/06/07/saudi-arabia-fashion-show-drones-lon-orig.cnn

Chapter 7

1   https://www.marieclaire.co.uk/reports/meet-the-millennial-god-squad-2451

2   https://www.forbes.com/sites/meghnasarkar/2019/04/04/its-time-we-stop-ignoring-modest-fashion-influencers/#455fda795da1

3   https://www.middleeasteye.net/in-depth/features/modest-fashion-shows-muslim-women-dolce-gabbana-instagram-1654612646

4   Shelina Janmohamed, *Generation M: Young Muslims Changing the World.* London: I.B. Tauris, 2016, 98

5   https://www.vogue.co.uk/article/dina-torkia-muslim-fashion-blogger-modesty-dressing

6   https://www.nytimes.com/2016/11/09/fashion/covergirl-beauty-hijab.html

7   https://www.vogue.co.uk/article/loreal-paris-elvive-campaign-amena-khan

8   Shelina Janmohamed, *Generation M: Young Muslims Changing the World.* London: I.B. Tauris, 2016, 86–87

9   Dina Torkia, *Modestly.* London: Ebury Press, 2018, 21

10 Pamela K. Taylor, 'I Just Want to Be Me: Issues in Identity for One American Muslim

Woman' in Jennifer Heath, *The Veil: Women Writers on Its History, Lore, and Politics.* Berkeley: University of California Press, 2008, 123

11 Amani Al-Khatahtbeh, *Muslim Girl: A Coming of Age.* New York: Simon & Schuster Paperbacks, 2016, 19

12 https://www.theguardian.com/fashion/2018/sep/02/shahira-yusuf-i-have-always-felt-beautiful-

13 https://www.amaliah.com/post/51130/hijab-no-hijab-turban-conversation-split-muslim-twitter

14 https://en.vogue.me/fashion/i-dont-consider-myself-a-hijabi-says-ascia-al-faraj/

15 Reina Lewis, *Muslim Fashion: Contemporary Style Cultures.* Durham: Duke University Press, 2015, 258

16 Reina Lewis, *Muslim Fashion: Contemporary Style Cultures.* Durham: Duke University Press, 2015, 267

17 https://www.thenational.ae/lifestyle/is-modest-modelling-an-oxymoron-1.614785

18 https://www.thenational.ae/lifestyle/fashion/dulce-by-safiya-is-modesty-that-s-a-la-mode-1.773752

19 https://www.thenational.ae/lifestyle/luxury/halima-aden-my-family-doesn-t-understand-modelling-is-a-real-job-1.874105

20 Annelies Moors, 'Discover the Beauty of Modesty: Islamic Fashion Online' in Reina Lewis, *Modest Fashion: Styling Bodies, Mediating Faith.* New York: I.B. Tauris, 2013, 27

Chapter 8

1 Faegheh Shirazi, *Brand Islam: The Marketing and Commodification of Piety.* Austin: The University of Texas Press, 2016, 155

2 https://www.refinery29.com/en-us/2017/01/134958/modest-clothing-fashion-trend

3 https://www.nytimes.com/2017/11/02/t-magazine/modest-fashion-clothes.html

4 Banu Gökarıksel, Anna Secor, 'Between Fashion and *Tesettür*: Marketing and Consuming Women's Islamic Dress' in *Journal of Middle East Women's Studies.* November 2010; 6 (3): 137. doi: https://doi.org/10.2979/MEW.2010.6.3.118

5 https://happymuslimfamily.org/modanisa-hijab-fashion/

6 https://www.huffingtonpost.com/2013/01/31/underwraps-muslim-models-maintain-modesty-with-fashion-agency_n_2585104.html

7 https://www.theguardian.com/sport/blog/2019/may/01/sports-illustrated-swimwear-issue-sex-beauty

8 https://www.vogue.co.uk/article/the-multibillion-dollar-modest-fashion-industry-thats-gone-global

9 https://www.thenational.ae/lifestyle/fashion/sass-brown-countering-consumption-with-a-new-look-approach-1.719137

10 https://www.telegraph.co.uk/women/life/how-the-hijab-went-high-fashion-and-divided-muslim-women/

11 https://www.thenational.ae/lifestyle/fashion/modestwear-collections-for-every-woman-in-pictures-1.853572

12 Pamela K. Taylor, 'I Just Want to Be Me: Issues in Identity for One American Muslim Woman' in Jennifer Heath, *The Veil: Women Writers on Its History, Lore, and Politics*. Berkeley: University of California Press, 2008, 128

13 Elizabeth Bucar, *Pious Fashion: How Muslim Women Dress*. Cambridge: Harvard University Press, 2017, 184

14 Reina Lewis, 'Marketing Muslim Lifestyle: A New Media Genre' in *Journal of Middle East Women's Studies*. November 2010; 6 (3): 72. doi: https://doi.org/10.2979/MEW.2010.6.3.58

15 Lauren Shields, *The Beauty Suit: How My Year of Religious Modesty Made Me a Better Feminist*. Boston: Beacon Press, 2018, 2

16 Lauren Shields, *The Beauty Suit: How My Year of Religious Modesty Made Me a Better Feminist*. Boston: Beacon Press, 2018, 3

17 Emma Tarlo and Annelies Moors, *Islamic Fashion and Anti-fashion: New Perspectives from Europe and North America*. London: Bloomsbury Academic, 2013, 205

18 https://www.epa.gov/sites/production/files/2016-11/documents/2014_smmfactsheet_508.pdf

19 https://www.washingtonpost.com/news/monkey-cage/wp/2017/04/24/four-years-after-one-of-the-worst-industrial-accidents-ever-what-have-we-learned/?noredirect=on&utm_term=.74fea3c6003d

20 https://www.thenational.ae/lifestyle/fashion/over-sized-and-on-trend-new-modest-styles-from-under-rapt-1.780304

21 http://issuu.com/fashionrevolution/docs/fr_fashiontransparencyindex2018?e=25766662/60458846

22 https://www.businessoffashion.com/articles/intelligence/top-industry-trends-2018-8-sustainability-credibility

Chapter 9

1 https://www.telegraph.co.uk/fashion/style/did-demure-dressing-become-biggest-trend-fashion

2 https://www.thenational.ae/lifestyle/fashion/modestwear-pioneer-mariah-idrissi-talks-faith-and-fashion-1.833871

3 Dina Torkia, *Modestly*. London: Ebury Press, 2018, 29

4 https://www.refinery29.com/en-us/2016/06/112630/mango-ramadan-criticism

5 https://www.bain.com/insights/luxury-goods-worldwide-market-study-fall-winter-2018/

6 Susan O. Michelman, 'Reveal or Conceal? American Religious Discourse With Fashion' in *Etnofoor* 2003; 16 (2): 86. Retrieved from http://www.jstor.org/stable/25758058

7 https://halalfocus.net/uae-ifdc-launchs-new-fashion-category/

8 Hafsa Lodi, 'Pret-A-Cover: A new approach to modesty' in *Mojeh Magazine*. United Arab Emirates: HS Media Group FZ LLC, April 2018, 99

9 http://bythefigandtheolive.com/male-modesty/

10 https://www.amaliah.com/post/47023/how-prophet-yusuf-can-empower-the-modern-man-towards-sexual-modesty

Conclusion

1   https://rebeccaamoore.com/2014/02/15/modest-is-not-hottest

2   http://www.patheos.com/blogs/unfundamentalistchristians/2015/07/why-we-shouldnt-say-modest-is-hottest/

3   Amani Al-Khatahtbeh, *Muslim Girl: A Coming of Age*. New York: Simon & Schuster Paperbacks, 2016, 136

4   https://www.independent.co.uk/news/world/europe/burqa-ban-netherlands-police-dutch-law-islam-muslim-a9033451.html

5   https://www.thenational.ae/lifestyle/fashion/veiled-and-vocal-charting-the-rise-of-the-niqab-wearing-influencer-1.882822

6   Mohja Kahf, 'From Her Royal Body the Robe Was Removed: The Blessings of the Veil and the Trauma of Forced Unveilings in the Middle East' in Jennifer Heath, *The Veil: Women Writers on Its History, Lore, and Politics*. Berkeley: University of California Press, 2008, 30

7   Maliha Masood, 'On the Road: Travels with My Hijab' in Jennifer Heath, *The Veil: Women Writers on Its History, Lore, and Politics*. Berkeley: University of California Press, 2008, 226

8   https://www.thenational.ae/lifestyle/fashion/veiled-and-vocal-charting-the-rise-of-the-niqab-wearing-influencer-1.882822

9   Pamela K. Taylor, 'I Just Want to Be Me: Issues in Identity for One American Muslim Woman' in Jennifer Heath, *The Veil: Women Writers on Its History, Lore, and Politics*. Berkeley: University of California Press, 2008, 120–121

10 http://muslimgirl.com/48724/modesty-is-not-the-most-important-thing-in-my-relationship-with-god/

11 Lauren Shields, *The Beauty Suit: How My Year of Religious Modesty Made Me a Better Feminist*. Boston: Beacon Press, 2018, 127

12 Rafia Zakaria, *Veil*. New York: Bloomsbury Academic, 2017, 38–39

13 Maliha Masood, 'On the Road: Travels with My Hijab' in Jennifer Heath, *The Veil: Women Writers on Its History, Lore, and Politics*. Berkeley: University of California Press, 2008, 225

14 https://www.thenational.ae/lifestyle/fashion/dulce-by-safiya-is-modesty-that-s-a-la-mode-1.773752

15 Amani Al-Khatahtbeh, *Muslim Girl: A Coming of Age*. New York: Simon & Schuster Paperbacks, 2016, 114

16 Susan O. Michelman, 'Reveal or Conceal? American Religious Discourse With Fashion' in *Etnofoor* 2003; 16 (2): 76. Retrieved from http://www.jstor.org/stable/25758058

17 https://www.telegraph.co.uk/fashion/style/did-demure-dressing-become-biggest-trend-fashion/

18 https://www.themodist.com/en/alamodist.html

ACKNOWLEDGMENTS

I'd like to give a heartfelt thank you to this book's cover girl Mariah Idrissi, and to the crew at *Hijab in Style* magazine (editor in chief: Shah Hatun, photographer: Ümit Taylan and makeup artist and stylist: Fatma Capkanman) for generously contributing the cover photograph.

Thank you to my editors at *The National* newspaper for giving me access to so many sources in the modest fashion industry over the years, and for carving out a space for these important stories in the paper. While styling and reporting about modest fashion has been a personal passion, I had never imagined writing an entire book about it – I'm immensely grateful to my publisher, for not only seeking me out and giving me this exhilarating opportunity, but also for providing a much-needed editing eye throughout the process.

I'd also like to express my gratitude to Modanisa for hosting me during Istanbul Modest Fashion Week, and connecting me with one of this book's key interviewees, Halima Aden. Halima – thank you for giving me your time and insight, and for squeezing me in before your trip to the hammam!

Maha Gorton, Rihab Nubi, Saira Arshad, Sameera Hussain, Safiya Abdallah, Nabilah Kariem and Kochkarova Tamila deserve a special mention for trudging around outdoors on a rare rainy day in Dubai to produce a beautiful campaign shoot reflecting unique interpretations of modest fashion. Your collective confidence, style and enthusiasm, shared by millennial modest fashion entrepreneurs, designers and bloggers across the globe, serves as the spirit fueling this book.

To all of the others who shared their personal stories, experiences and expertise for this project: Aima Warriach, Akil Desai, Alia Khan, Alexa

Sue-Anne Dudley, Cynthia Jreige, Daniel James Cole, Deanna Khalil, Dian Pelangi, Faiza Bouguessa, Fatma Al Mulla, Franka Soeria, Kerim Türe, Lisa Vogl, Marriam Mossalli, Marwa Atik, Melanie Elturk, Nafisa Bakkar, Nicole Najmah Abraham, Nuriddeen Knight, Ozlem Sahin, Rachelle Yadegar, Romanna Bint Abu-Bakr, Ruby Aslam, Sabrina Salhi, Shagoofa Ali, Wafeeqa Azeem, Yasmin Sobeih, Zaahid Ahmed, Zaf Shabir, Zahra Valji and any others I may have missed – your voices were critical in chronicling the modest fashion revolution, and I sincerely hope you enjoy reading this book.

To the brilliant women who previously opened the doors to analyzing, exploring and writing about contemporary Muslims and modest fashion: the studies, articles and books compiled by Reina Lewis, Elizabeth Bucar, Emma Tarlo, Annelies Moors, Faegheh Shirazi, Lauren Shields, Rafia Zakaria, Fadwa El Guindi, Leila Ahmed, Carla Jones, Mohja Kahf, Pamela K. Taylor, Amani Al-Khatahtbeh and Shelina Janmohamed, provided invaluable research for this project.

I'm thankful to my family for sharing my enthusiasm for this project (especially my mother for taking on helpful babysitting duties) and to my husband Omair, for spending hours changing diapers, rocking our little one to sleep, hanging the endless laundry loads to dry and tackling the towering piles of dirty dishes in the sink, while I was consumed with writing. Thank you for your unwavering patience.